TORCHWOOD

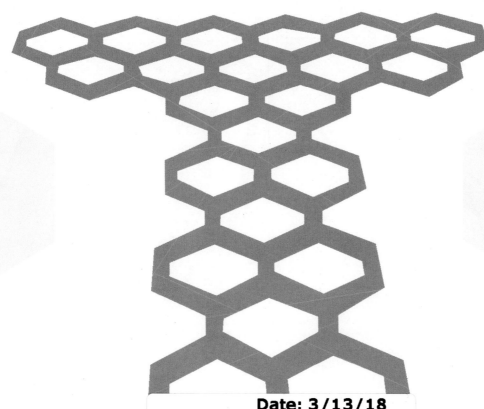

ARCHIVES VOL.1

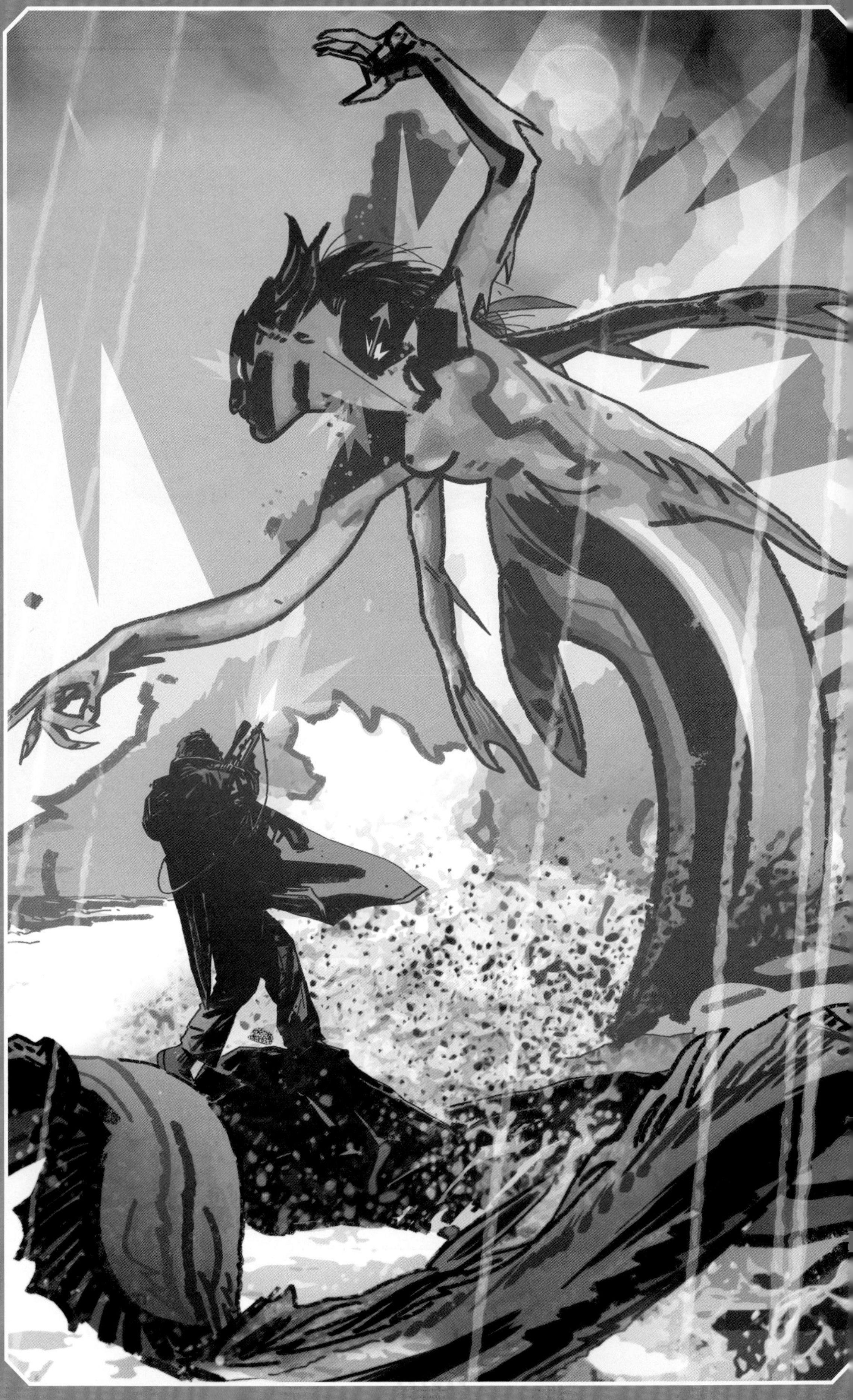

TORCHWOOD
ARCHIVES VOL. 1

'THE LEGACY OF TORCHWOOD ONE!'
WRITER: SIMON FURMAN; ARTIST: SL GALLANT

'THE SELKIE'
WRITERS: JOHN BARROWMAN
AND CAROLE BARROWMAN;
ARTIST: TOMMY LEE EDWARDS

'FATED TO PRETEND'
WRITER: BRIAN MINCHIN; ARTIST: STEVE YEOWELL

'SHROUDED PARTS 1 AND 2'
WRITER: GARETH DAVID-LLOYD; ARTIST: PIA GUERRA

'SOMEBODY ELSE'S PROBLEM'
WRITER: CHRISTOPHER COOPER;
ARTIST: STEPHEN DOWNEY

'THE RETURN OF THE VOSTOK'
WRITER: BRIAN MINCHIN; ARTIST: ADRIAN SALMON

'CULTURAL FIRSTS'
WRITER: RICHARD STOKES; ARTIST: MIKE DOWLING

'THE MAN WHO DREAMED OF STARS'
WRITER: BRIAN MINCHIN; ARTIST: BEN WILLSHER

'THEY KEEP KILLING ANDY'
WRITER: TREVOR BAXENDALE; ARTIST: BEN WILLSHER

COLOURISTS: PHIL ELLIOTT, HI-FI DESIGN
LETTERERS: JOHN WORKMAN, RICHARD
STARKINGS/COMICRAFT

TORCHWOOD ARCHIVES VOL 1

ISBN: 9781785861611

Torchwood Archives Vol 1, July 2017. Published by Titan Comics, a division of Titan Publishing Group, Ltd., 144 Southwark Street, London SE1 0UP.

Torchwood is a BBC Worldwide Production for the BBC. Executive Producers: Russell T. Davies, Julie Gardner, and Jane Tranter. Original series created by Russell T. Davies, and developed and produced by BBC Cymru Wales.

Front cover artwork by Tommy Lee Edwards.

Printed in China.

Titan Comics does not read or accept unsolicited TORCHWOOD submissions or ideas, stories, or artwork.

10 9 8 7 6 5 4 3 2 1

A CIP catalogue record for this title is available from the British Library.

First edition: First published July 2017

TITAN COMICS

COLLECTION EDITOR Neil D. Edwards **SENIOR EDITOR** Martin Eden
COLLECTION DESIGNER Wilfried Tshikana-Ekutshu
SENIOR PRODUCTION CONTROLLER Jackie Flook
PRODUCTION CONTROLLER Peter James **PRODUCTION SUPERVISOR** Maria Pearson
ART DIRECTOR Oz Browne **PUBLISHING MANAGER** Darryl Tothill
PUBLISHING DIRECTOR Chris Teather **OPERATIONS DIRECTOR** Leigh Baulch
EXECUTIVE DIRECTOR Vivian Cheung
PUBLISHER Nick Landau

www.titan-comics.com
Follow us on **Twitter: @comicstitan**
Become a fan on Facebook: **facebook.com/comicstitan**

CARDIFF

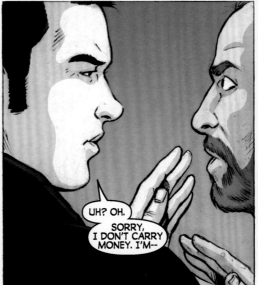

UH? OH.

SORRY, I DON'T CARRY MONEY. I'M--

IANTO-- I *NEED* YOUR HELP.

...

RUPERT? *RUPERT HOWARTH*?! BUT YOU'RE DEAD! I SAW--

YOU SAW WHAT I WANTED YOU TO SEE, IANTO. YOU *ALL* DID. BUT HERE I AM...

"THE LEGACY OF TORCHWOOD ONE!"

TORCHWOOD THREE

CREVGWIN·IN·THESE·
ELGWYDR·HORIZ
OFWRNAIS·AWEN

"OKAY. JUST SO I HAVE THIS STRAIGHT..."

YOU WERE HEAD OF TORCHWOOD ONE'S BIO-CHEMICAL RESEARCH DIVISION, UP TO THE POINT YOU *FAKED* YOUR OWN DEATH AND DISAPPEARED?

RIGHT.

WHICH BEGS THE QUESTION: *WHY?*

I WAS ON THE VERGE OF A *MASSIVE* BREAKTHROUGH IN IMMUNITY-BOOSTING DRUGS! WE WERE READY TO WIPE OUT ALL VIRAL DISEASE! THEN THE BIG PHARMACEUTICAL COMPANIES FOUND OUT. FIRST THEY TRIED TO *BRIBE* ME...

THEN THEY TRIED TO *KILL* ME!

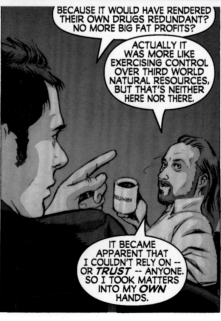

BECAUSE IT WOULD HAVE RENDERED THEIR OWN DRUGS REDUNDANT? NO MORE BIG FAT PROFITS?

ACTUALLY IT WAS MORE LIKE EXERCISING CONTROL OVER THIRD WORLD NATURAL RESOURCES, BUT THAT'S NEITHER HERE NOR THERE.

IT BECAME APPARENT THAT I COULDN'T RELY ON -- OR *TRUST* -- ANYONE. SO I TOOK MATTERS INTO MY *OWN* HANDS.

AND YET HERE YOU ARE NOW, LARGE AS LIFE AND IN REAL NEED OF A BATH. WHAT'S CHANGED?

EVERYTHING CHANGED, CAPTAIN, WHEN I MADE MY BREAKTHROUGH.

WORK LIKE MINE CAN'T STAY HIDDEN FOREVER.

I CAN'T STAY HIDDEN FOREVER.

HE'S A BRILLIANT MAN, JACK. HE *MENTORED* ME WHEN STARTED AT TORCHWOOD O I CAN *VOUCH* FOR HIM

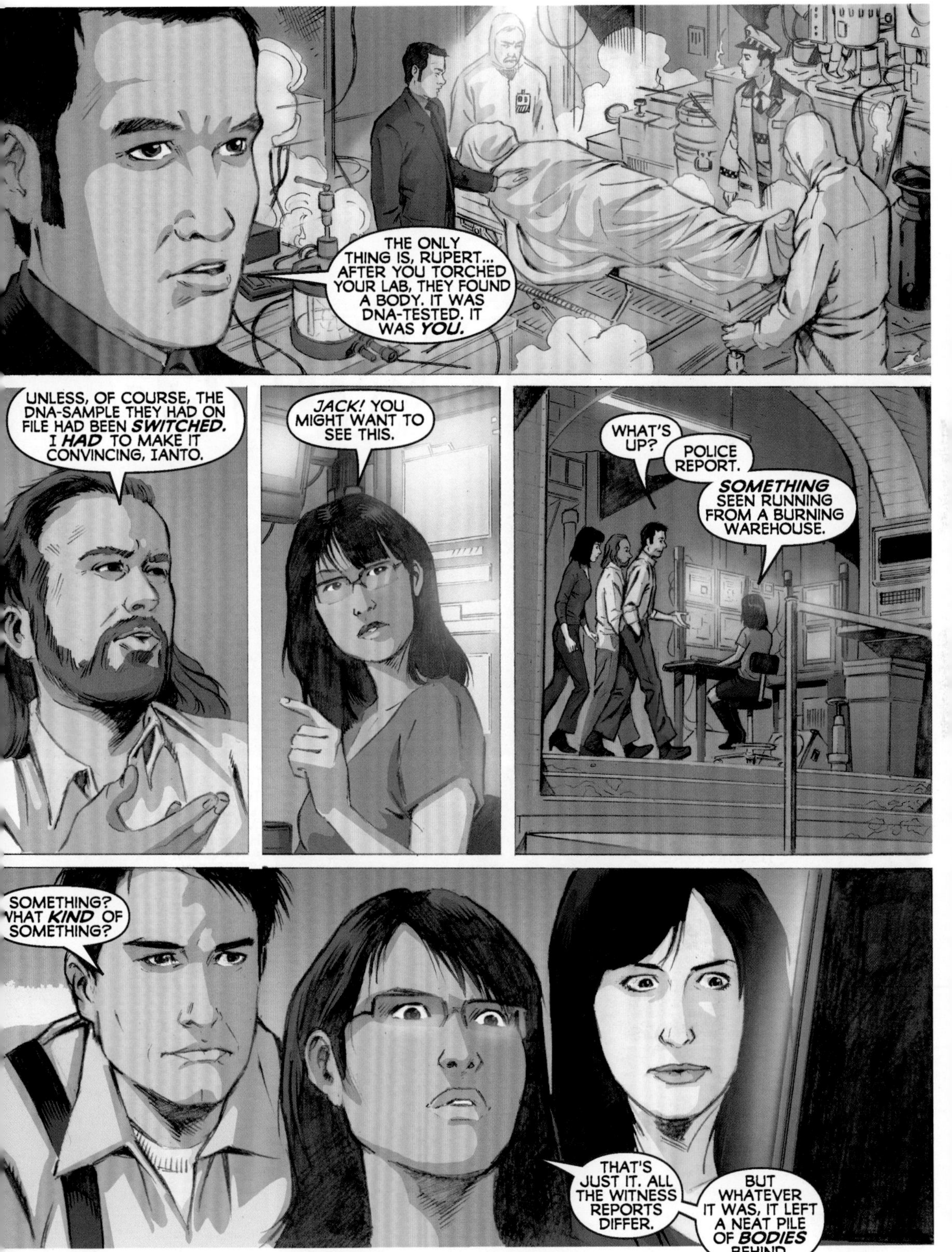
THE ONLY THING IS, RUPERT... AFTER YOU TORCHED YOUR LAB, THEY FOUND A BODY. IT WAS DNA-TESTED. IT WAS *YOU.*
UNLESS, OF COURSE, THE DNA-SAMPLE THEY HAD ON FILE HAD BEEN *SWITCHED.* I *HAD* TO MAKE IT CONVINCING, IANTO.
JACK! YOU MIGHT WANT TO SEE THIS.
WHAT'S UP?
POLICE REPORT.
SOMETHING SEEN RUNNING FROM A BURNING WAREHOUSE.
SOMETHING? WHAT *KIND* OF SOMETHING?
THAT'S JUST IT. ALL THE WITNESS REPORTS DIFFER.
BUT WHATEVER IT WAS, IT LEFT A NEAT PILE OF *BODIES* BEHIND.

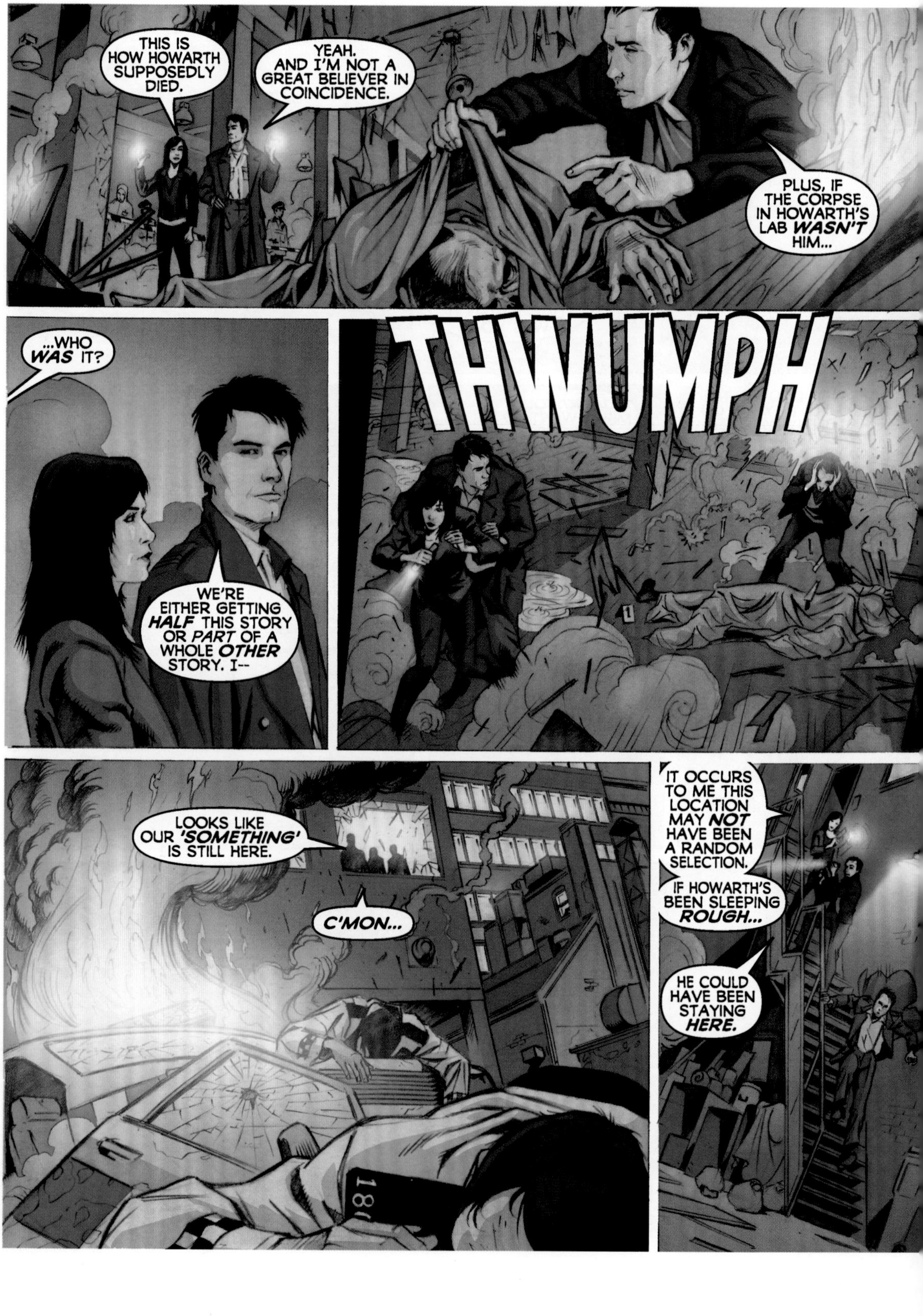
THIS IS HOW HOWARTH SUPPOSEDLY DIED.
YEAH. AND I'M NOT A GREAT BELIEVER IN COINCIDENCE.
PLUS, IF THE CORPSE IN HOWARTH'S LAB *WASN'T* HIM...
...WHO *WAS* IT?
WE'RE EITHER GETTING *HALF* THIS STORY OR *PART* OF A WHOLE *OTHER* STORY. I--
THWUMPH
LOOKS LIKE OUR *'SOMETHING'* IS STILL HERE.
C'MON...
IT OCCURS TO ME THIS LOCATION MAY *NOT* HAVE BEEN A RANDOM SELECTION.
IF HOWARTH'S BEEN SLEEPING *ROUGH...*
HE COULD HAVE BEEN STAYING *HERE.*

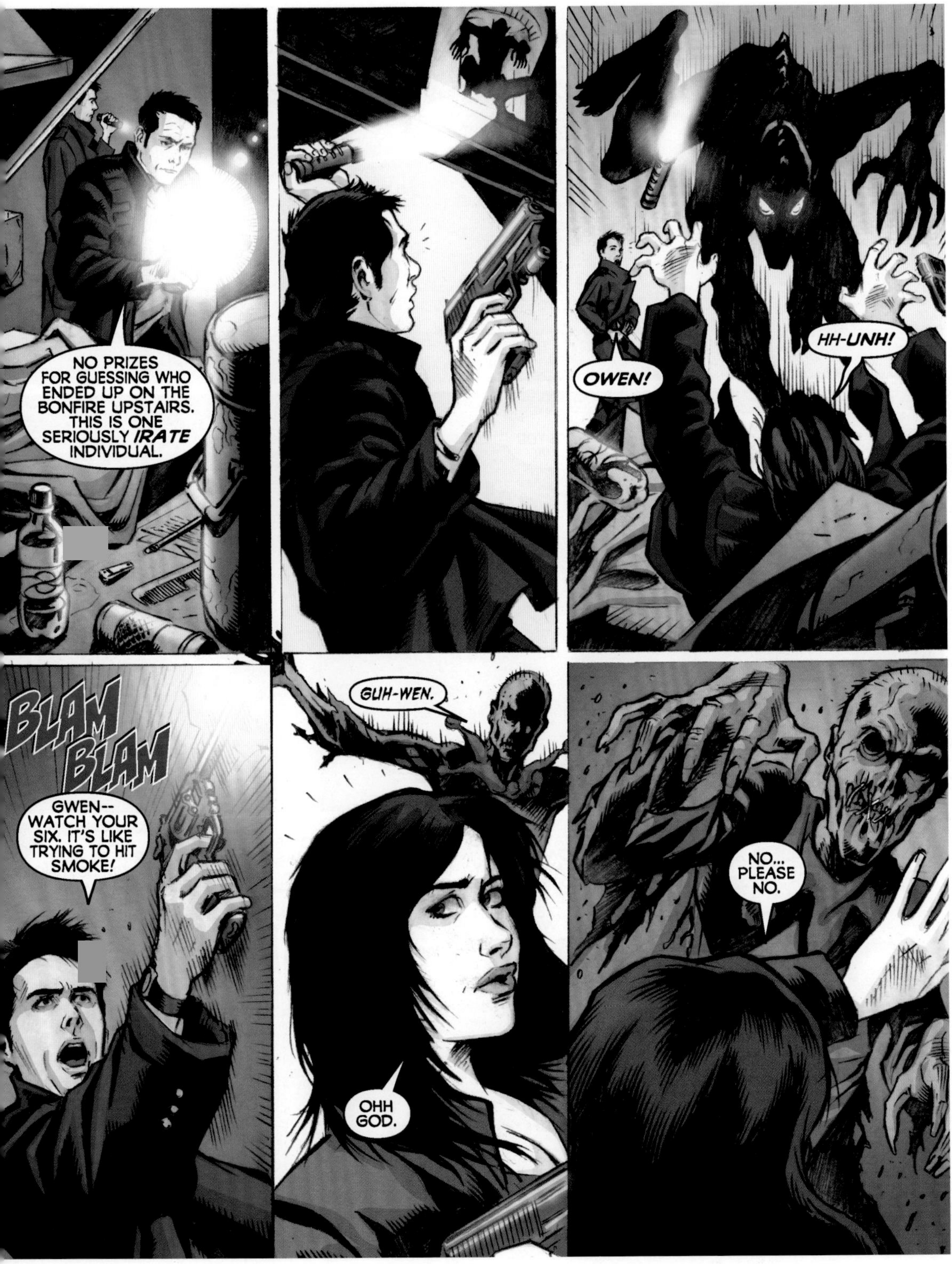
NO PRIZES FOR GUESSING WHO ENDED UP ON THE BONFIRE UPSTAIRS. THIS IS ONE SERIOUSLY *IRATE* INDIVIDUAL.
OWEN!
HH-UNH!
BLAM BLAM
GWEN-- WATCH YOUR SIX. IT'S LIKE TRYING TO HIT SMOKE!
GUH-WEN.
OHH GOD.
NO... PLEASE NO.

GWEN, BACK *AWAY* -- NOW. DON'T --

JAH-ACK.

DAMN YOU! WHAT DO YOU WANT?

THE CRE-AHT-TOR. HOW-ARTH.

OR THO-OSE YOU LOVE... DIE.

GWEN!

JACK! *JACK!*

GWEN? I --

IT'S GONE.

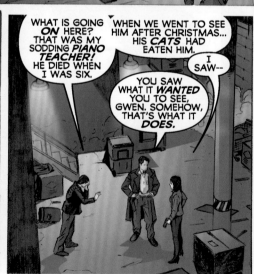

WHAT IS GOING *ON* HERE? THAT WAS MY SODDING *PIANO TEACHER!* HE DIED WHEN I WAS SIX.

WHEN WE WENT TO SEE HIM AFTER CHRISTMAS... HIS *CATS* HAD EATEN HIM.

I SAW--

YOU SAW WHAT IT *WANTED* YOU TO SEE, GWEN. SOMEHOW, THAT'S WHAT IT *DOES.*

AS FOR HOW AND WHY... I'M BETTING HOWARTH CAN GIVE US *CHAPTER AND VERSE.*

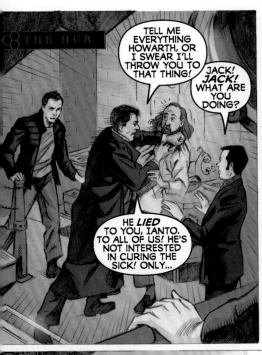

TELL ME EVERYTHING HOWARTH, OR I SWEAR I'LL THROW YOU TO THAT THING!

JACK! JACK! WHAT ARE YOU DOING?

HE *LIED* TO YOU, IANTO. TO ALL OF US! HE'S NOT INTERESTED IN CURING THE SICK! ONLY...

...WHAT?!

EFF! CH-*CHIMERA!*

IT'S CALLED CHIMERA.

WE... *ACQUIRED* SOME ALIEN TISSUE SAMPLES. EXPOSURE TO THEM PROVOKED A *PRIMAL FEAR* RESPONSE. THE IDEA WAS...

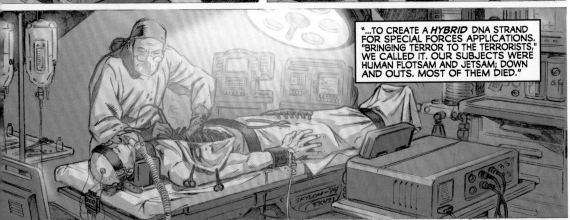

"...TO CREATE A *HYBRID* DNA STRAND FOR SPECIAL FORCES APPLICATIONS. "BRINGING TERROR TO THE TERRORISTS," WE CALLED IT. OUR SUBJECTS WERE HUMAN FLOTSAM AND JETSAM; DOWN AND OUTS. MOST OF THEM DIED."

BUT ONE DIDN'T?

HE WAS A CRACK ADDICT -- A NO-ONE. BUT THE END RESULT WAS UNCONTROLLABLE. IT ESCAPED. IT CAME *BACK.*

SO YOU FAKED YOUR DEATH USING ONE OF YOUR VICTIMS AND HID AMONG THE PEOPLE YOU'D PREYED ON.

WHOOT WHOOT

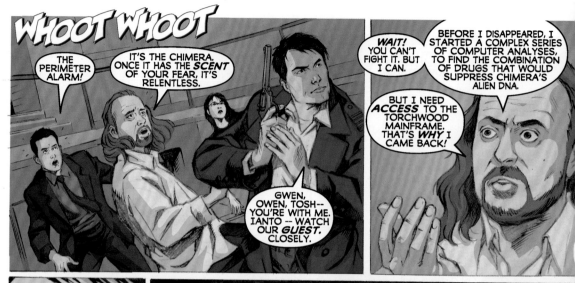

THE PERIMETER ALARM!

IT'S THE CHIMERA. ONCE IT HAS THE *SCENT* OF YOUR FEAR, IT'S RELENTLESS.

WAIT! YOU CAN'T FIGHT IT. BUT I CAN.

BEFORE I DISAPPEARED, I STARTED A COMPLEX SERIES OF COMPUTER ANALYSES, TO FIND THE COMBINATION OF DRUGS THAT WOULD SUPPRESS CHIMERA'S ALIEN DNA.

BUT I NEED *ACCESS* TO THE TORCHWOOD MAINFRAME. THAT'S *WHY* I CAME BACK!

GWEN, OWEN, TOSH-- YOU'RE WITH ME. IANTO -- WATCH OUR *GUEST*. CLOSELY.

DO IT. TOSH, GWEN, LET'S SEE IF WE CAN'T BUY THEM SOME TIME.

REMEMBER – IT'S TAPPING INTO YOUR FEARS. WHATEVER YOU SEE, THAT'S *NOT* WHAT IT REALLY IS!

EASY FOR YOU TO SAY... HOWARTH, WHAT AM I LOOKING FOR?

THE FILE NAME IS 'CHANGELING.' IT'S IN A LOW PRIORITY MAINTENANCE SUB-FOLDER ON THE TERTIARY LONDON MANIFOLD.

I TRUSTED YOU.

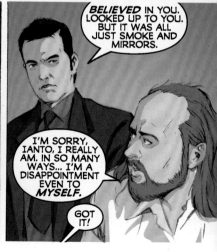

BELIEVED IN YOU. LOOKED UP TO YOU. BUT IT WAS ALL JUST SMOKE AND MIRRORS.

I'M SORRY, IANTO, I REALLY AM. IN SO MANY WAYS... I'M A DISAPPOINTMENT EVEN TO *MYSELF*.

GOT IT!

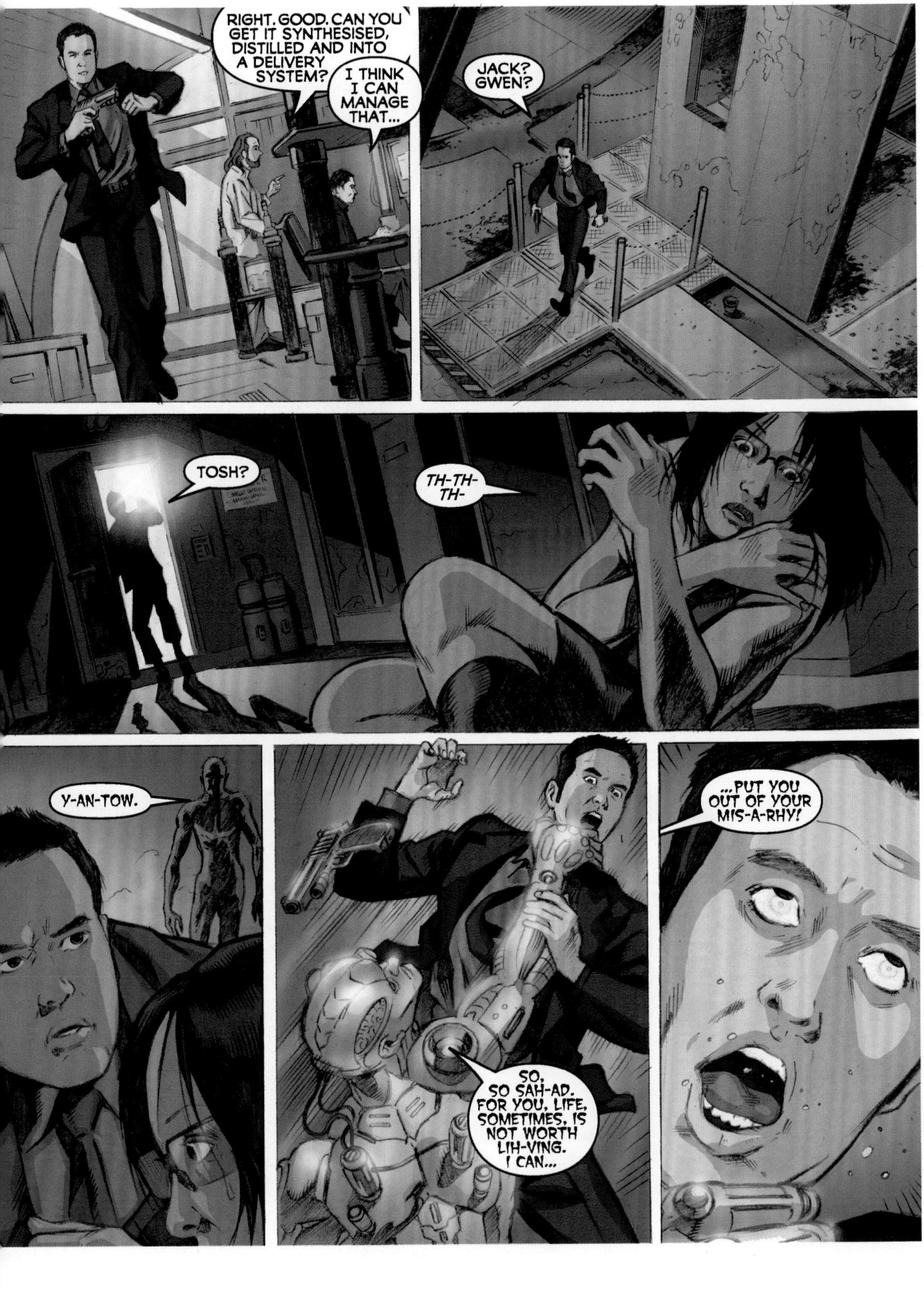
RIGHT. GOOD. CAN YOU GET IT SYNTHESISED, DISTILLED AND INTO A DELIVERY SYSTEM?
I THINK I CAN MANAGE THAT...
JACK? GWEN?
TOSH?
TH-TH-TH-
Y-AN-TOW.
SO, SO SAH-AD. FOR YOU, LIFE, SOMETIMES, IS NOT WORTH LIH-VING. I CAN...
...PUT YOU OUT OF YOUR MIS-A-RHY!

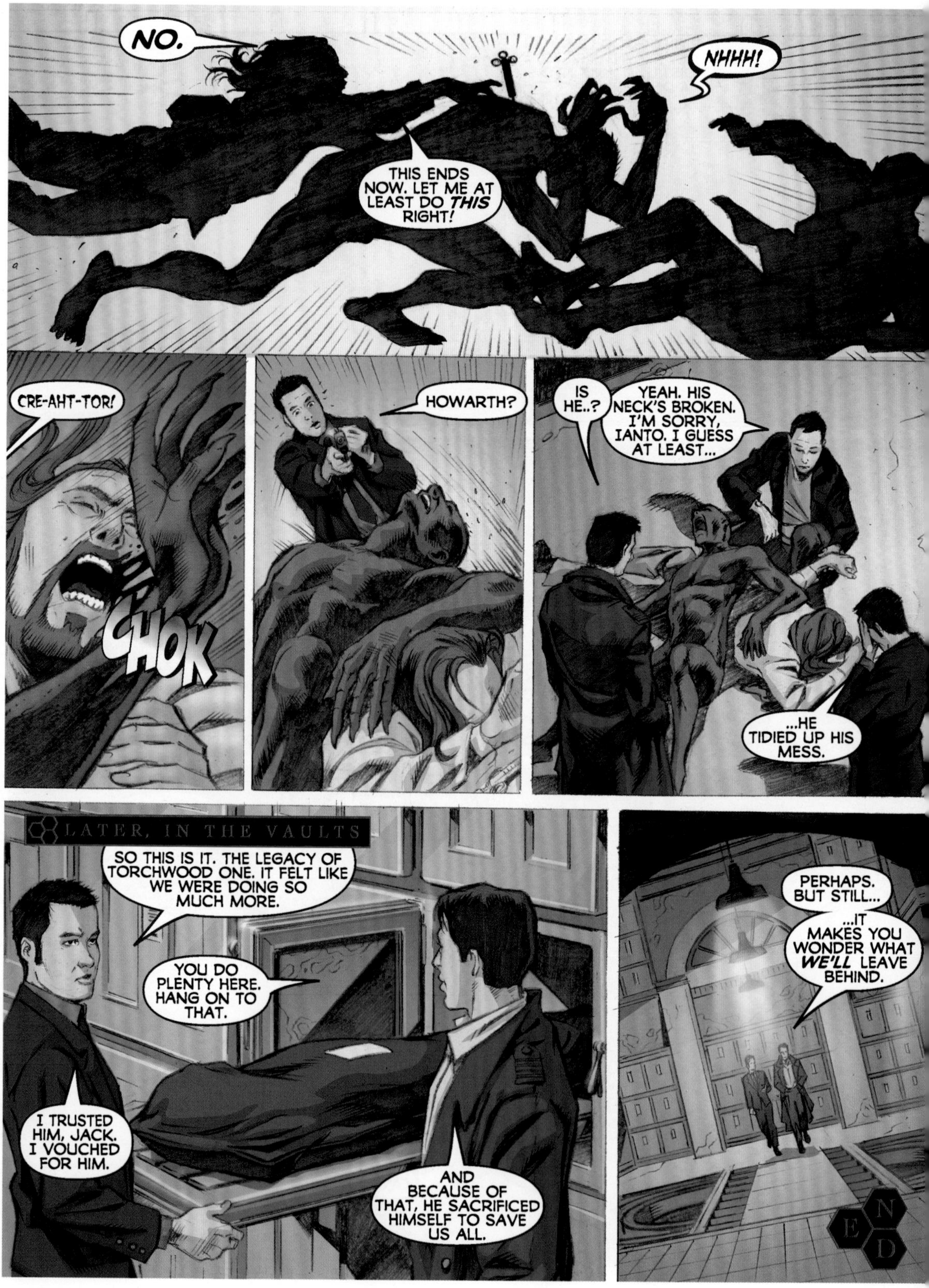
NO.
NHHH!
THIS ENDS NOW. LET ME AT LEAST DO *THIS* RIGHT!
CRE-AHT-TOR!
CHOK
HOWARTH?
IS HE..?
YEAH. HIS NECK'S BROKEN. I'M SORRY, IANTO. I GUESS AT LEAST...
...HE TIDIED UP HIS MESS.
LATER, IN THE VAULTS
SO THIS IS IT. THE LEGACY OF TORCHWOOD ONE. IT FELT LIKE WE WERE DOING SO MUCH MORE.
YOU DO PLENTY HERE. HANG ON TO THAT.
I TRUSTED HIM, JACK. I VOUCHED FOR HIM.
AND BECAUSE OF THAT, HE SACRIFICED HIMSELF TO SAVE US ALL.
PERHAPS. BUT STILL...
...IT MAKES YOU WONDER WHAT *WE'LL* LEAVE BEHIND.
END

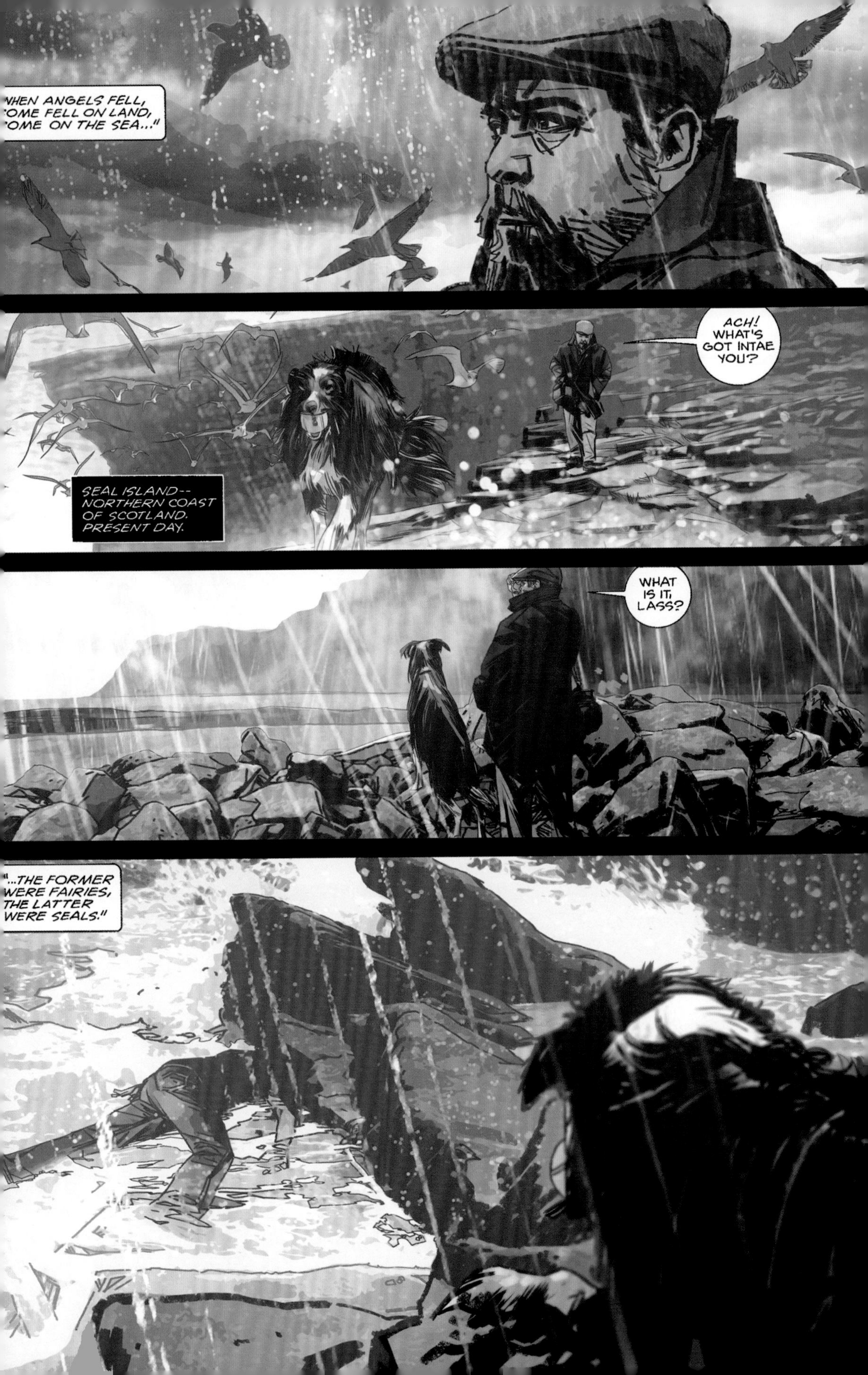
"WHEN ANGELS FELL, SOME FELL ON LAND, SOME ON THE SEA..."
ACH! WHAT'S GOT INTAE YOU?
SEAL ISLAND-- NORTHERN COAST OF SCOTLAND. PRESENT DAY.
WHAT IS IT, LASS?
"...THE FORMER WERE FAIRIES, THE LATTER WERE SEALS."

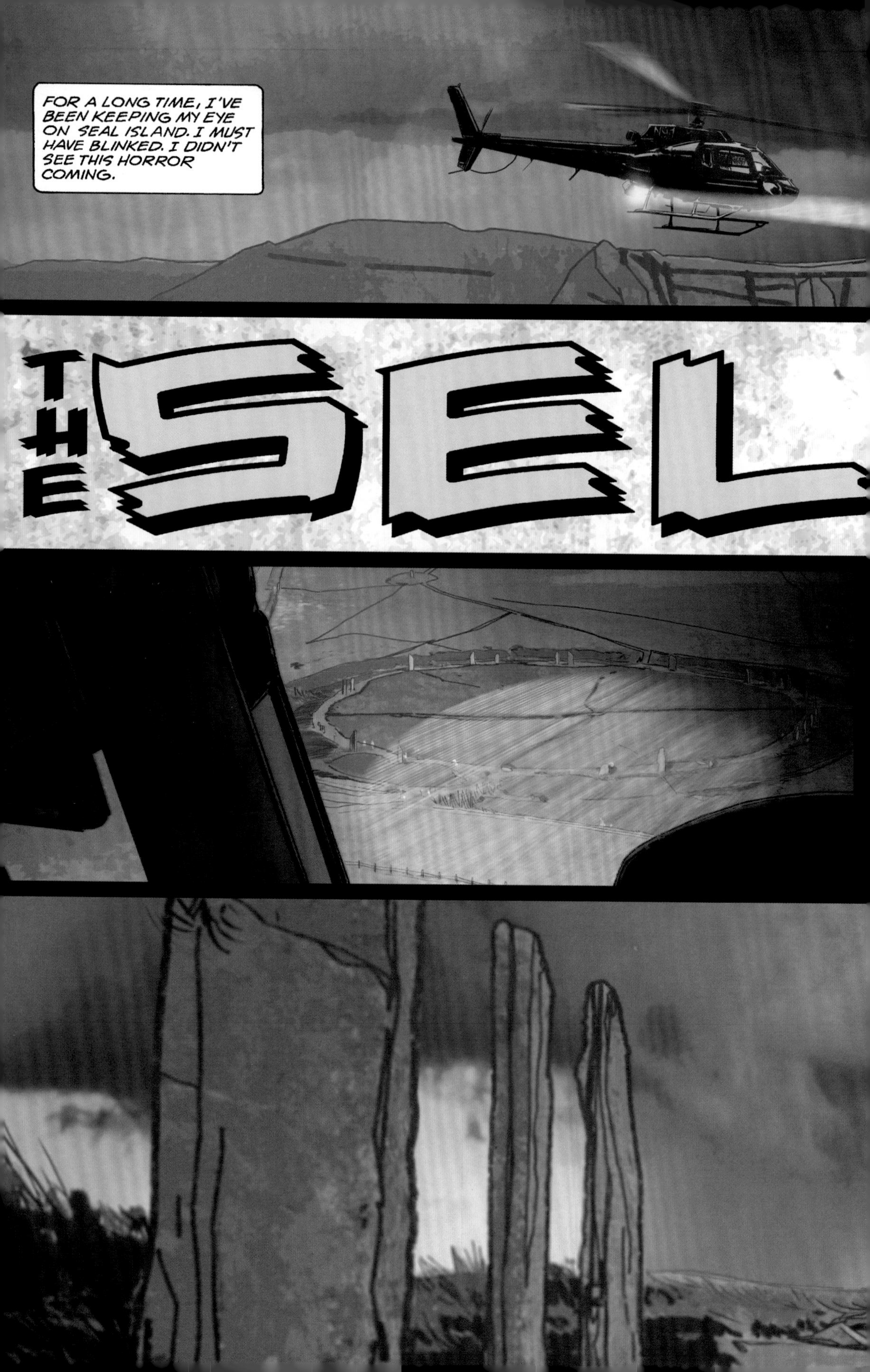
FOR A LONG TIME, I'VE BEEN KEEPING MY EYE ON SEAL ISLAND. I MUST HAVE BLINKED. I DIDN'T SEE THIS HORROR COMING.
THE SEL

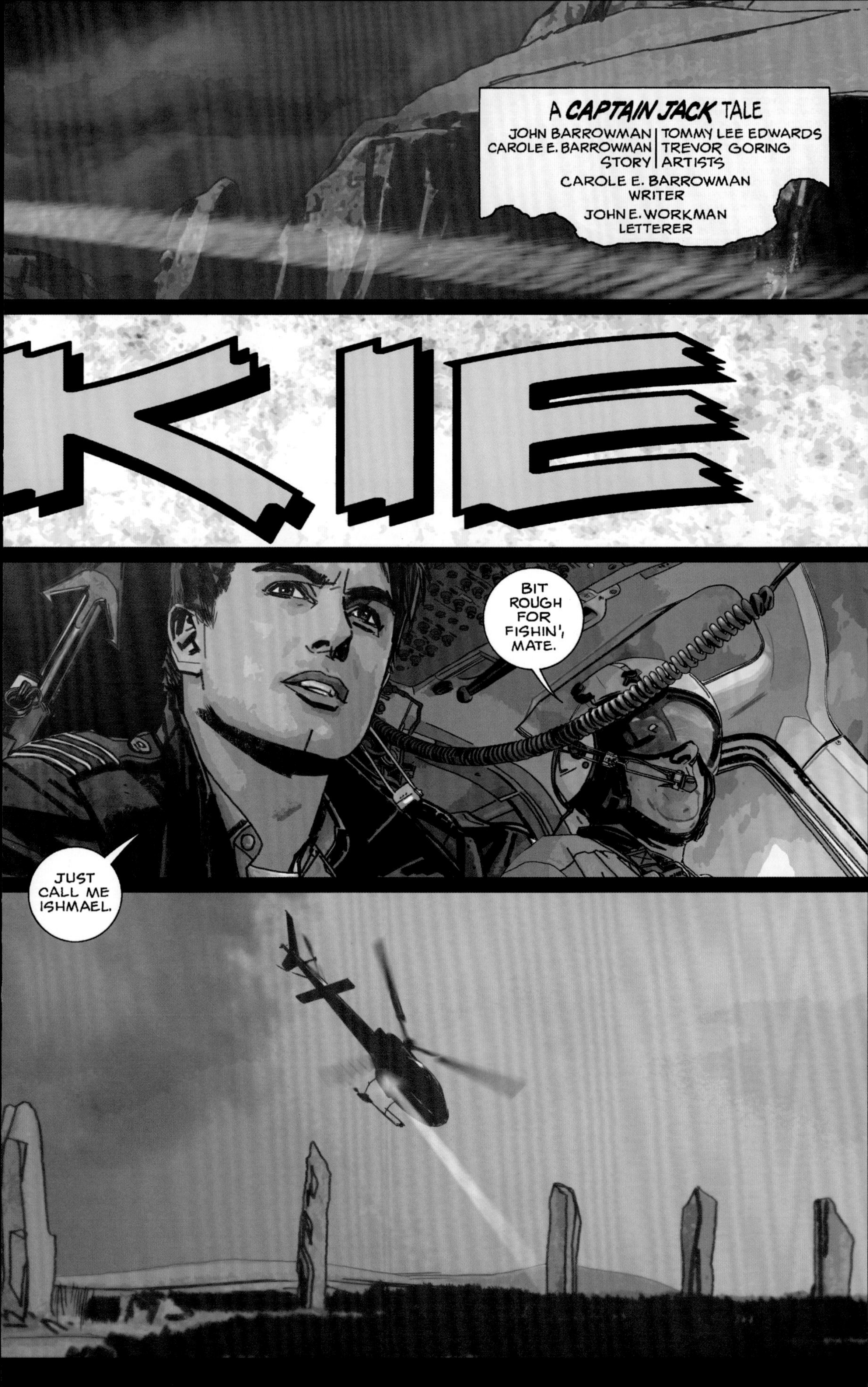
A CAPTAIN JACK TALE
JOHN BARROWMAN CAROLE E. BARROWMAN STORY
TOMMY LEE EDWARDS TREVOR GORING ARTISTS
CAROLE E. BARROWMAN WRITER
JOHN E. WORKMAN LETTERER
KIE
BIT ROUGH FOR FISHIN', MATE.
JUST CALL ME ISHMAEL.

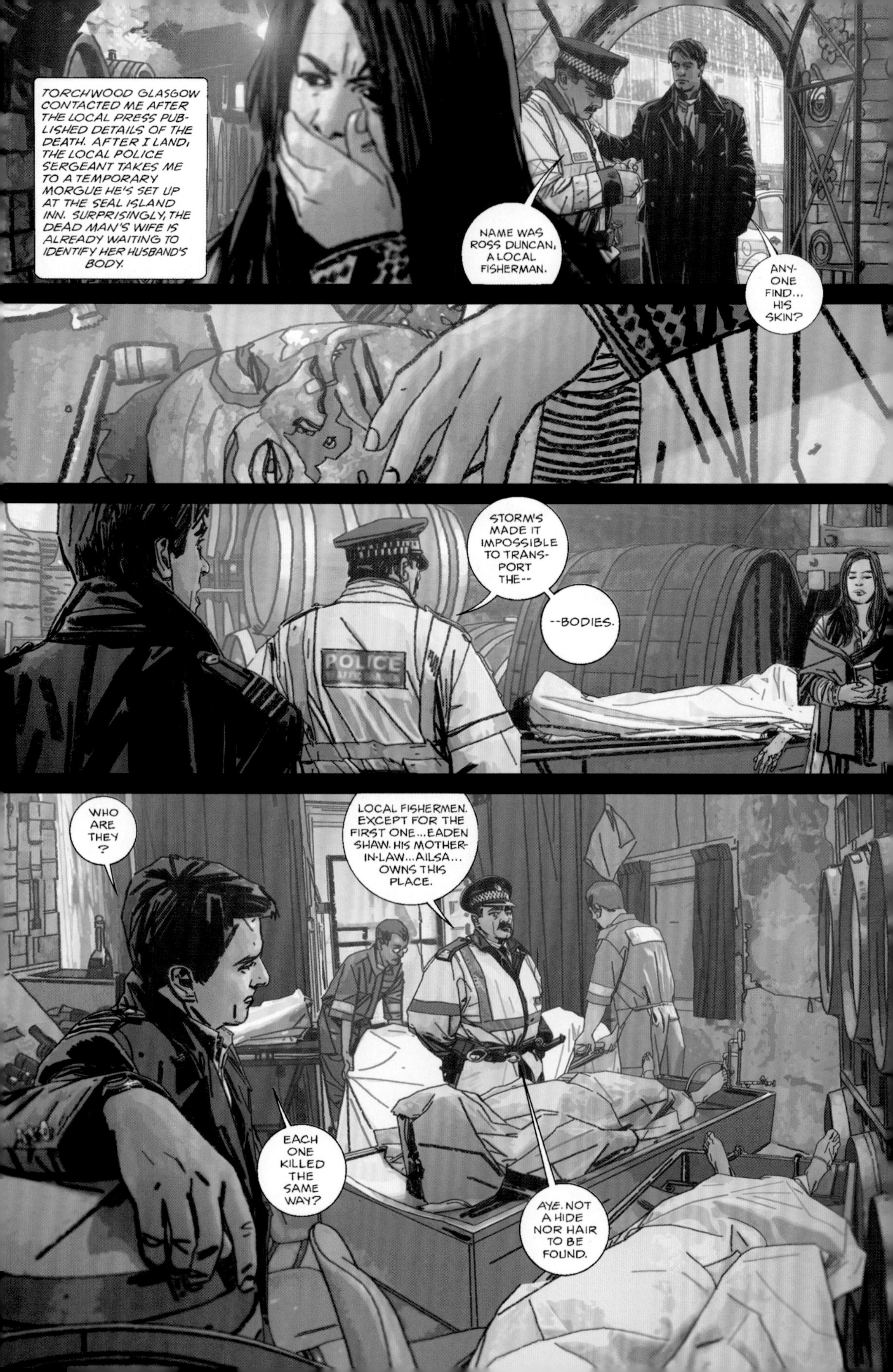
TORCHWOOD GLASGOW CONTACTED ME AFTER THE LOCAL PRESS PUBLISHED DETAILS OF THE DEATH. AFTER I LAND, THE LOCAL POLICE SERGEANT TAKES ME TO A TEMPORARY MORGUE HE'S SET UP AT THE SEAL ISLAND INN. SURPRISINGLY, THE DEAD MAN'S WIFE IS ALREADY WAITING TO IDENTIFY HER HUSBAND'S BODY.
NAME WAS ROSS DUNCAN, A LOCAL FISHERMAN.
ANY-ONE FIND... HIS SKIN?
STORM'S MADE IT IMPOSSIBLE TO TRANS-PORT THE--
--BODIES.
POLICE
WHO ARE THEY ?
LOCAL FISHERMEN. EXCEPT FOR THE FIRST ONE...EADEN SHAW. HIS MOTHER-IN-LAW...AILSA... OWNS THIS PLACE.
EACH ONE KILLED THE SAME WAY?
AYE. NOT A HIDE NOR HAIR TO BE FOUND.

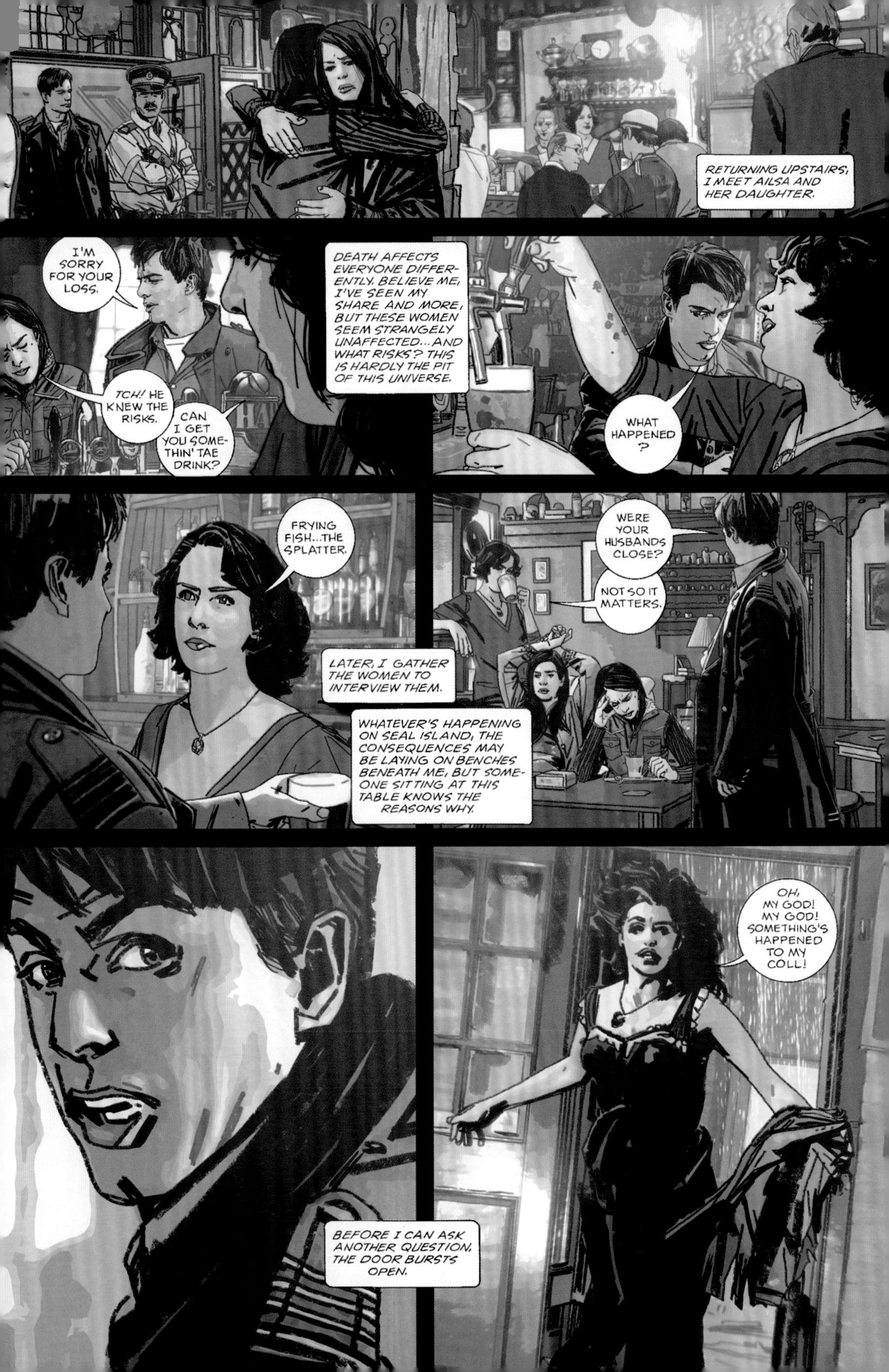

RETURNING UPSTAIRS, I MEET AILSA AND HER DAUGHTER.
I'M SORRY FOR YOUR LOSS.
TCH! HE KNEW THE RISKS.
CAN I GET YOU SOMETHIN' TAE DRINK?
DEATH AFFECTS EVERYONE DIFFERENTLY. BELIEVE ME, I'VE SEEN MY SHARE AND MORE, BUT THESE WOMEN SEEM STRANGELY UNAFFECTED... AND WHAT RISKS? THIS IS HARDLY THE PIT OF THIS UNIVERSE.
WHAT HAPPENED?
FRYING FISH... THE SPLATTER.
LATER, I GATHER THE WOMEN TO INTERVIEW THEM.
WHATEVER'S HAPPENING ON SEAL ISLAND, THE CONSEQUENCES MAY BE LAYING ON BENCHES BENEATH ME, BUT SOMEONE SITTING AT THIS TABLE KNOWS THE REASONS WHY.
WERE YOUR HUSBANDS CLOSE?
NOT SO IT MATTERS.
BEFORE I CAN ASK ANOTHER QUESTION, THE DOOR BURSTS OPEN.
OH, MY GOD! MY GOD! SOMETHING'S HAPPENED TO MY COLL!

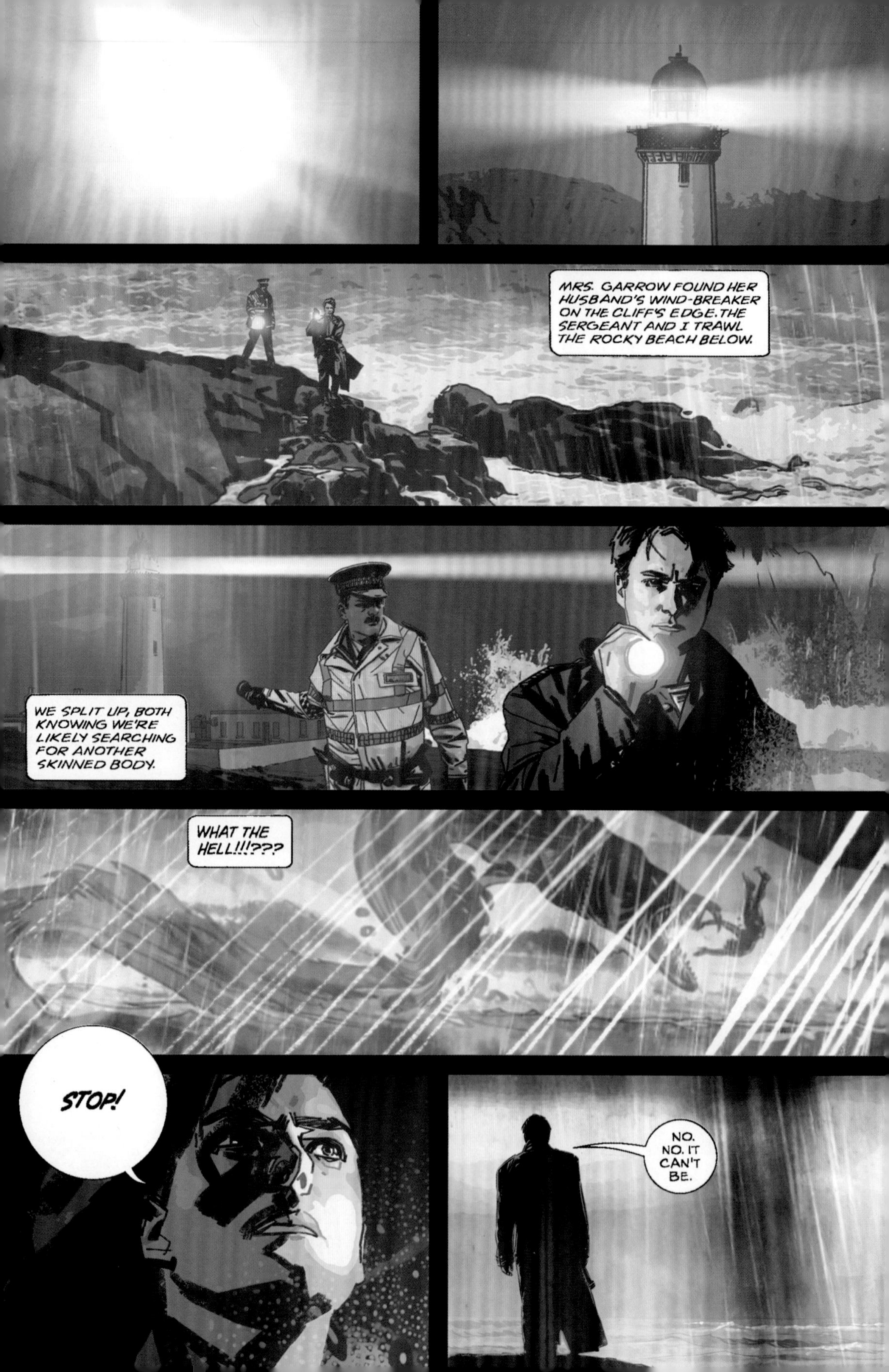
MRS. GARROW FOUND HER HUSBAND'S WIND-BREAKER ON THE CLIFF'S EDGE. THE SERGEANT AND I TRAWL THE ROCKY BEACH BELOW.
WE SPLIT UP, BOTH KNOWING WE'RE LIKELY SEARCHING FOR ANOTHER SKINNED BODY.
WHAT THE HELL!!!???
STOP!
NO. NO. IT CAN'T BE.

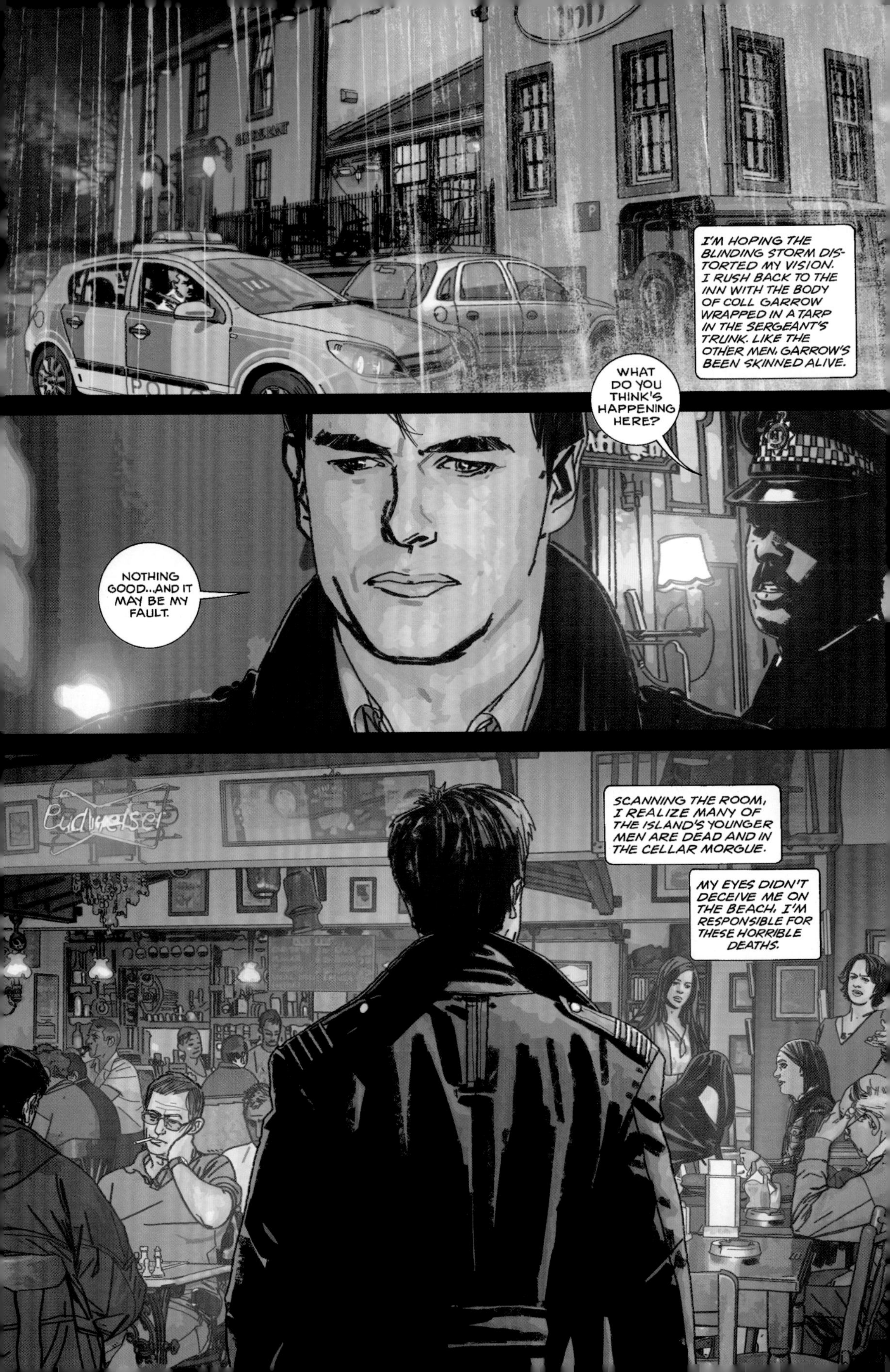
I'M HOPING THE BLINDING STORM DISTORTED MY VISION. I RUSH BACK TO THE INN WITH THE BODY OF COLL GARROW WRAPPED IN A TARP IN THE SERGEANT'S TRUNK. LIKE THE OTHER MEN, GARROW'S BEEN SKINNED ALIVE.
WHAT DO YOU THINK'S HAPPENING HERE?
NOTHING GOOD...AND IT MAY BE MY FAULT.
SCANNING THE ROOM, I REALIZE MANY OF THE ISLAND'S YOUNGER MEN ARE DEAD AND IN THE CELLAR MORGUE.
MY EYES DIDN'T DECEIVE ME ON THE BEACH. I'M RESPONSIBLE FOR THESE HORRIBLE DEATHS.

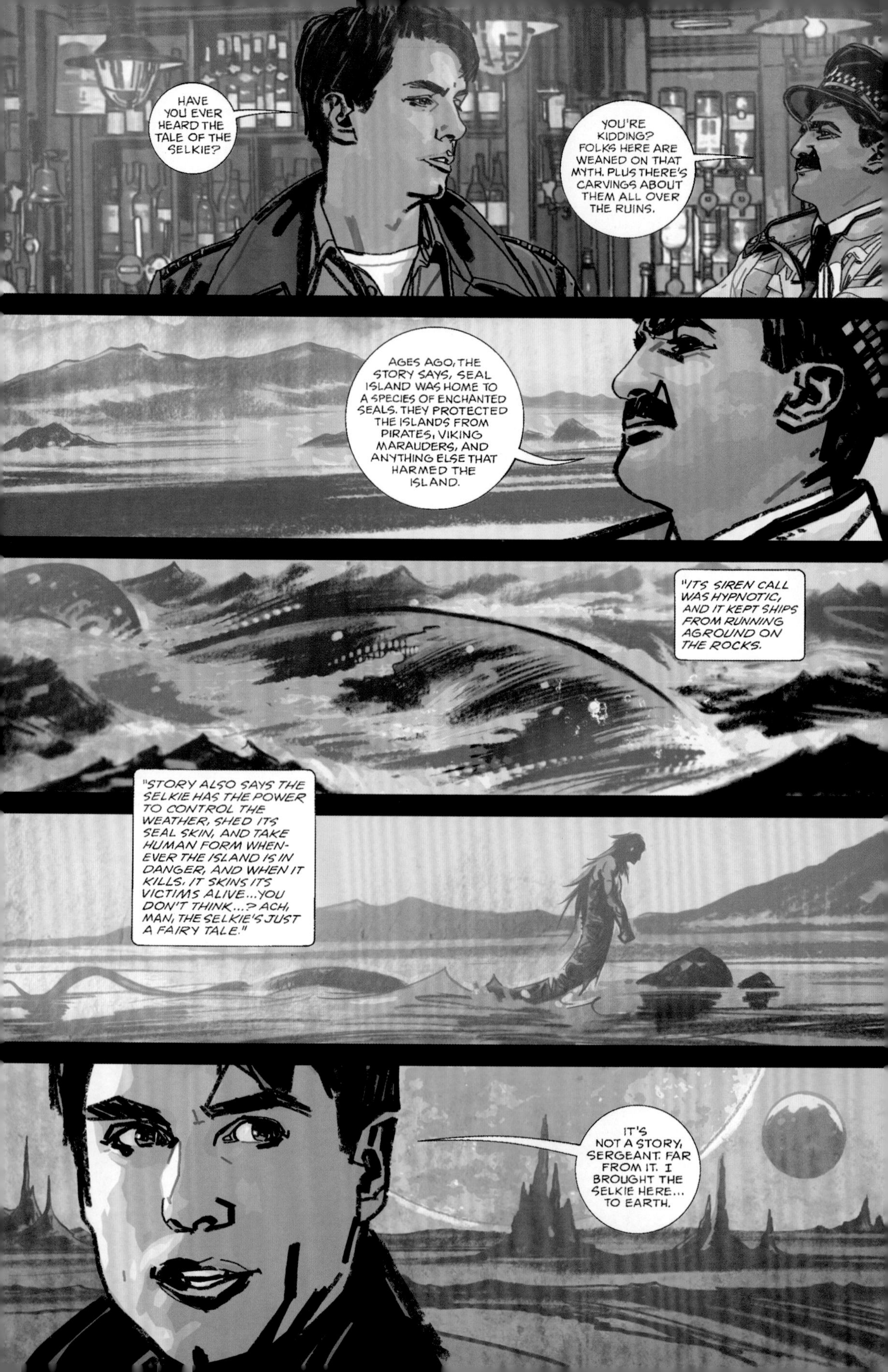
HAVE YOU EVER HEARD THE TALE OF THE SELKIE?
YOU'RE KIDDING? FOLKS HERE ARE WEANED ON THAT MYTH. PLUS THERE'S CARVINGS ABOUT THEM ALL OVER THE RUINS.
AGES AGO, THE STORY SAYS, SEAL ISLAND WAS HOME TO A SPECIES OF ENCHANTED SEALS. THEY PROTECTED THE ISLANDS FROM PIRATES, VIKING MARAUDERS, AND ANYTHING ELSE THAT HARMED THE ISLAND.
"ITS SIREN CALL WAS HYPNOTIC, AND IT KEPT SHIPS FROM RUNNING AGROUND ON THE ROCKS.
"STORY ALSO SAYS THE SELKIE HAS THE POWER TO CONTROL THE WEATHER, SHED ITS SEAL SKIN, AND TAKE HUMAN FORM WHENEVER THE ISLAND IS IN DANGER, AND WHEN IT KILLS, IT SKINS ITS VICTIMS ALIVE...YOU DON'T THINK...? ACH, MAN, THE SELKIE'S JUST A FAIRY TALE."
IT'S NOT A STORY, SERGEANT. FAR FROM IT. I BROUGHT THE SELKIE HERE... TO EARTH.

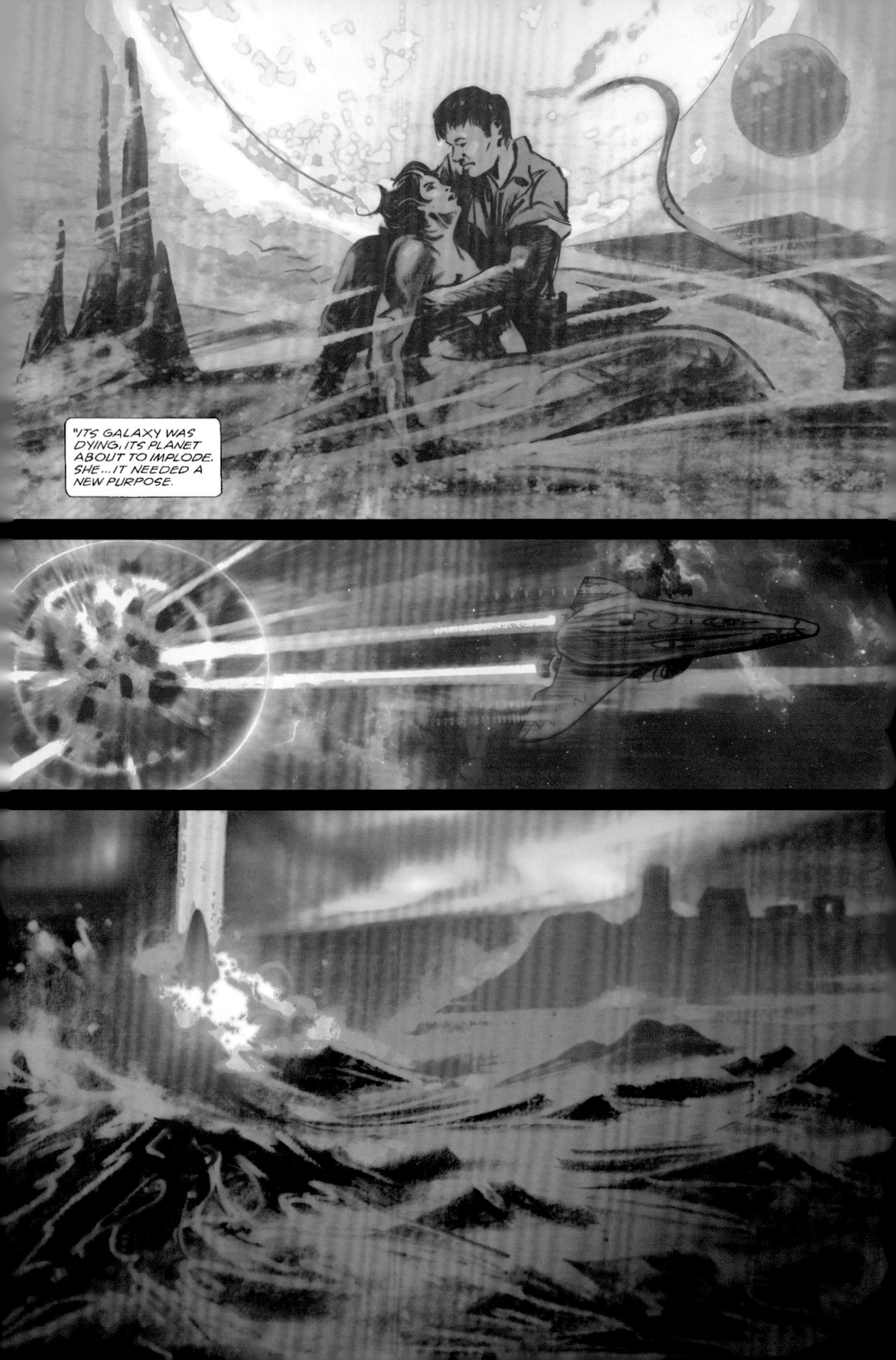
"ITS GALAXY WAS DYING, ITS PLANET ABOUT TO IMPLODE. SHE... IT NEEDED A NEW PURPOSE.

"I KNOW NOW IT WAS THE WRONG THING TO DO--SELFISH OF ME--BECAUSE IT'S EVOLVED --BUT I COULDN'T LET HER DIE."

Husband Released

MILE FRONT
CIFIC NEW
TER OF WAR

The Kirkwall Police have released Eaden Shaw, 23, after his wife refused to press charges

prior arrests

TOM NESBIT

Assault (DV) 8-11-8
DUI 22-9-8
DUI 7-7-7
OCCUPATION:
North Shore Fisheries

ROSS DUNCAN

Assault (DV) 5-7-5

served 6 months

OCCUPATION:
North Shore Fisheries

IT'S FOUND A NEW PURPOSE.

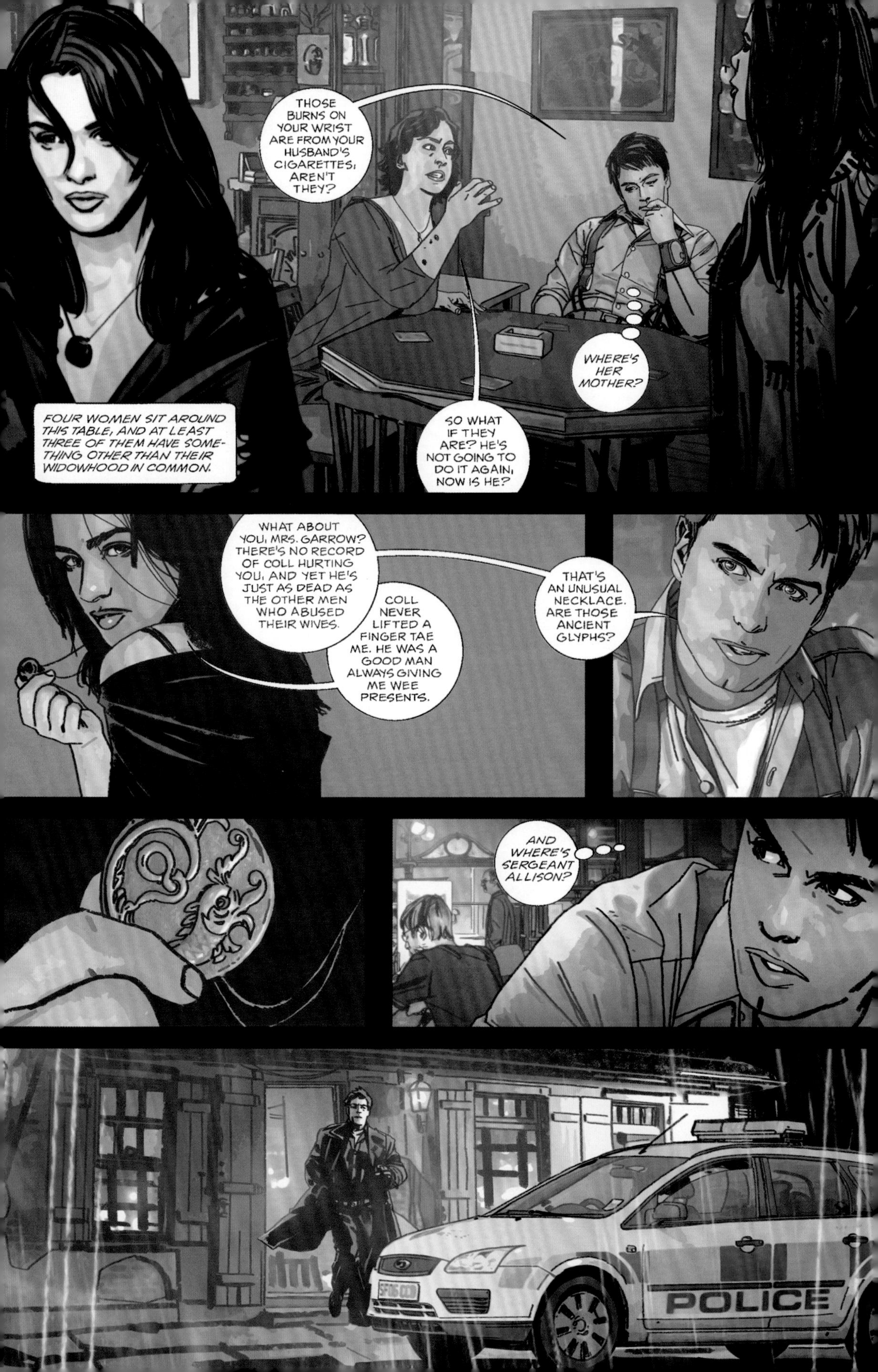

FOUR WOMEN SIT AROUND THIS TABLE, AND AT LEAST THREE OF THEM HAVE SOMETHING OTHER THAN THEIR WIDOWHOOD IN COMMON.
THOSE BURNS ON YOUR WRIST ARE FROM YOUR HUSBAND'S CIGARETTES, AREN'T THEY?
SO WHAT IF THEY ARE? HE'S NOT GOING TO DO IT AGAIN, NOW IS HE?
WHERE'S HER MOTHER?
WHAT ABOUT YOU, MRS. GARROW? THERE'S NO RECORD OF COLL HURTING YOU, AND YET HE'S JUST AS DEAD AS THE OTHER MEN WHO ABUSED THEIR WIVES.
COLL NEVER LIFTED A FINGER TAE ME. HE WAS A GOOD MAN ALWAYS GIVING ME WEE PRESENTS.
THAT'S AN UNUSUAL NECKLACE. ARE THOSE ANCIENT GLYPHS?
AND WHERE'S SERGEANT ALLISON?
POLICE

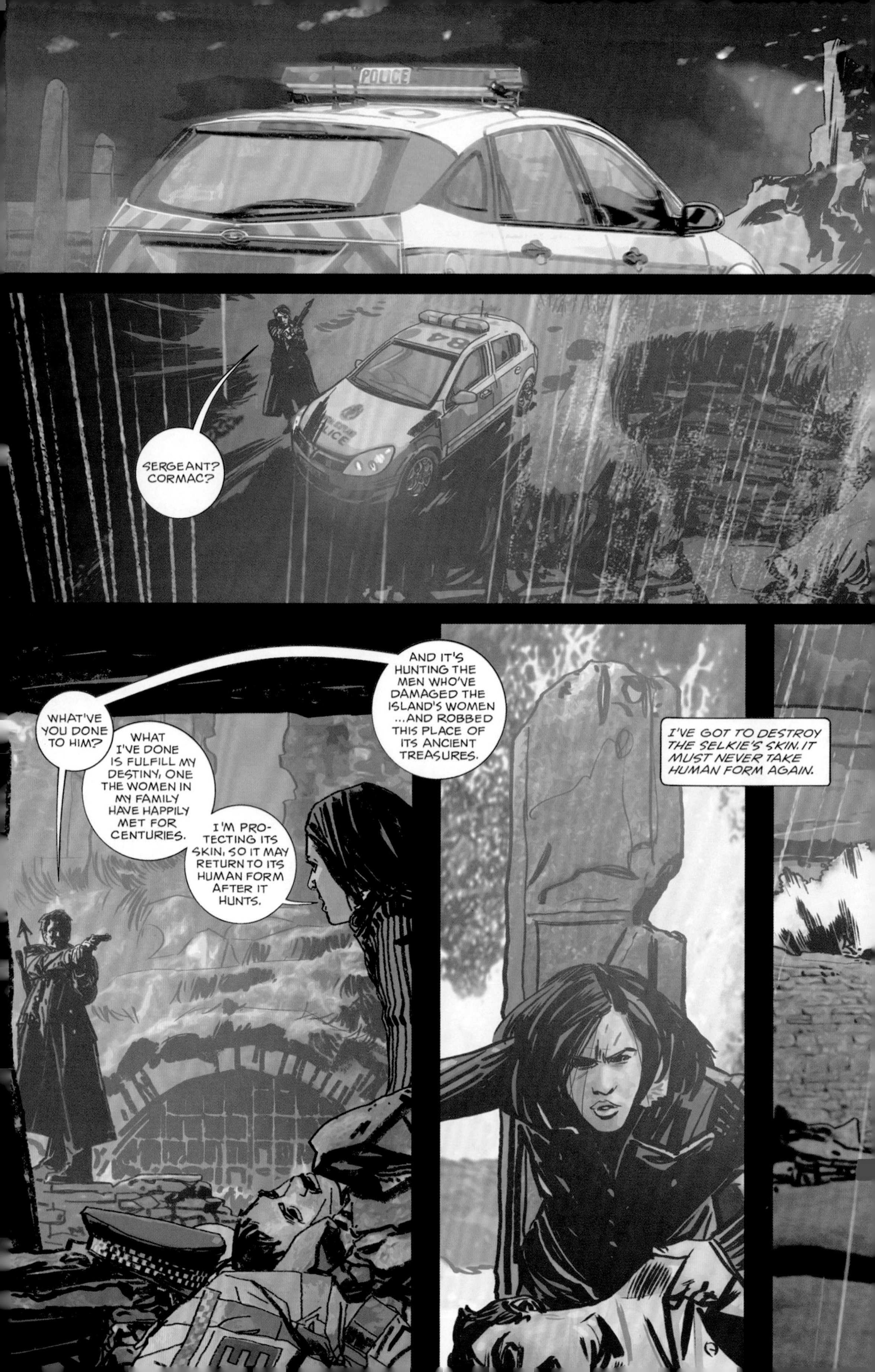
POLICE
SERGEANT? CORMAC?
WHAT'VE YOU DONE TO HIM?
WHAT I'VE DONE IS FULFILL MY DESTINY, ONE THE WOMEN IN MY FAMILY HAVE HAPPILY MET FOR CENTURIES.
I'M PROTECTING ITS SKIN, SO IT MAY RETURN TO ITS HUMAN FORM AFTER IT HUNTS.
AND IT'S HUNTING THE MEN WHO'VE DAMAGED THE ISLAND'S WOMEN ...AND ROBBED THIS PLACE OF ITS ANCIENT TREASURES.
I'VE GOT TO DESTROY THE SELKIE'S SKIN. IT MUST NEVER TAKE HUMAN FORM AGAIN.

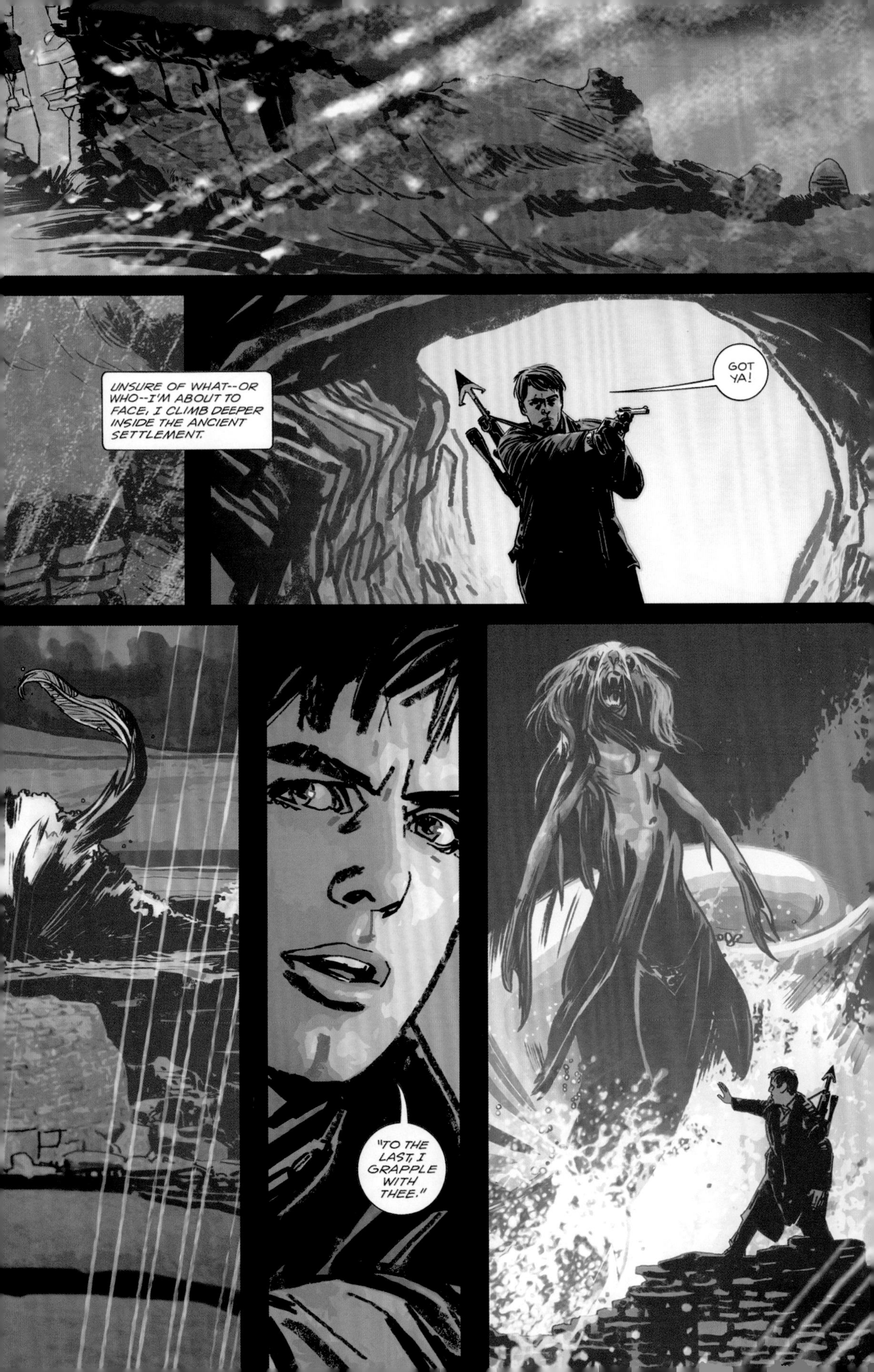
UNSURE OF WHAT--OR WHO--I'M ABOUT TO FACE, I CLIMB DEEPER INSIDE THE ANCIENT SETTLEMENT.
GOT YA!
"TO THE LAST, I GRAPPLE WITH THEE."

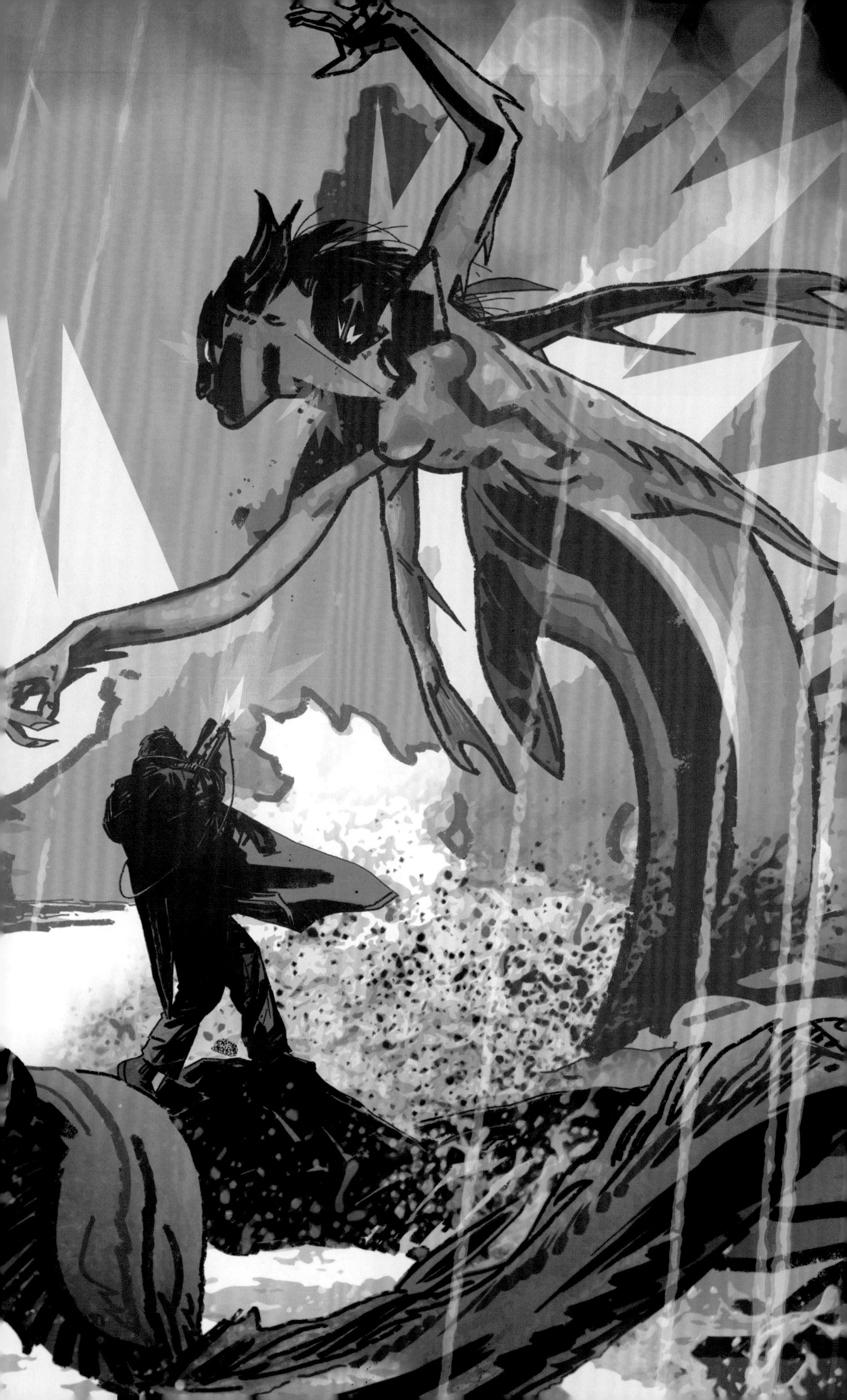

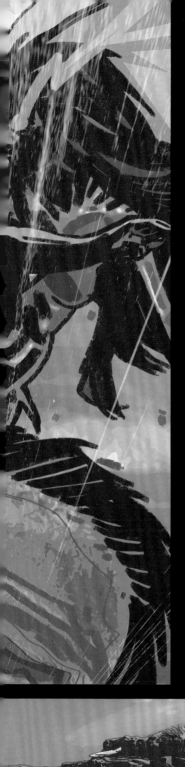

"THEN THE GREAT SHROUD OF THE SEA ROLLED ON AS IT ROLLED FIVE THOUSAND YEARS AGO."

END

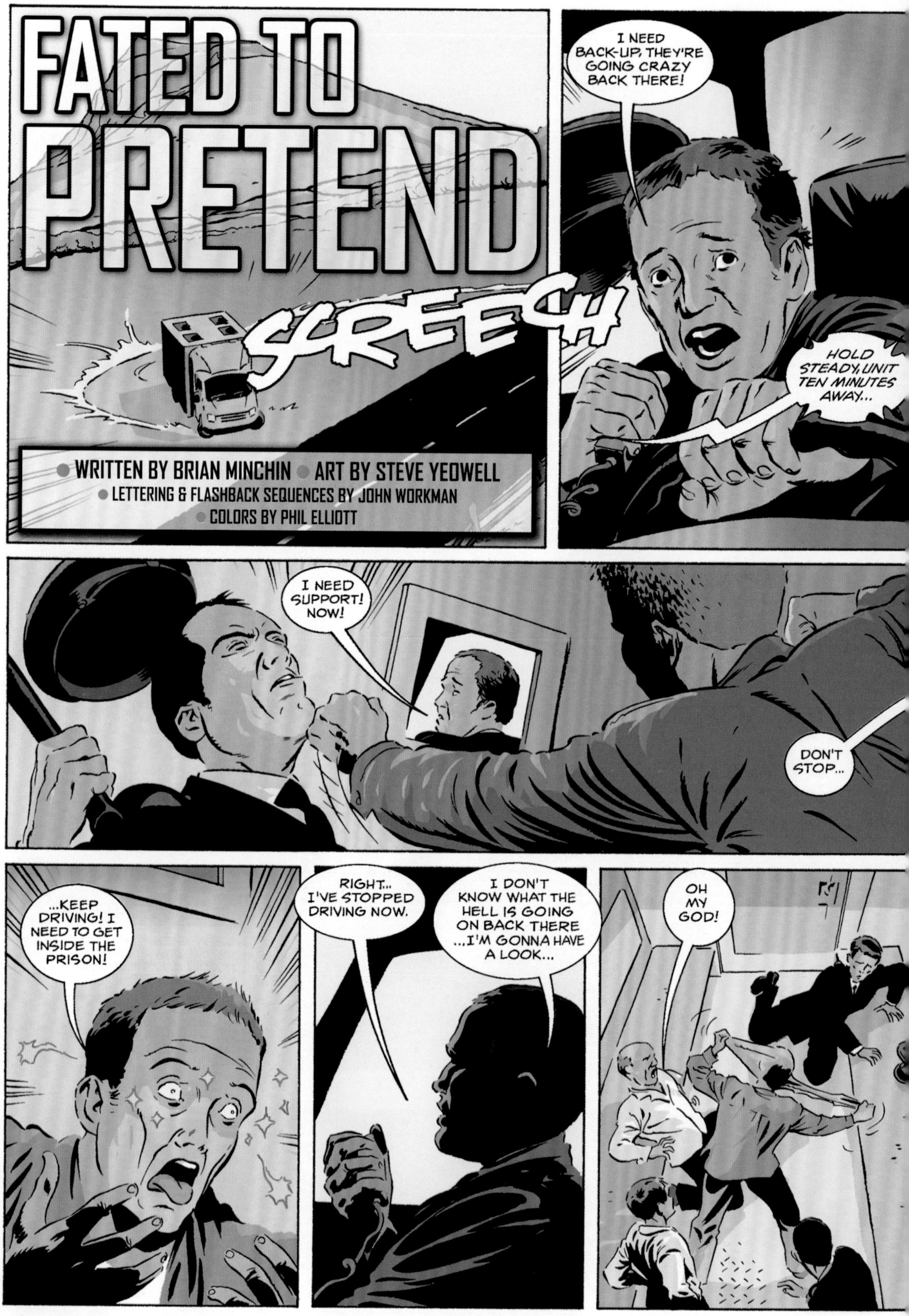
FATED TO PRETEND
SCREECH
WRITTEN BY BRIAN MINCHIN
ART BY STEVE YEOWELL
LETTERING & FLASHBACK SEQUENCES BY JOHN WORKMAN
COLORS BY PHIL ELLIOTT
I NEED BACK-UP, THEY'RE GOING CRAZY BACK THERE!
HOLD STEADY, UNIT TEN MINUTES AWAY...
I NEED SUPPORT! NOW!
DON'T STOP...
...KEEP DRIVING! I NEED TO GET INSIDE THE PRISON!
RIGHT... I'VE STOPPED DRIVING NOW.
I DON'T KNOW WHAT THE HELL IS GOING ON BACK THERE ...I'M GONNA HAVE A LOOK...
OH MY GOD!

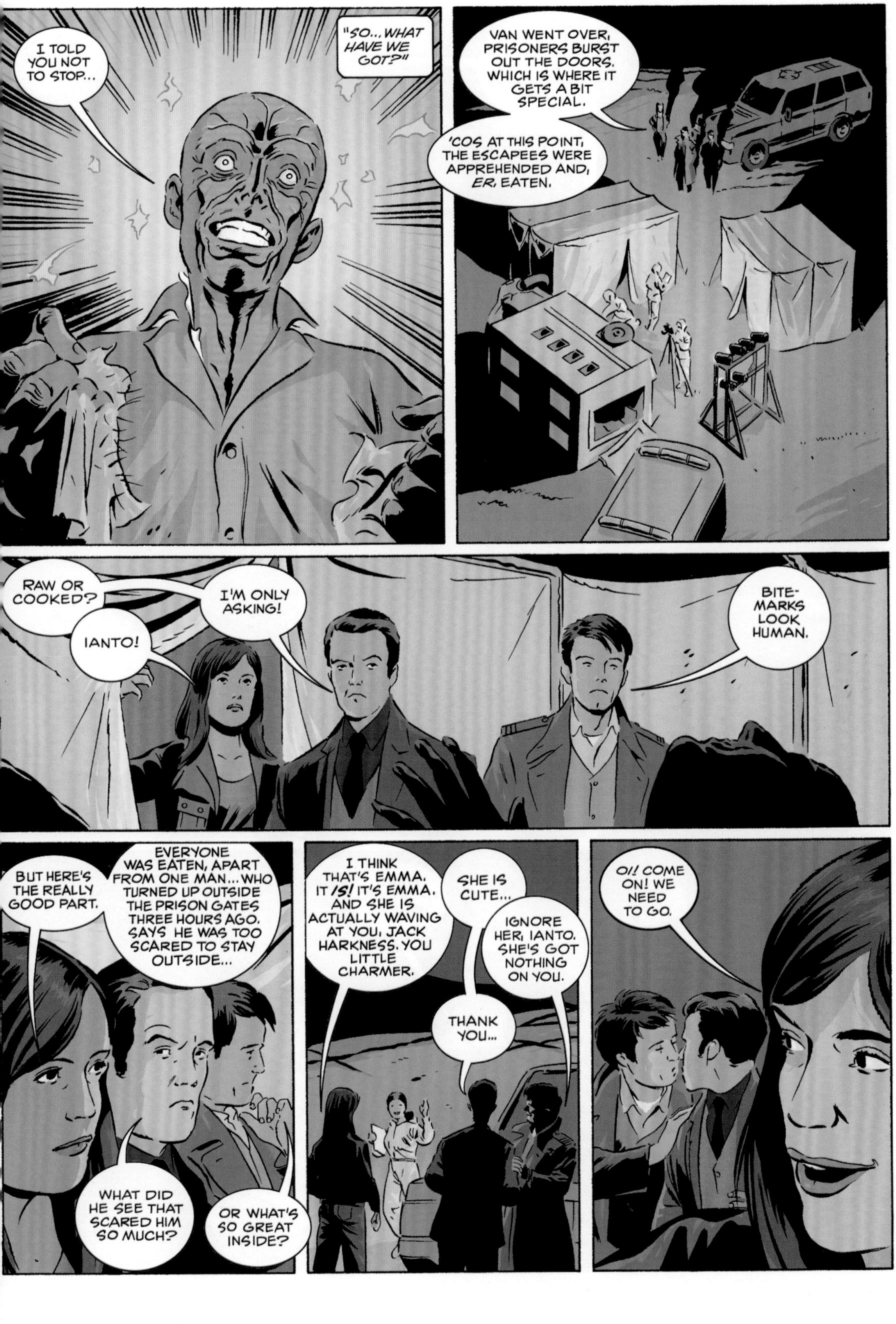
"SO... WHAT HAVE WE GOT?"
I TOLD YOU NOT TO STOP...
VAN WENT OVER, PRISONERS BURST OUT THE DOORS. WHICH IS WHERE IT GETS A BIT SPECIAL.
'COS AT THIS POINT, THE ESCAPEES WERE APPREHENDED AND, ER, EATEN.
RAW OR COOKED?
IANTO!
I'M ONLY ASKING!
BITE-MARKS LOOK HUMAN.
BUT HERE'S THE REALLY GOOD PART.
EVERYONE WAS EATEN, APART FROM ONE MAN... WHO TURNED UP OUTSIDE THE PRISON GATES THREE HOURS AGO. SAYS HE WAS TOO SCARED TO STAY OUTSIDE...
WHAT DID HE SEE THAT SCARED HIM SO MUCH?
OR WHAT'S SO GREAT INSIDE?
I THINK THAT'S EMMA. IT IS! IT'S EMMA. AND SHE IS ACTUALLY WAVING AT YOU, JACK HARKNESS. YOU LITTLE CHARMER.
SHE IS CUTE...
IGNORE HER, IANTO. SHE'S GOT NOTHING ON YOU.
THANK YOU...
OI! COME ON! WE NEED TO GO.

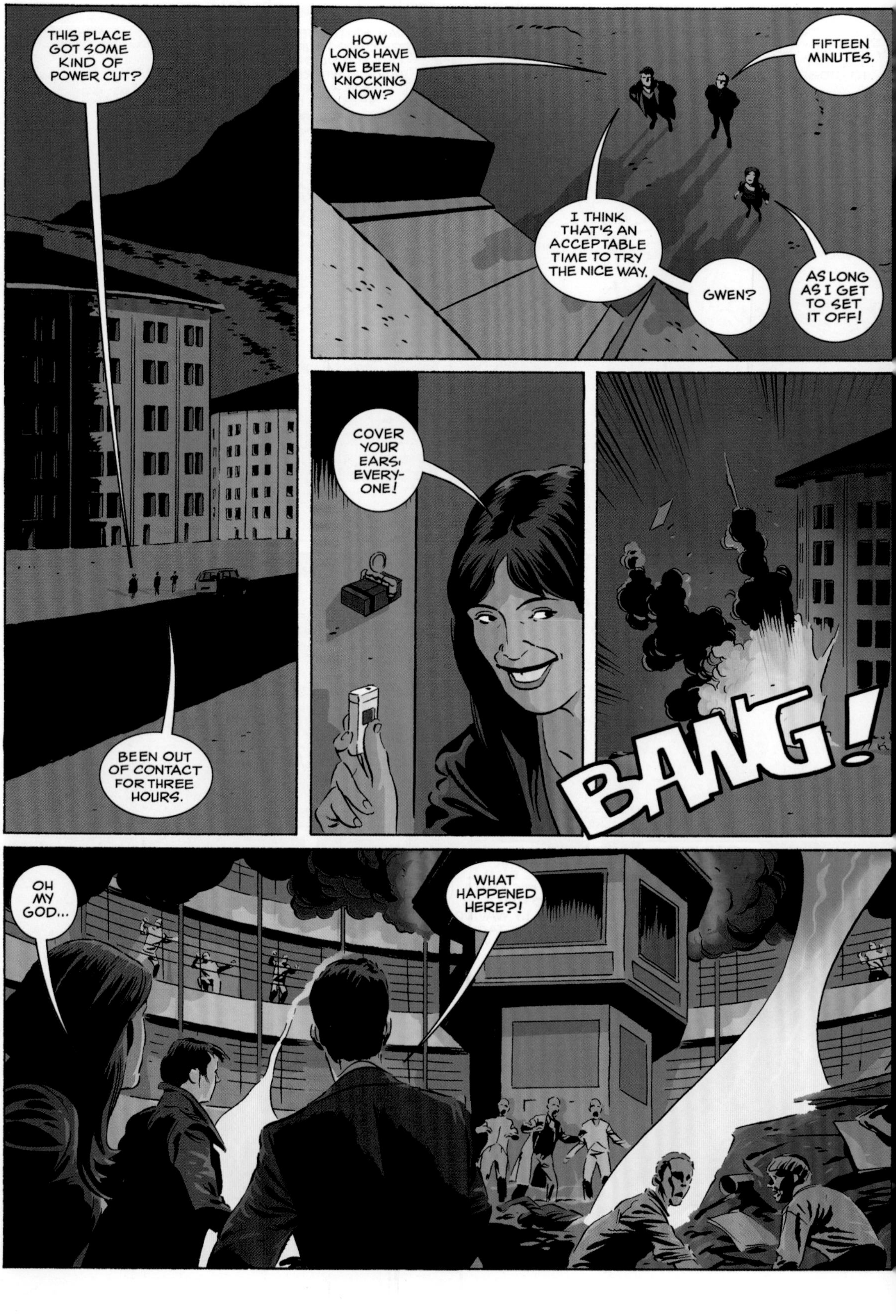
THIS PLACE GOT SOME KIND OF POWER CUT?
BEEN OUT OF CONTACT FOR THREE HOURS.
HOW LONG HAVE WE BEEN KNOCKING NOW?
FIFTEEN MINUTES.
I THINK THAT'S AN ACCEPTABLE TIME TO TRY THE NICE WAY.
GWEN?
AS LONG AS I GET TO SET IT OFF!
COVER YOUR EARS, EVERY-ONE!
BANG!
OH MY GOD...
WHAT HAPPENED HERE?!

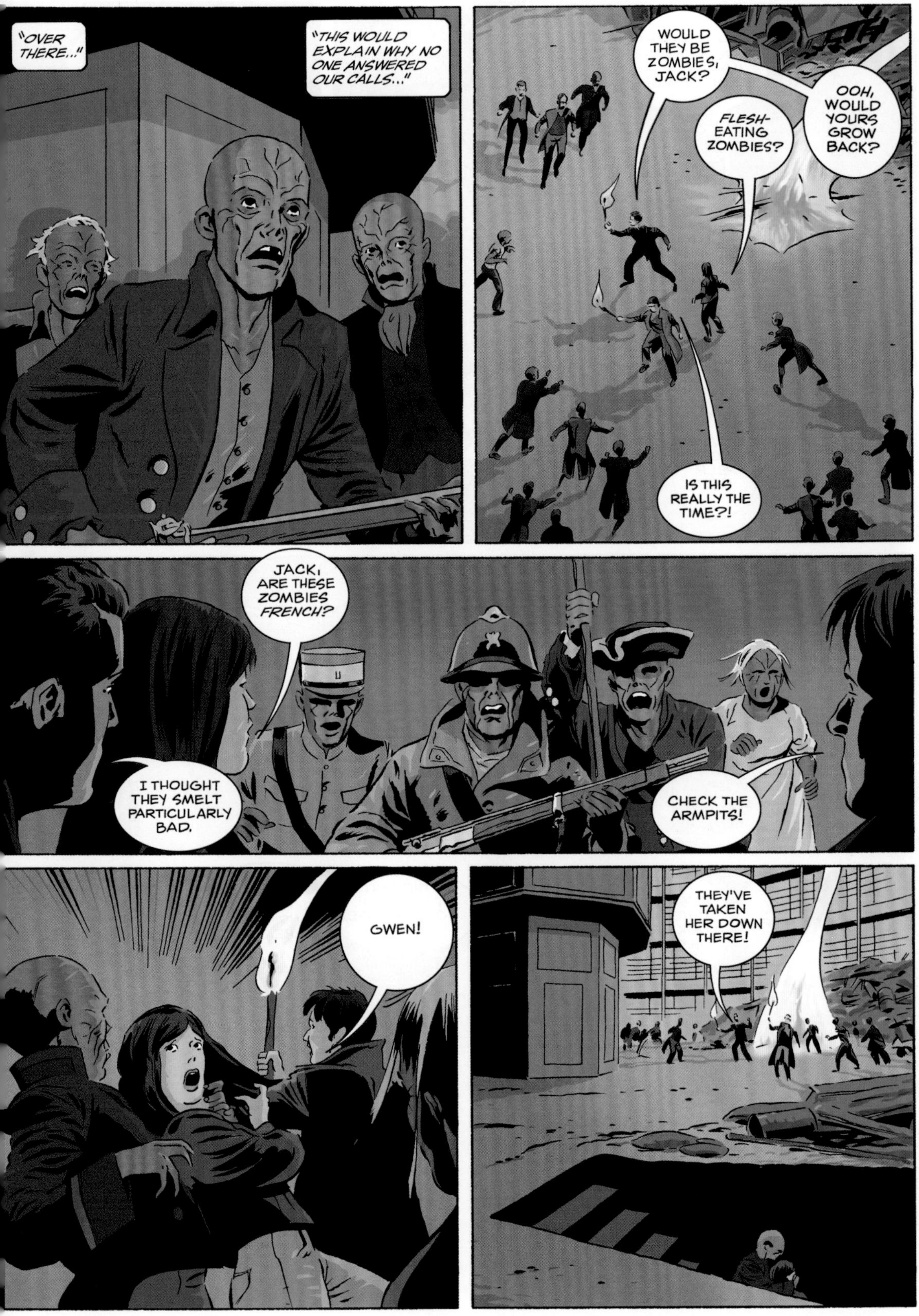
"OVER THERE..."
"THIS WOULD EXPLAIN WHY NO ONE ANSWERED OUR CALLS..."
WOULD THEY BE ZOMBIES, JACK?
OOH, WOULD YOURS GROW BACK?
FLESH-EATING ZOMBIES?
IS THIS REALLY THE TIME?!
JACK, ARE THESE ZOMBIES FRENCH?
I THOUGHT THEY SMELT PARTICULARLY BAD.
CHECK THE ARMPITS!
GWEN!
THEY'VE TAKEN HER DOWN THERE!

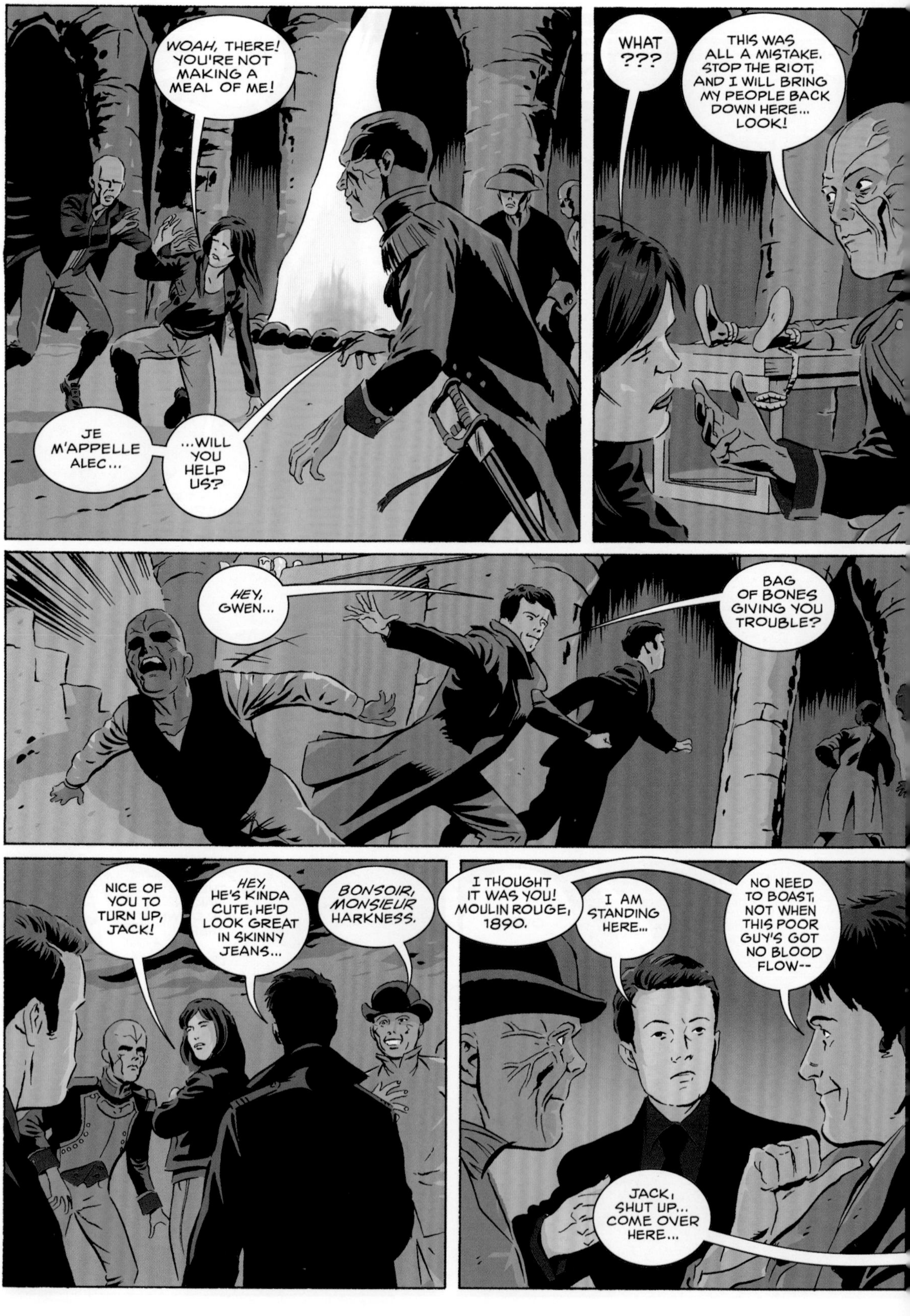
WOAH, THERE! YOU'RE NOT MAKING A MEAL OF ME!
JE M'APPELLE ALEC...
...WILL YOU HELP US?
WHAT ???
THIS WAS ALL A MISTAKE. STOP THE RIOT, AND I WILL BRING MY PEOPLE BACK DOWN HERE... LOOK!
HEY, GWEN...
BAG OF BONES GIVING YOU TROUBLE?
NICE OF YOU TO TURN UP, JACK!
HEY, HE'S KINDA CUTE, HE'D LOOK GREAT IN SKINNY JEANS...
BONSOIR, MONSIEUR HARKNESS.
I THOUGHT IT WAS YOU! MOULIN ROUGE, 1890.
I AM STANDING HERE...
NO NEED TO BOAST, NOT WHEN THIS POOR GUY'S GOT NO BLOOD FLOW--
JACK, SHUT UP... COME OVER HERE...

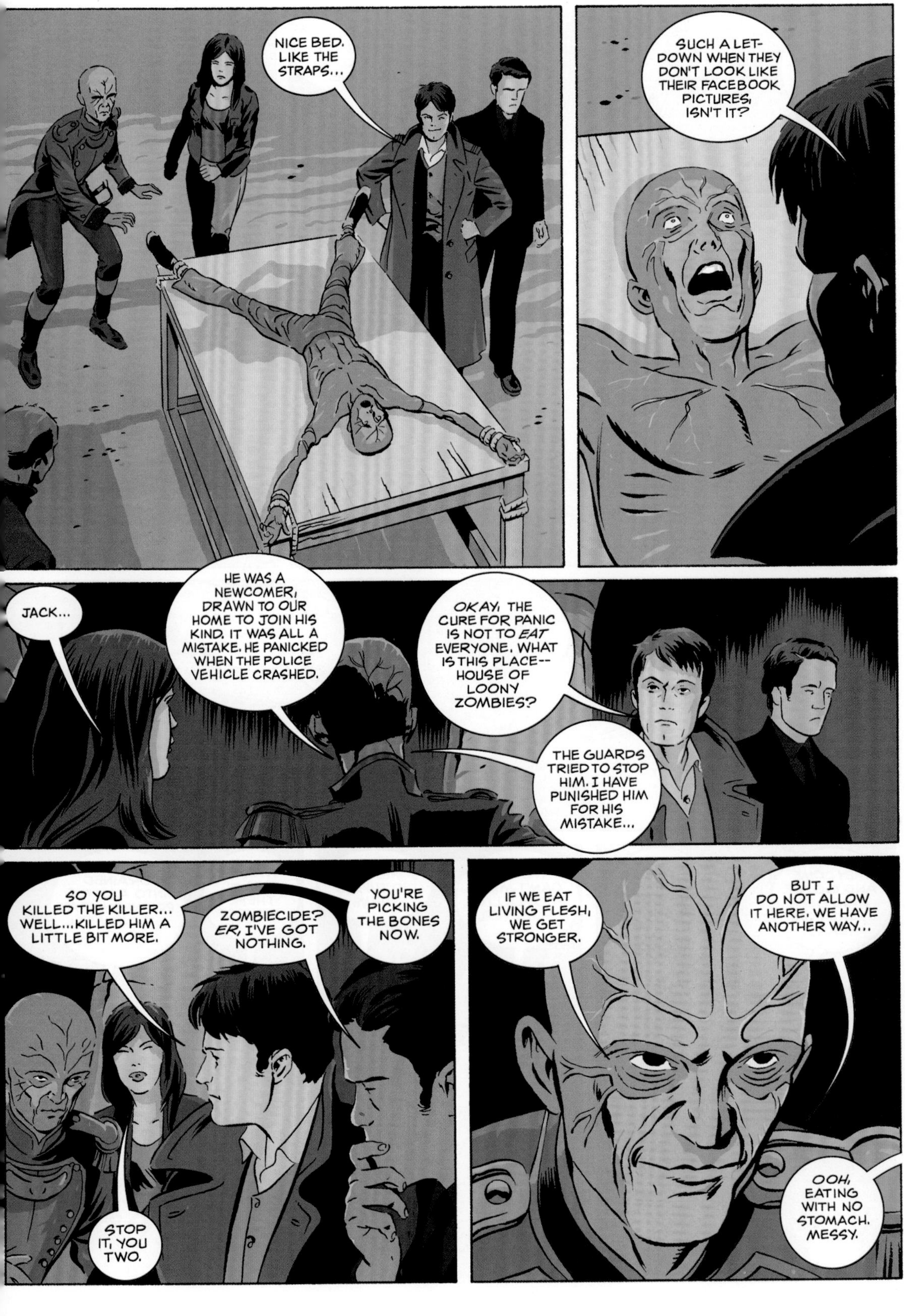
NICE BED. LIKE THE STRAPS...
SUCH A LET-DOWN WHEN THEY DON'T LOOK LIKE THEIR FACEBOOK PICTURES, ISN'T IT?
JACK...
HE WAS A NEWCOMER, DRAWN TO OUR HOME TO JOIN HIS KIND. IT WAS ALL A MISTAKE. HE PANICKED WHEN THE POLICE VEHICLE CRASHED.
OKAY, THE CURE FOR PANIC IS NOT TO EAT EVERYONE. WHAT IS THIS PLACE-- HOUSE OF LOONY ZOMBIES?
THE GUARDS TRIED TO STOP HIM. I HAVE PUNISHED HIM FOR HIS MISTAKE...
SO YOU KILLED THE KILLER... WELL...KILLED HIM A LITTLE BIT MORE.
ZOMBIECIDE? ER, I'VE GOT NOTHING.
YOU'RE PICKING THE BONES NOW.
STOP IT, YOU TWO.
IF WE EAT LIVING FLESH, WE GET STRONGER.
BUT I DO NOT ALLOW IT HERE. WE HAVE ANOTHER WAY...
OOH, EATING WITH NO STOMACH. MESSY.

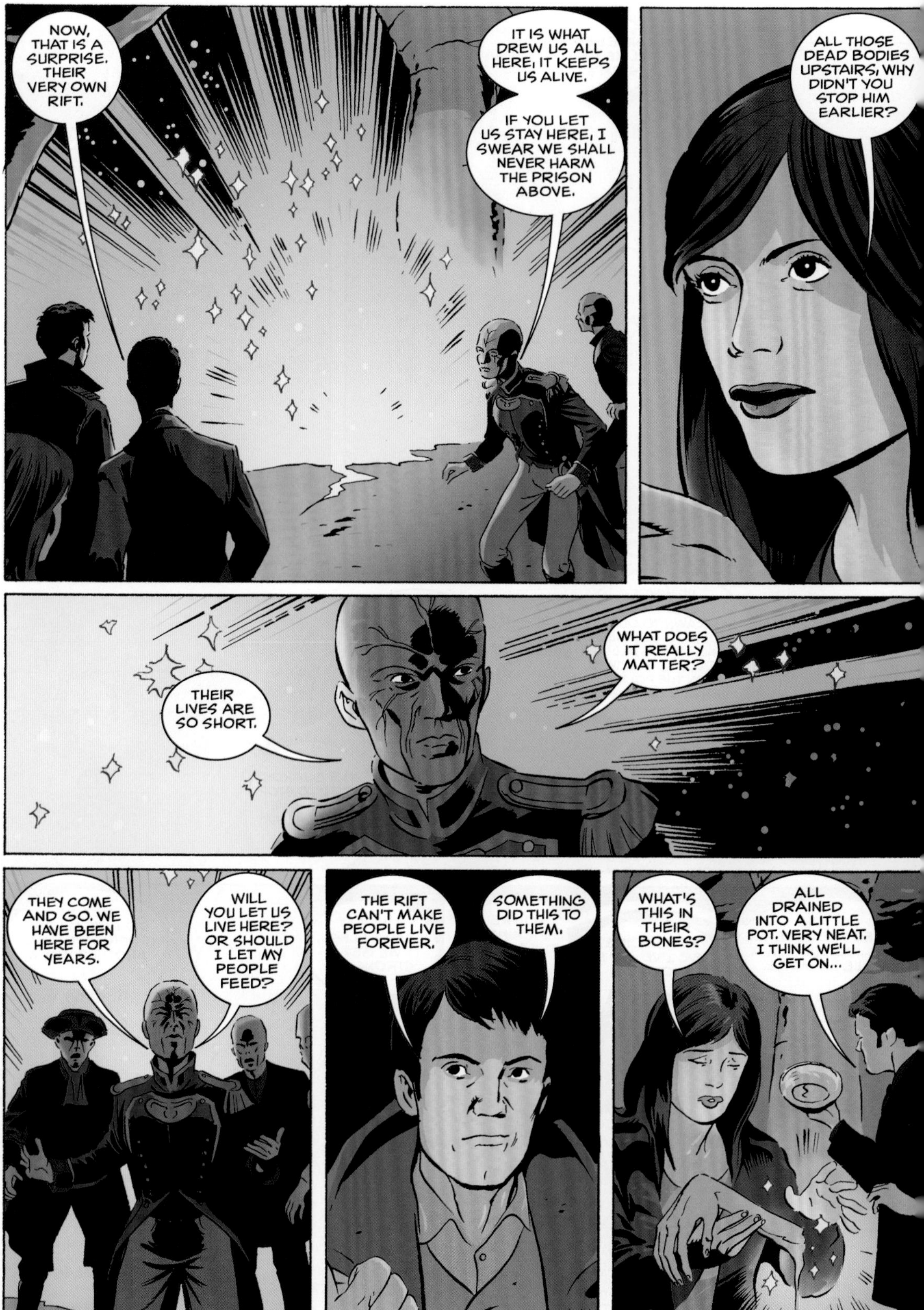
NOW, THAT IS A SURPRISE. THEIR VERY OWN RIFT.
IT IS WHAT DREW US ALL HERE, IT KEEPS US ALIVE.
IF YOU LET US STAY HERE, I SWEAR WE SHALL NEVER HARM THE PRISON ABOVE.
ALL THOSE DEAD BODIES UPSTAIRS, WHY DIDN'T YOU STOP HIM EARLIER?
THEIR LIVES ARE SO SHORT.
WHAT DOES IT REALLY MATTER?
THEY COME AND GO. WE HAVE BEEN HERE FOR YEARS.
WILL YOU LET US LIVE HERE? OR SHOULD I LET MY PEOPLE FEED?
THE RIFT CAN'T MAKE PEOPLE LIVE FOREVER.
SOMETHING DID THIS TO THEM.
WHAT'S THIS IN THEIR BONES?
ALL DRAINED INTO A LITTLE POT. VERY NEAT. I THINK WE'LL GET ON...

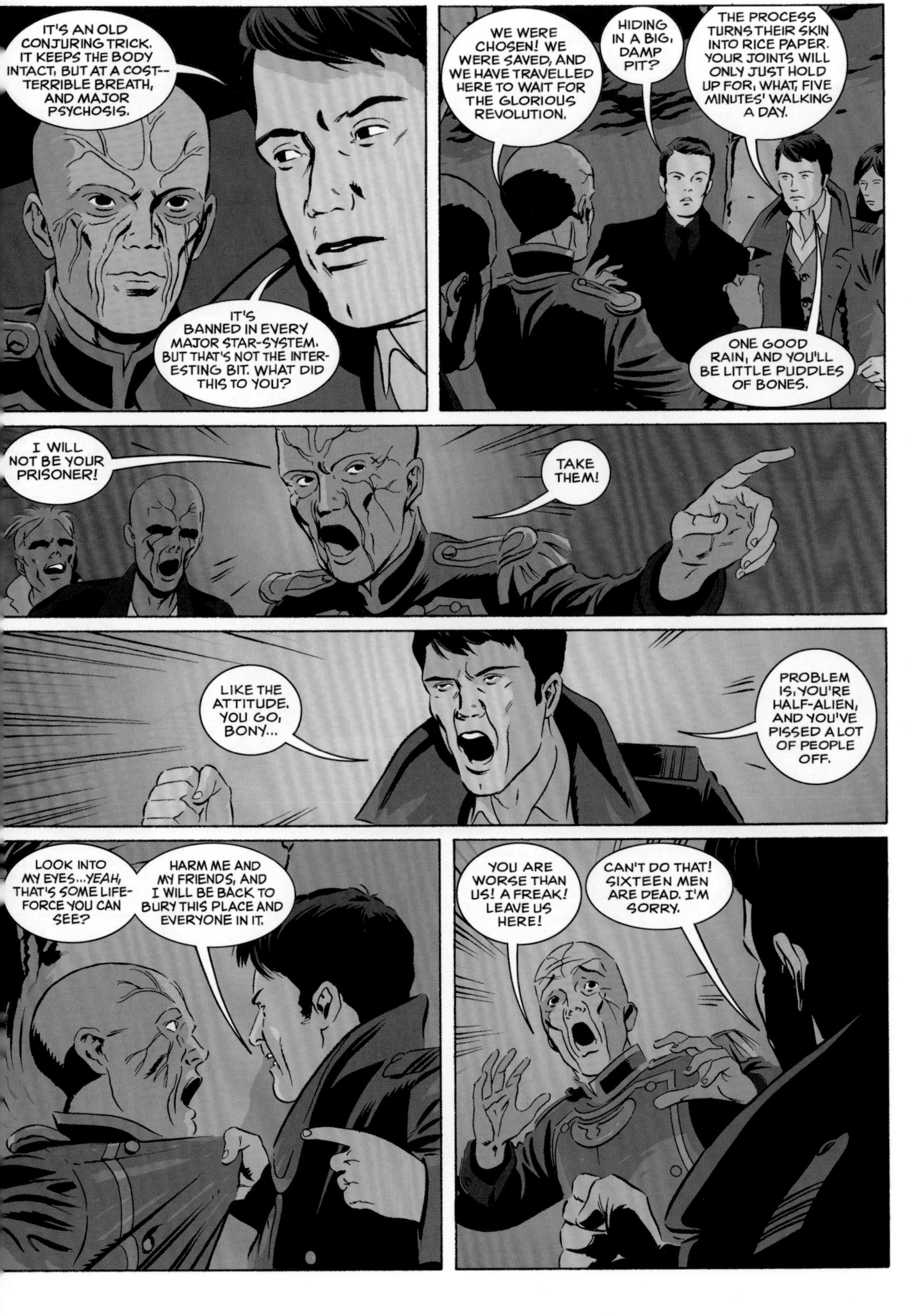
IT'S AN OLD CONJURING TRICK. IT KEEPS THE BODY INTACT, BUT AT A COST-- TERRIBLE BREATH, AND MAJOR PSYCHOSIS.
IT'S BANNED IN EVERY MAJOR STAR-SYSTEM. BUT THAT'S NOT THE INTERESTING BIT. WHAT DID THIS TO YOU?
WE WERE CHOSEN! WE WERE SAVED, AND WE HAVE TRAVELLED HERE TO WAIT FOR THE GLORIOUS REVOLUTION.
HIDING IN A BIG, DAMP PIT?
THE PROCESS TURNS THEIR SKIN INTO RICE PAPER. YOUR JOINTS WILL ONLY JUST HOLD UP FOR, WHAT, FIVE MINUTES' WALKING A DAY.
ONE GOOD RAIN, AND YOU'LL BE LITTLE PUDDLES OF BONES.
I WILL NOT BE YOUR PRISONER!
TAKE THEM!
LIKE THE ATTITUDE. YOU GO, BONY...
PROBLEM IS, YOU'RE HALF-ALIEN, AND YOU'VE PISSED A LOT OF PEOPLE OFF.
LOOK INTO MY EYES...*YEAH*, THAT'S SOME LIFE-FORCE YOU CAN SEE?
HARM ME AND MY FRIENDS, AND I WILL BE BACK TO BURY THIS PLACE AND EVERYONE IN IT.
YOU ARE WORSE THAN US! A FREAK! LEAVE US HERE!
CAN'T DO THAT! SIXTEEN MEN ARE DEAD. I'M SORRY.

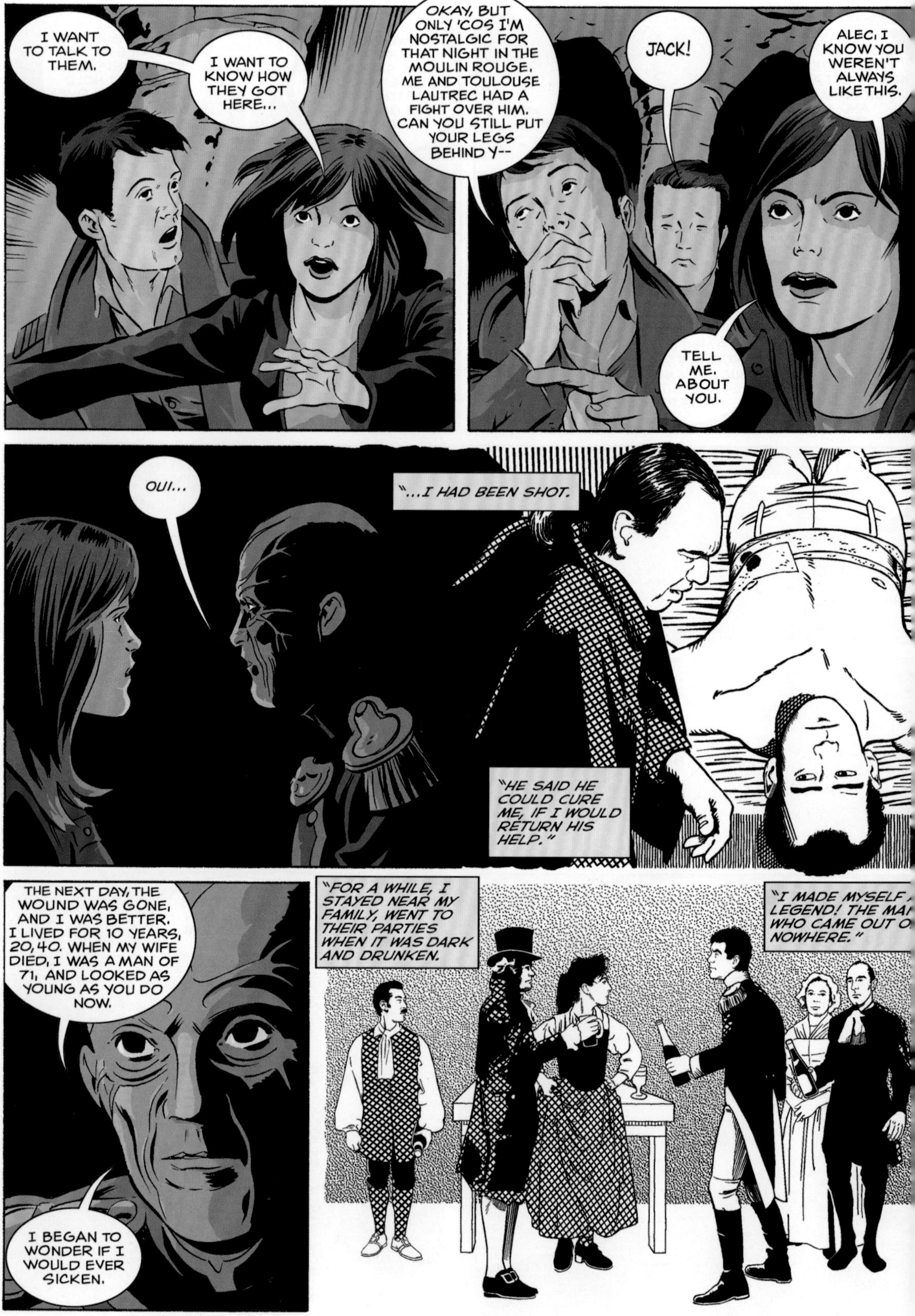

I WANT TO TALK TO THEM.
I WANT TO KNOW HOW THEY GOT HERE...
OKAY, BUT ONLY 'COS I'M NOSTALGIC FOR THAT NIGHT IN THE MOULIN ROUGE. ME AND TOULOUSE LAUTREC HAD A FIGHT OVER HIM. CAN YOU STILL PUT YOUR LEGS BEHIND Y--
JACK!
ALEC, I KNOW YOU WEREN'T ALWAYS LIKE THIS.
TELL ME. ABOUT YOU.
OUI...
"...I HAD BEEN SHOT.
"HE SAID HE COULD CURE ME, IF I WOULD RETURN HIS HELP."
THE NEXT DAY, THE WOUND WAS GONE, AND I WAS BETTER. I LIVED FOR 10 YEARS, 20, 40. WHEN MY WIFE DIED, I WAS A MAN OF 71, AND LOOKED AS YOUNG AS YOU DO NOW.
I BEGAN TO WONDER IF I WOULD EVER SICKEN.
"FOR A WHILE, I STAYED NEAR MY FAMILY, WENT TO THEIR PARTIES WHEN IT WAS DARK AND DRUNKEN.

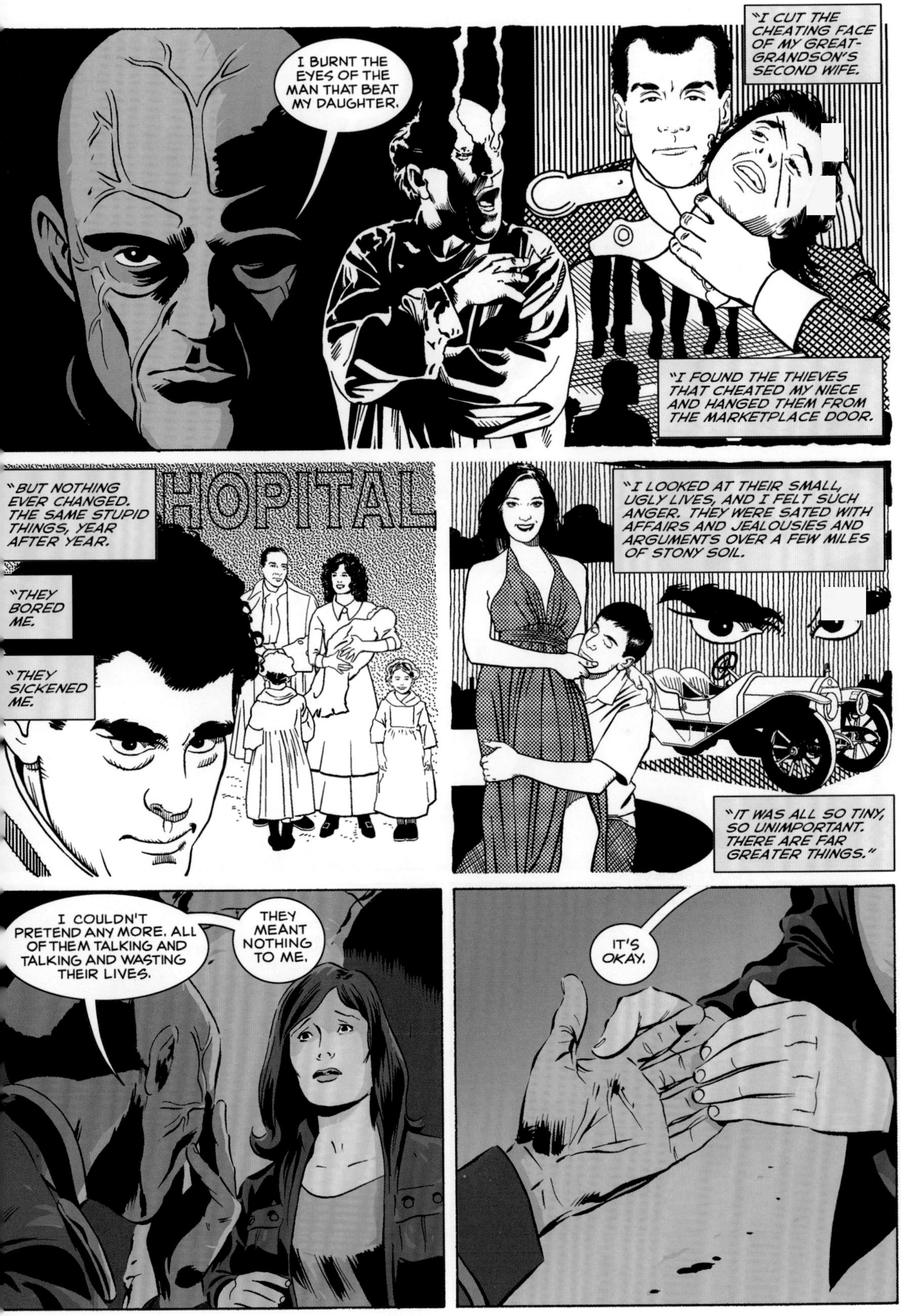
I BURNT THE EYES OF THE MAN THAT BEAT MY DAUGHTER.
"I CUT THE CHEATING FACE OF MY GREAT-GRANDSON'S SECOND WIFE.
"I FOUND THE THIEVES THAT CHEATED MY NIECE AND HANGED THEM FROM THE MARKETPLACE DOOR.
HOPITAL
"BUT NOTHING EVER CHANGED. THE SAME STUPID THINGS, YEAR AFTER YEAR.
"THEY BORED ME.
"THEY SICKENED ME.
"I LOOKED AT THEIR SMALL, UGLY LIVES, AND I FELT SUCH ANGER. THEY WERE SATED WITH AFFAIRS AND JEALOUSIES AND ARGUMENTS OVER A FEW MILES OF STONY SOIL.
"IT WAS ALL SO TINY, SO UNIMPORTANT. THERE ARE FAR GREATER THINGS."
I COULDN'T PRETEND ANY MORE. ALL OF THEM TALKING AND TALKING AND WASTING THEIR LIVES.
THEY MEANT NOTHING TO ME.
IT'S OKAY.

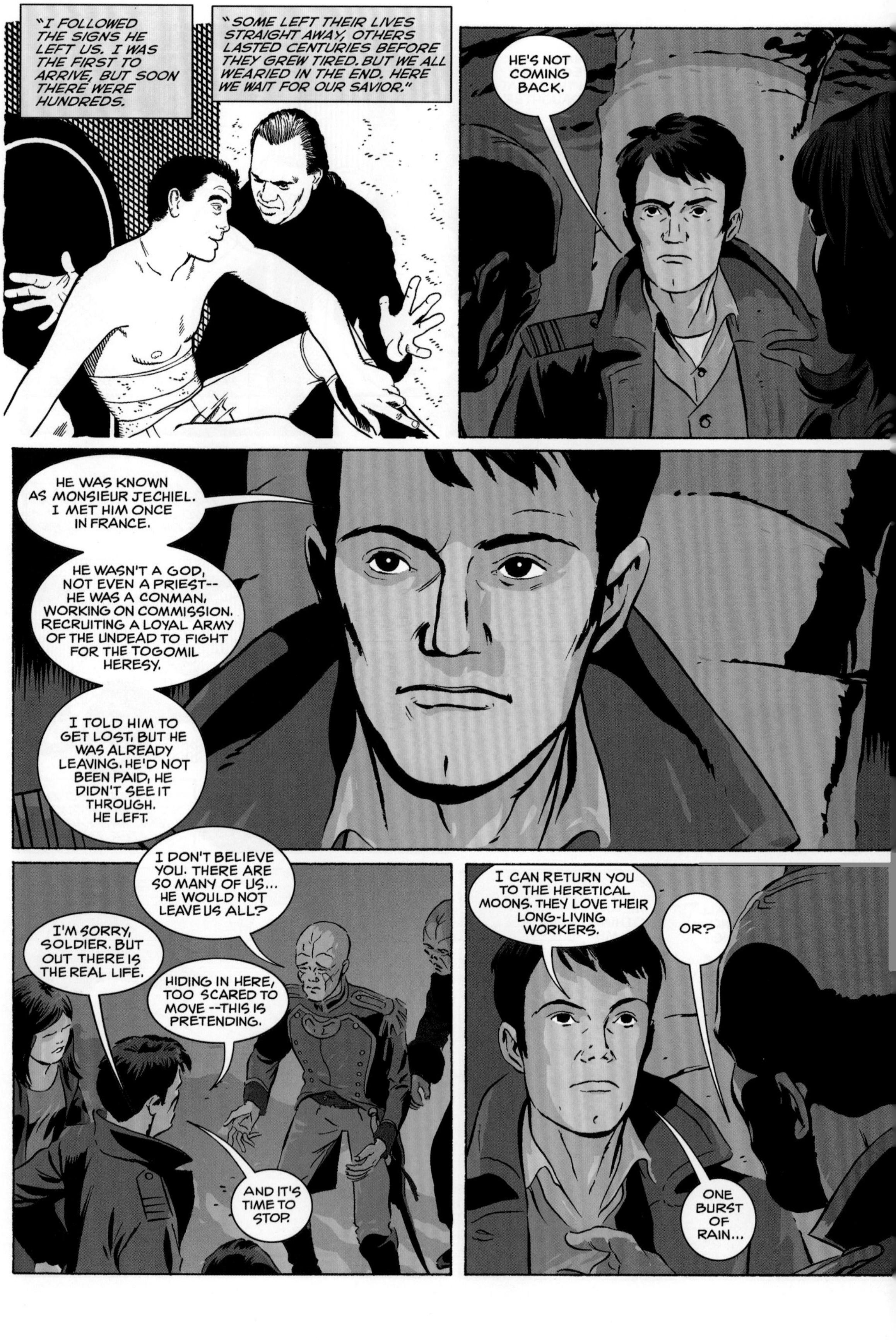
"I FOLLOWED THE SIGNS HE LEFT US. I WAS THE FIRST TO ARRIVE, BUT SOON THERE WERE HUNDREDS.
"SOME LEFT THEIR LIVES STRAIGHT AWAY, OTHERS LASTED CENTURIES BEFORE THEY GREW TIRED. BUT WE ALL WEARIED IN THE END. HERE WE WAIT FOR OUR SAVIOR."
HE'S NOT COMING BACK.
HE WAS KNOWN AS MONSIEUR JECHIEL. I MET HIM ONCE IN FRANCE.
HE WASN'T A GOD, NOT EVEN A PRIEST-- HE WAS A CONMAN, WORKING ON COMMISSION. RECRUITING A LOYAL ARMY OF THE UNDEAD TO FIGHT FOR THE TOGOMIL HERESY.
I TOLD HIM TO GET LOST, BUT HE WAS ALREADY LEAVING. HE'D NOT BEEN PAID, HE DIDN'T SEE IT THROUGH. HE LEFT.
I DON'T BELIEVE YOU. THERE ARE SO MANY OF US... HE WOULD NOT LEAVE US ALL?
I'M SORRY, SOLDIER. BUT OUT THERE IS THE REAL LIFE.
HIDING IN HERE, TOO SCARED TO MOVE --THIS IS PRETENDING.
AND IT'S TIME TO STOP.
I CAN RETURN YOU TO THE HERETICAL MOONS. THEY LOVE THEIR LONG-LIVING WORKERS.
OR?
ONE BURST OF RAIN...

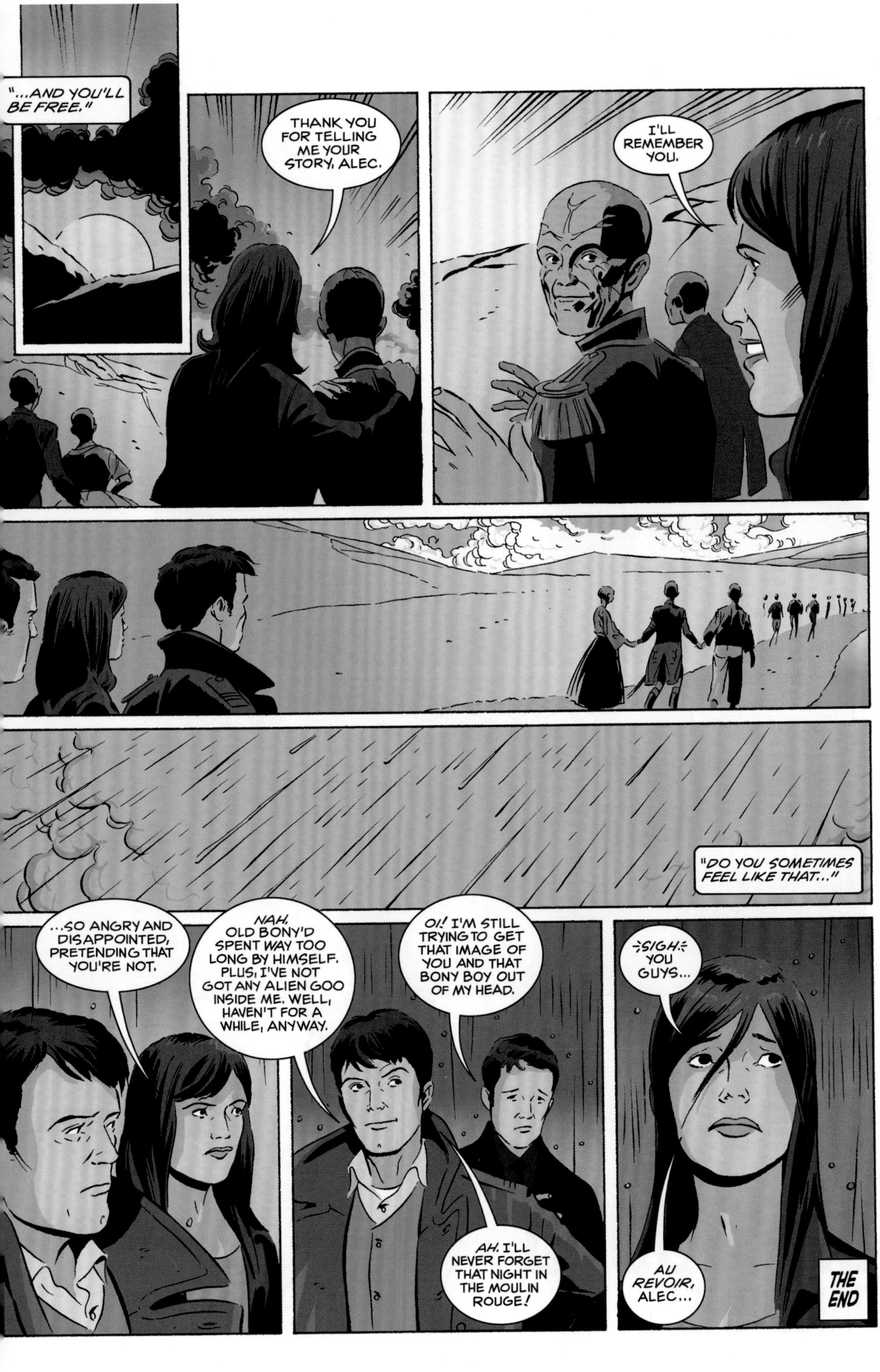
"...AND YOU'LL BE FREE."
THANK YOU FOR TELLING ME YOUR STORY, ALEC.
I'LL REMEMBER YOU.
"DO YOU SOMETIMES FEEL LIKE THAT..."
...SO ANGRY AND DISAPPOINTED, PRETENDING THAT YOU'RE NOT.
NAH. OLD BONY'D SPENT WAY TOO LONG BY HIMSELF. PLUS, I'VE NOT GOT ANY ALIEN GOO INSIDE ME. WELL, HAVEN'T FOR A WHILE, ANYWAY.
OI! I'M STILL TRYING TO GET THAT IMAGE OF YOU AND THAT BONY BOY OUT OF MY HEAD.
AH. I'LL NEVER FORGET THAT NIGHT IN THE MOULIN ROUGE!
SIGH YOU GUYS...
AU REVOIR, ALEC...
THE END

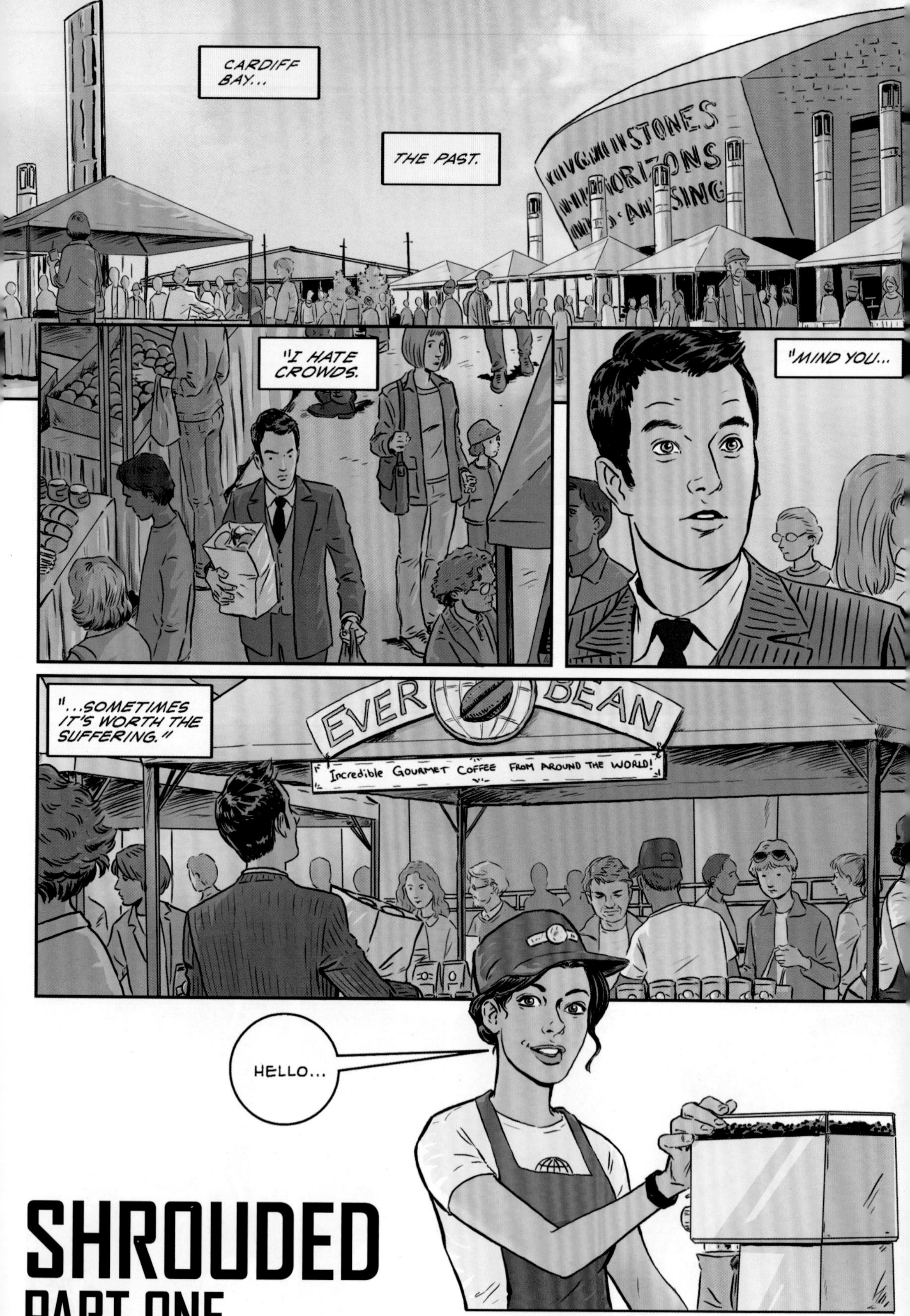
CARDIFF BAY...
THE PAST.
"I HATE CROWDS.
"MIND YOU...
"...SOMETIMES IT'S WORTH THE SUFFERING."
EVER BEAN
Incredible GOURMET COFFEE FROM AROUND THE WORLD!
HELLO...

SHROUDED
PART ONE

● WRITTEN BY GARETH DAVID-LLOYD ● ART BY PIA GUERRA
● COLORS BY PHIL ELLIOTT ● LETTERS BY JOHN WORKMAN

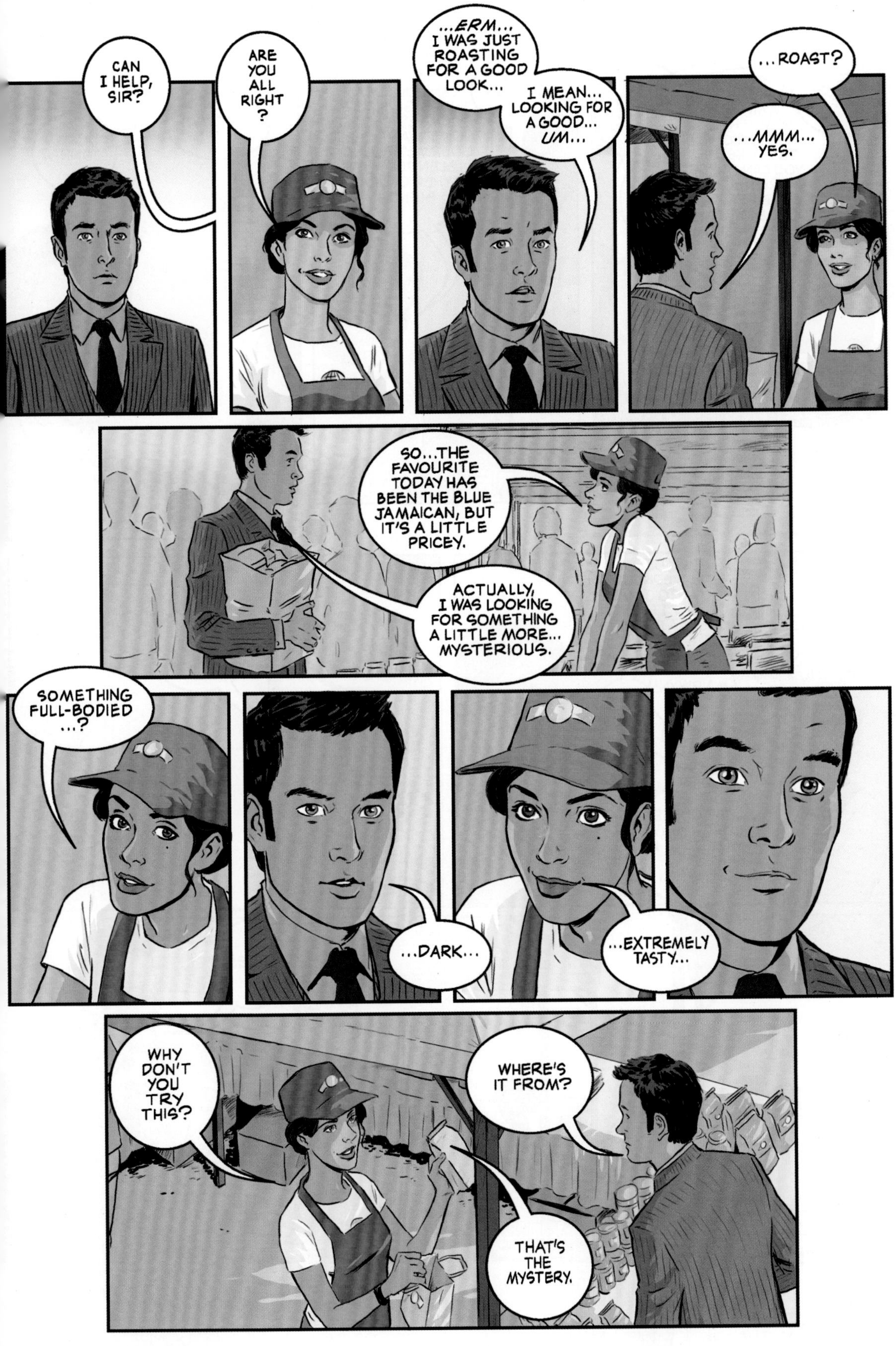
CAN I HELP, SIR?
ARE YOU ALL RIGHT?
...ERM... I WAS JUST ROASTING FOR A GOOD LOOK...
I MEAN... LOOKING FOR A GOOD... UM...
...ROAST?
...MMM... YES.
SO...THE FAVOURITE TODAY HAS BEEN THE BLUE JAMAICAN, BUT IT'S A LITTLE PRICEY.
ACTUALLY, I WAS LOOKING FOR SOMETHING A LITTLE MORE... MYSTERIOUS.
SOMETHING FULL-BODIED ...?
...DARK...
...EXTREMELY TASTY...
WHY DON'T YOU TRY THIS?
WHERE'S IT FROM?
THAT'S THE MYSTERY.

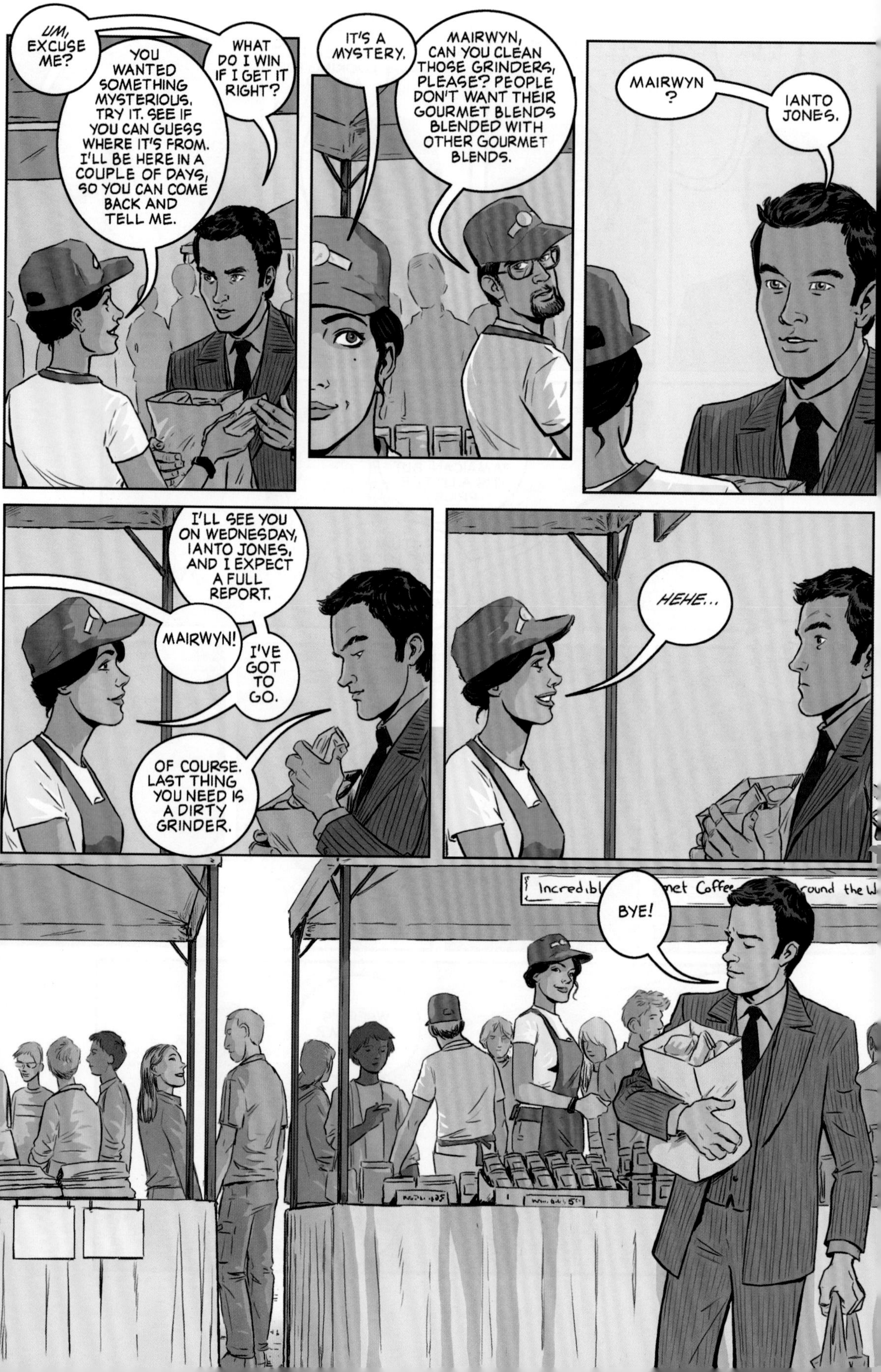
UM, EXCUSE ME?
WHAT DO I WIN IF I GET IT RIGHT?
YOU WANTED SOMETHING MYSTERIOUS. TRY IT. SEE IF YOU CAN GUESS WHERE IT'S FROM. I'LL BE HERE IN A COUPLE OF DAYS, SO YOU CAN COME BACK AND TELL ME.
IT'S A MYSTERY.
MAIRWYN, CAN YOU CLEAN THOSE GRINDERS, PLEASE? PEOPLE DON'T WANT THEIR GOURMET BLENDS BLENDED WITH OTHER GOURMET BLENDS.
MAIRWYN?
IANTO JONES.
I'LL SEE YOU ON WEDNESDAY, IANTO JONES, AND I EXPECT A FULL REPORT.
MAIRWYN!
I'VE GOT TO GO.
OF COURSE. LAST THING YOU NEED IS A DIRTY GRINDER.
HEHE...
BYE!

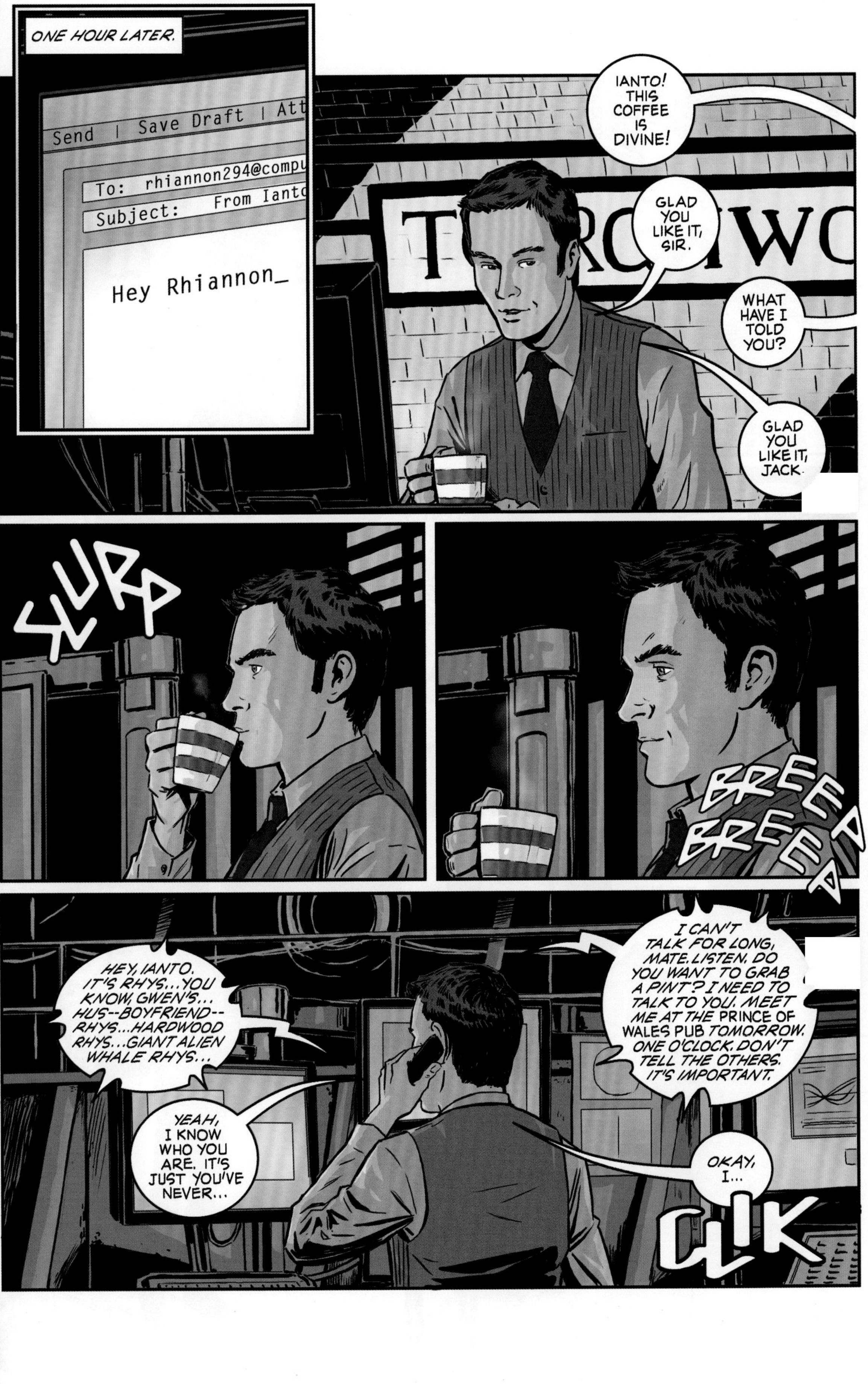
ONE HOUR LATER.
Send | Save Draft | Att
To: rhiannon294@compu
Subject: From Ianto
Hey Rhiannon_
IANTO! THIS COFFEE IS DIVINE!
GLAD YOU LIKE IT, SIR.
WHAT HAVE I TOLD YOU?
GLAD YOU LIKE IT, JACK.
SLURP
BREEP BREEP
HEY, IANTO. IT'S RHYS... YOU KNOW, GWEN'S... HUS--BOYFRIEND--RHYS...HARDWOOD RHYS...GIANT ALIEN WHALE RHYS...
YEAH, I KNOW WHO YOU ARE. IT'S JUST YOU'VE NEVER...
I CAN'T TALK FOR LONG, MATE. LISTEN. DO YOU WANT TO GRAB A PINT? I NEED TO TALK TO YOU. MEET ME AT THE PRINCE OF WALES PUB TOMORROW. ONE O'CLOCK. DON'T TELL THE OTHERS. IT'S IMPORTANT.
OKAY, I...
CLIK

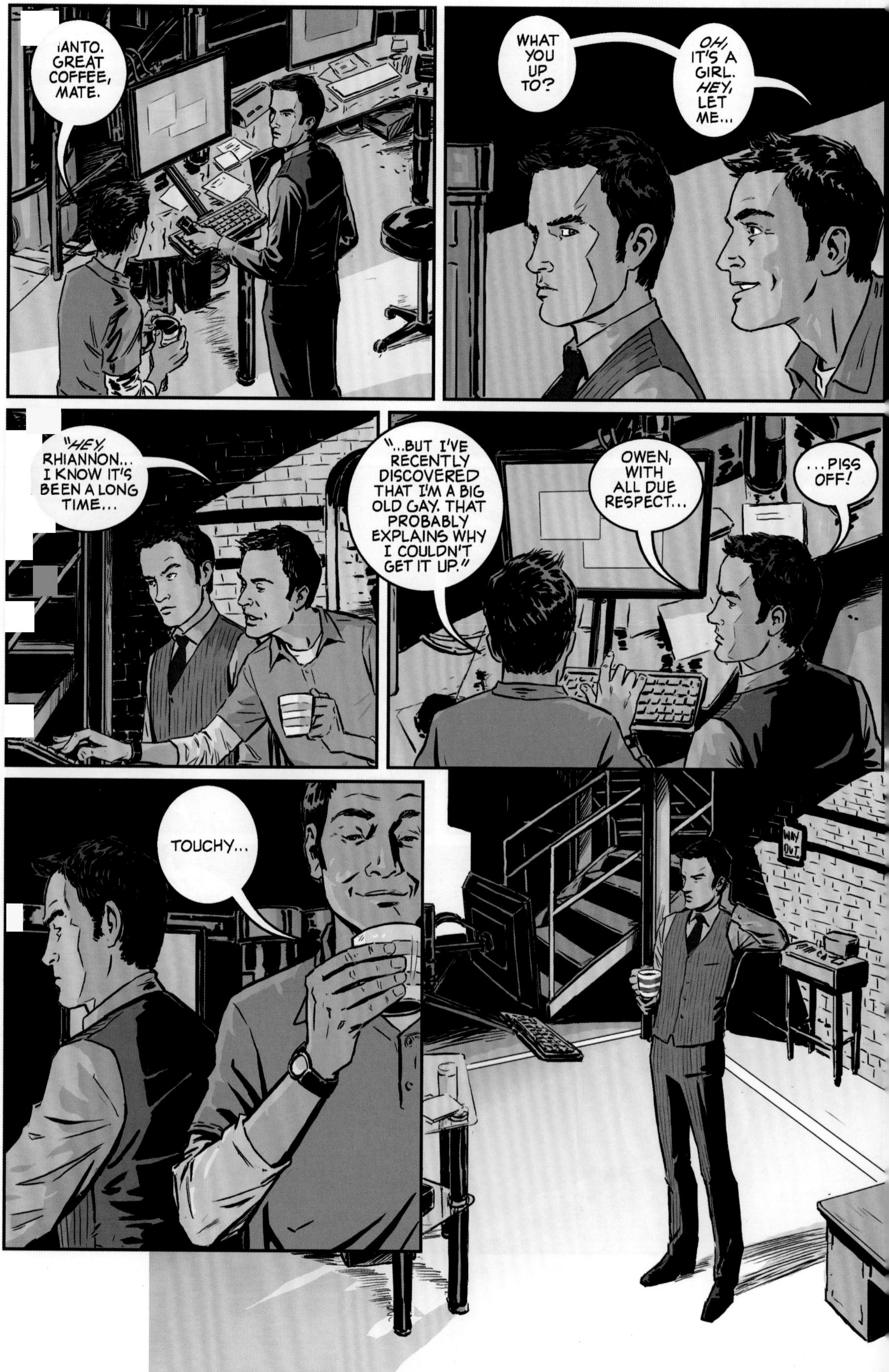
IANTO. GREAT COFFEE, MATE.
WHAT YOU UP TO?
OH, IT'S A GIRL. HEY, LET ME...
"HEY, RHIANNON... I KNOW IT'S BEEN A LONG TIME...
"...BUT I'VE RECENTLY DISCOVERED THAT I'M A BIG OLD GAY. THAT PROBABLY EXPLAINS WHY I COULDN'T GET IT UP."
OWEN, WITH ALL DUE RESPECT...
...PISS OFF!
TOUCHY...
WAY OUT.

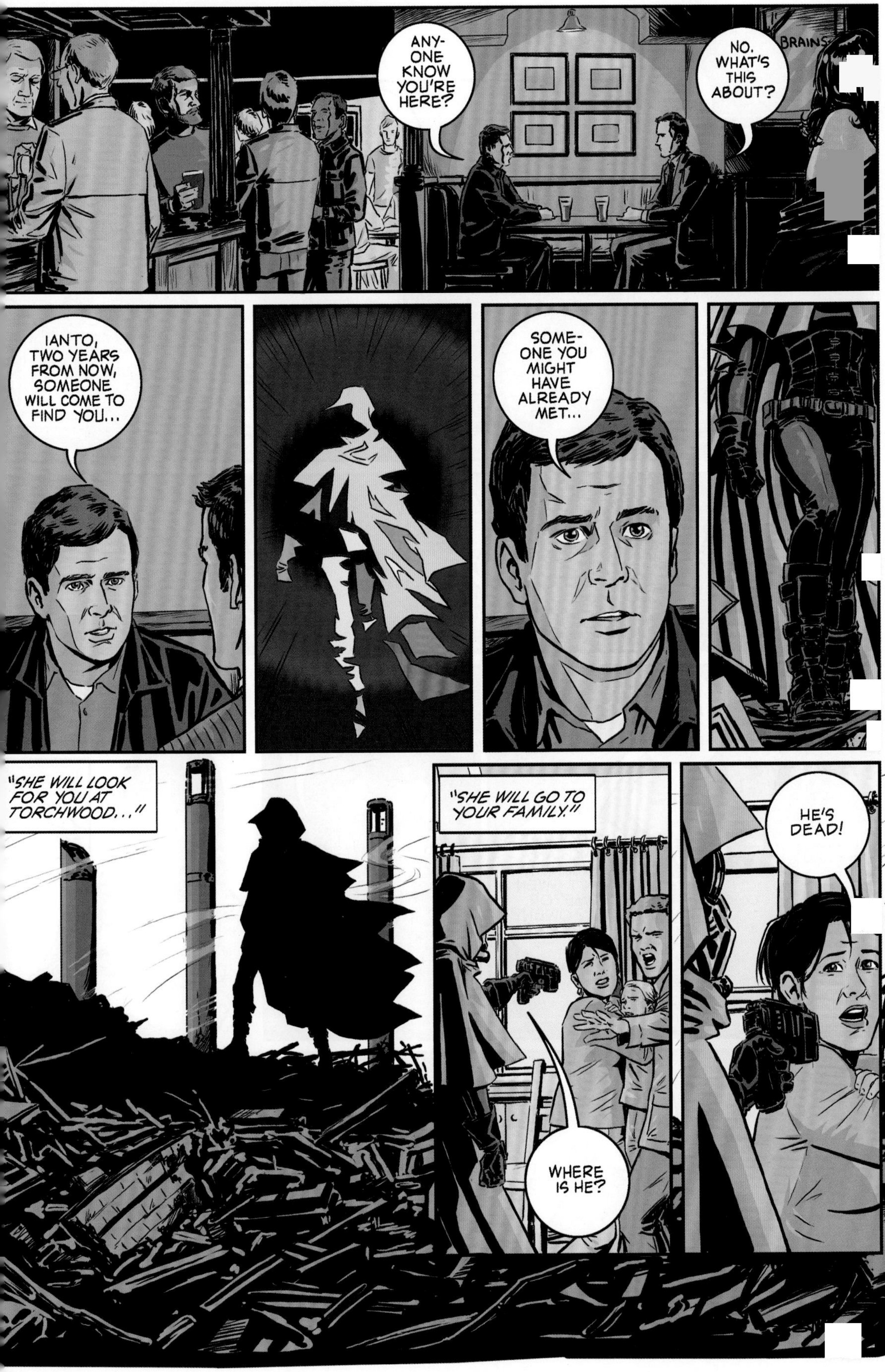
ANY-ONE KNOW YOU'RE HERE?
NO. WHAT'S THIS ABOUT?
BRAINS
IANTO, TWO YEARS FROM NOW, SOMEONE WILL COME TO FIND YOU...
SOME-ONE YOU MIGHT HAVE ALREADY MET...
"SHE WILL LOOK FOR YOU AT TORCHWOOD..."
"SHE WILL GO TO YOUR FAMILY."
WHERE IS HE?
HE'S DEAD!

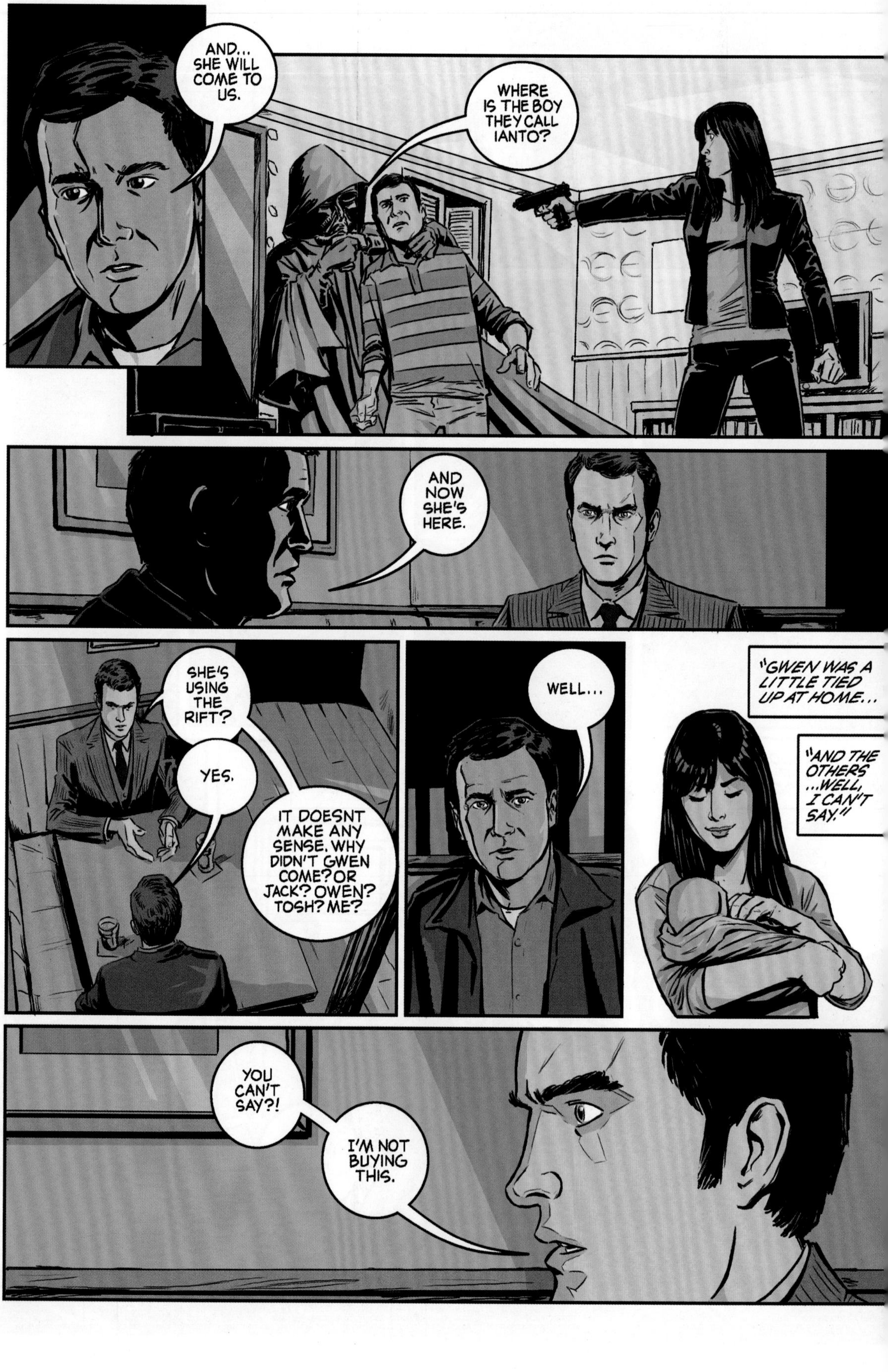
AND... SHE WILL COME TO US.
WHERE IS THE BOY THEY CALL IANTO?
AND NOW SHE'S HERE.
SHE'S USING THE RIFT?
YES.
IT DOESNT MAKE ANY SENSE. WHY DIDN'T GWEN COME? OR JACK? OWEN? TOSH? ME?
WELL...
"GWEN WAS A LITTLE TIED UP AT HOME...
"AND THE OTHERS ...WELL, I CAN'T SAY."
YOU CAN'T SAY?!
I'M NOT BUYING THIS.

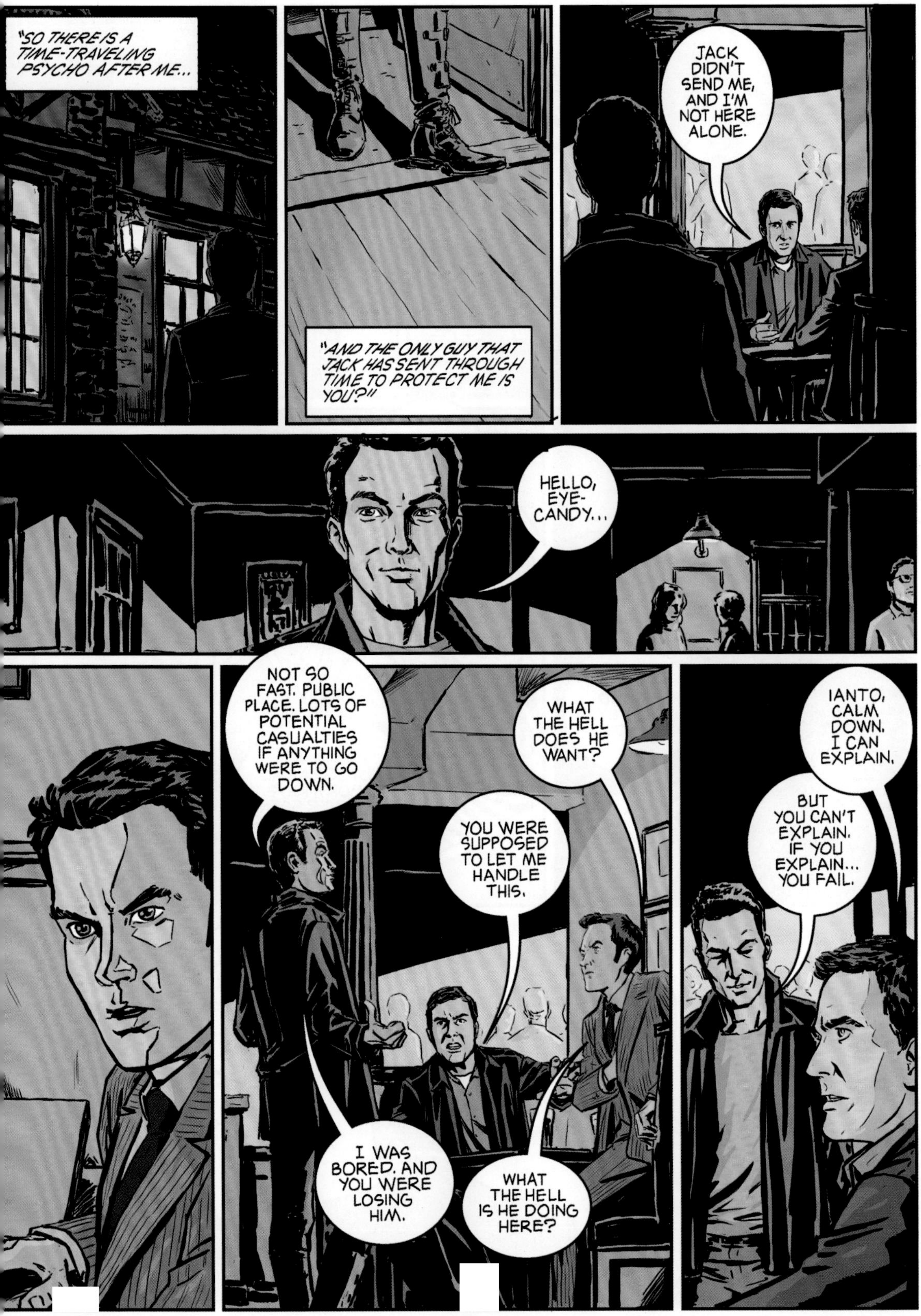
"SO THERE IS A TIME-TRAVELING PSYCHO AFTER ME...
"AND THE ONLY GUY THAT JACK HAS SENT THROUGH TIME TO PROTECT ME IS YOU?"
JACK DIDN'T SEND ME, AND I'M NOT HERE ALONE.
HELLO, EYE-CANDY...
NOT SO FAST. PUBLIC PLACE. LOTS OF POTENTIAL CASUALTIES IF ANYTHING WERE TO GO DOWN.
WHAT THE HELL DOES HE WANT?
YOU WERE SUPPOSED TO LET ME HANDLE THIS.
I WAS BORED. AND YOU WERE LOSING HIM.
WHAT THE HELL IS HE DOING HERE?
IANTO, CALM DOWN. I CAN EXPLAIN.
BUT YOU CAN'T EXPLAIN. IF YOU EXPLAIN... YOU FAIL.

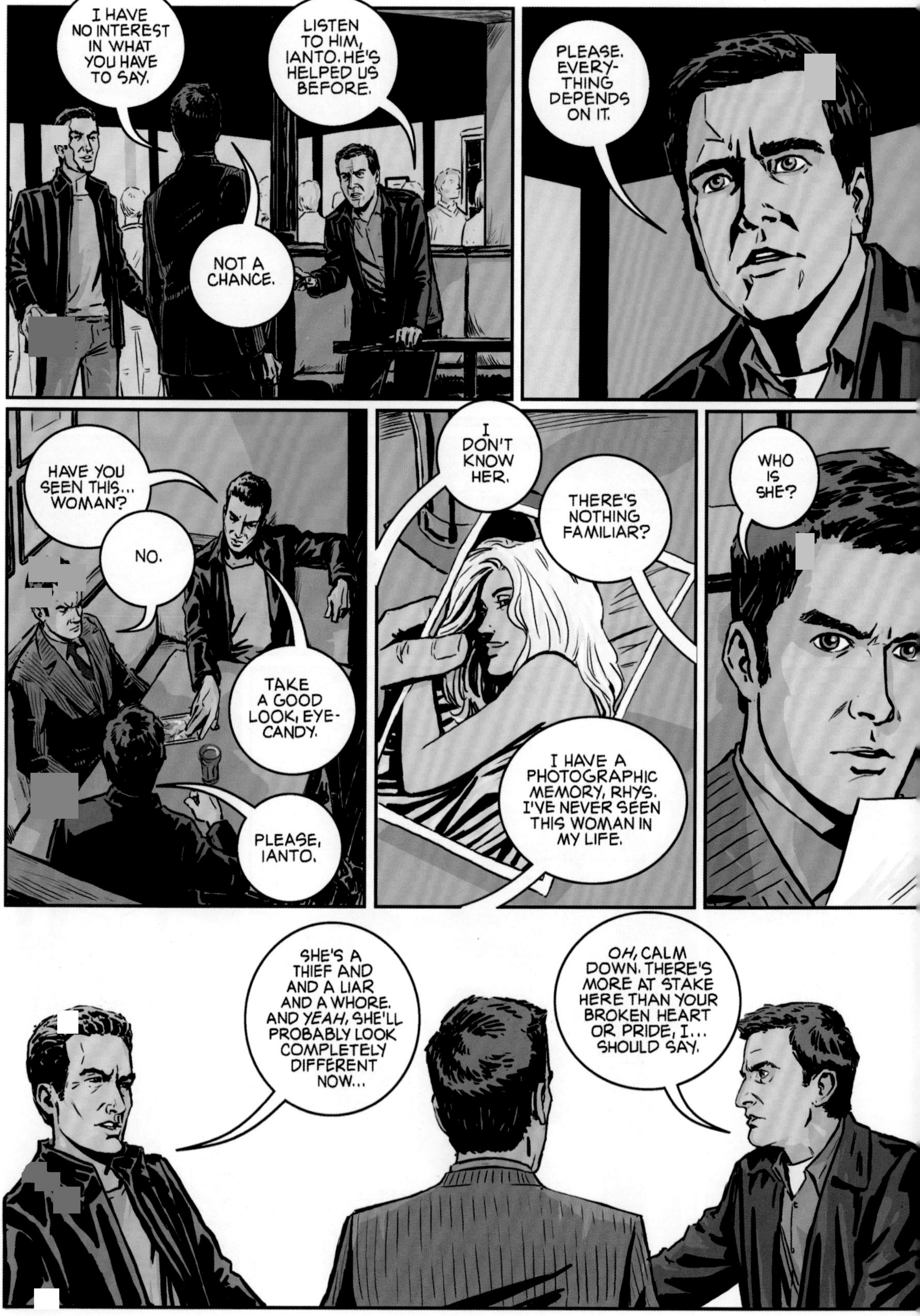
I HAVE NO INTEREST IN WHAT YOU HAVE TO SAY.
LISTEN TO HIM, IANTO. HE'S HELPED US BEFORE.
NOT A CHANCE.
PLEASE. EVERY-THING DEPENDS ON IT.
HAVE YOU SEEN THIS... WOMAN?
NO.
TAKE A GOOD LOOK, EYE-CANDY.
PLEASE, IANTO.
I DON'T KNOW HER.
THERE'S NOTHING FAMILIAR?
I HAVE A PHOTOGRAPHIC MEMORY, RHYS. I'VE NEVER SEEN THIS WOMAN IN MY LIFE.
WHO IS SHE?
SHE'S A THIEF AND AND A LIAR AND A WHORE. AND *YEAH*, SHE'LL PROBABLY LOOK COMPLETELY DIFFERENT NOW...
OH, CALM DOWN. THERE'S MORE AT STAKE HERE THAN YOUR BROKEN HEART OR PRIDE, I... SHOULD SAY.

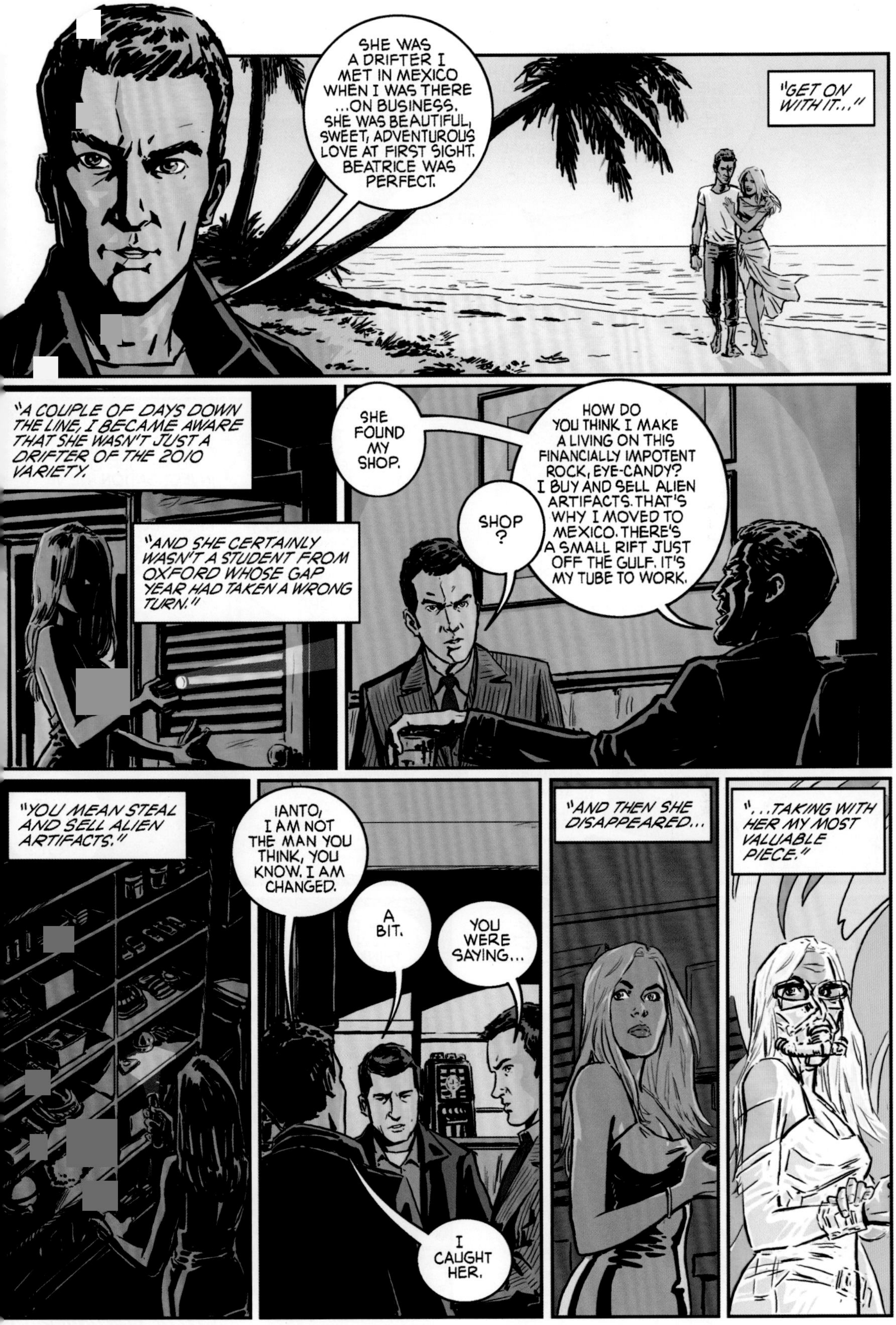
SHE WAS A DRIFTER I MET IN MEXICO WHEN I WAS THERE ...ON BUSINESS. SHE WAS BEAUTIFUL, SWEET, ADVENTUROUS LOVE AT FIRST SIGHT. BEATRICE WAS PERFECT.
"GET ON WITH IT..."
"A COUPLE OF DAYS DOWN THE LINE, I BECAME AWARE THAT SHE WASN'T JUST A DRIFTER OF THE 2010 VARIETY.
"AND SHE CERTAINLY WASN'T A STUDENT FROM OXFORD WHOSE GAP YEAR HAD TAKEN A WRONG TURN."
SHE FOUND MY SHOP.
SHOP?
HOW DO YOU THINK I MAKE A LIVING ON THIS FINANCIALLY IMPOTENT ROCK, EYE-CANDY? I BUY AND SELL ALIEN ARTIFACTS. THAT'S WHY I MOVED TO MEXICO. THERE'S A SMALL RIFT JUST OFF THE GULF. IT'S MY TUBE TO WORK.
"YOU MEAN STEAL AND SELL ALIEN ARTIFACTS."
IANTO, I AM NOT THE MAN YOU THINK, YOU KNOW. I AM CHANGED.
A BIT.
YOU WERE SAYING...
I CAUGHT HER.
"AND THEN SHE DISAPPEARED...
"...TAKING WITH HER MY MOST VALUABLE PIECE."

HOW DID SHE USE THE RIFT?

SHE USED ONE OF THESE. BUT AN OLDER DESIGN. AND WITH A FEW STRANGE ADD-ONS. THE ONE THING THOSE OLDER MODELS LEAVE IS A SORT OF SIGNAL. A FAINT IMPRINT, LIKE AN ECHO.

THAT'S WHY THOSE OLDER MODELS WERE SCRAPPED. EASY TO TRACK. THE ECHO BROUGHT ME TO HIM, AND NOW IT'S BROUGHT ME TO YOU.

"I WANT MY PROPERTY BACK...AND I WANT TO HELP YOU BOYS, OF COURSE.

"IF I'M GONNA HANG AROUND, THEN YOUR FUTURE IS MY FUTURE."

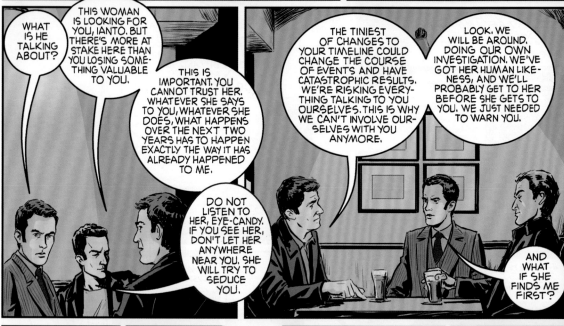

WHAT IS HE TALKING ABOUT?

THIS WOMAN IS LOOKING FOR YOU, IANTO. BUT THERE'S MORE AT STAKE HERE THAN YOU LOSING SOMETHING VALUABLE TO YOU.

THIS IS IMPORTANT. YOU CANNOT TRUST HER. WHATEVER SHE SAYS TO YOU, WHATEVER SHE DOES, WHAT HAPPENS OVER THE NEXT TWO YEARS HAS TO HAPPEN EXACTLY THE WAY IT HAS ALREADY HAPPENED TO ME.

DO NOT LISTEN TO HER, EYE-CANDY. IF YOU SEE HER, DON'T LET HER ANYWHERE NEAR YOU. SHE WILL TRY TO SEDUCE YOU.

THE TINIEST OF CHANGES TO YOUR TIMELINE COULD CHANGE THE COURSE OF EVENTS AND HAVE CATASTROPHIC RESULTS. WE'RE RISKING EVERYTHING TALKING TO YOU OURSELVES. THIS IS WHY WE CAN'T INVOLVE OURSELVES WITH YOU ANYMORE.

LOOK, WE WILL BE AROUND, DOING OUR OWN INVESTIGATION. WE'VE GOT HER HUMAN LIKENESS, AND WE'LL PROBABLY GET TO HER BEFORE SHE GETS TO YOU. WE JUST NEEDED TO WARN YOU.

AND WHAT IF SHE FINDS ME FIRST?

KILL HER.

"JOHN, IF SHE USES THAT DEVICE ON IANTO..."

DON'T EVEN THINK ABOUT THE CONSEQUENCES...

JUST DON'T EVEN GO THERE...

TO BE CONTINUED...

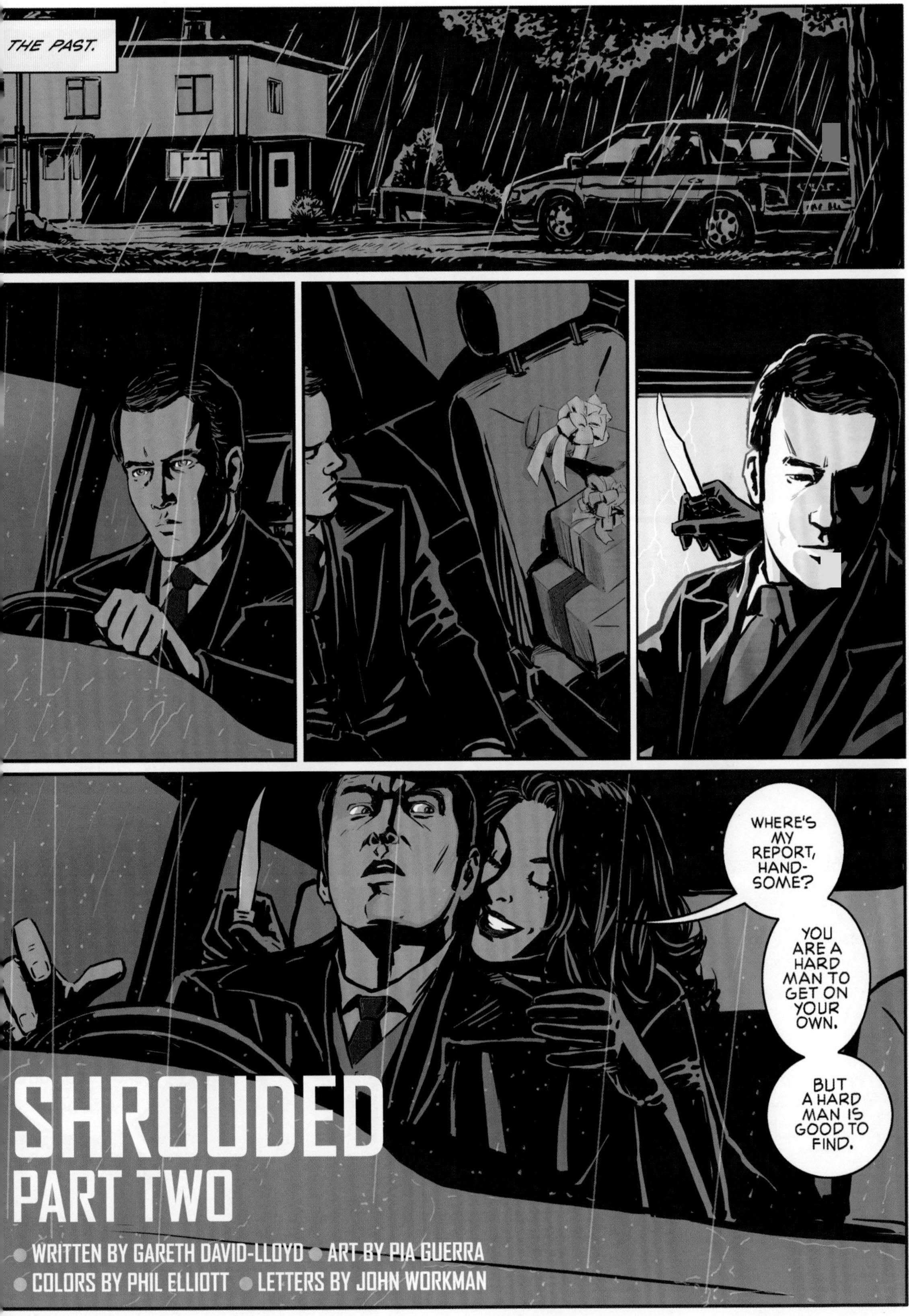
THE PAST.
WHERE'S MY REPORT, HANDSOME?
YOU ARE A HARD MAN TO GET ON YOUR OWN.
BUT A HARD MAN IS GOOD TO FIND.
SHROUDED
PART TWO
WRITTEN BY GARETH DAVID-LLOYD
ART BY PIA GUERRA
COLORS BY PHIL ELLIOTT
LETTERS BY JOHN WORKMAN

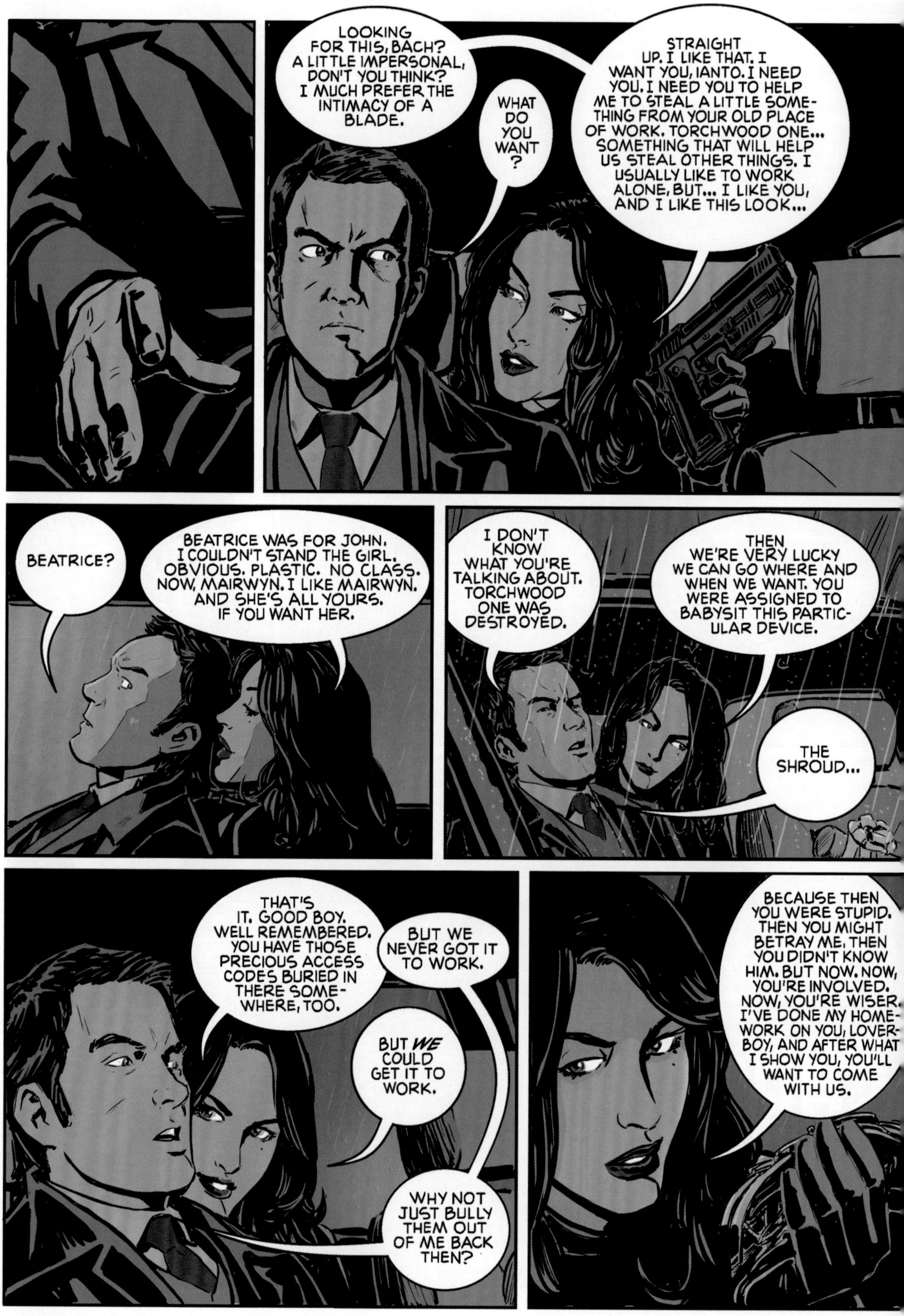
LOOKING FOR THIS, BACH? A LITTLE IMPERSONAL, DON'T YOU THINK? I MUCH PREFER THE INTIMACY OF A BLADE.
WHAT DO YOU WANT?
STRAIGHT UP. I LIKE THAT. I WANT YOU, IANTO. I NEED YOU. I NEED YOU TO HELP ME TO STEAL A LITTLE SOMETHING FROM YOUR OLD PLACE OF WORK. TORCHWOOD ONE... SOMETHING THAT WILL HELP US STEAL OTHER THINGS. I USUALLY LIKE TO WORK ALONE, BUT... I LIKE YOU, AND I LIKE THIS LOOK...
BEATRICE?
BEATRICE WAS FOR JOHN. I COULDN'T STAND THE GIRL. OBVIOUS. PLASTIC. NO CLASS. NOW, MAIRWYN. I LIKE MAIRWYN. AND SHE'S ALL YOURS. IF YOU WANT HER.
I DON'T KNOW WHAT YOU'RE TALKING ABOUT. TORCHWOOD ONE WAS DESTROYED.
THEN WE'RE VERY LUCKY WE CAN GO WHERE AND WHEN WE WANT. YOU WERE ASSIGNED TO BABYSIT THIS PARTICULAR DEVICE.
THE SHROUD...
THAT'S IT. GOOD BOY. WELL REMEMBERED. YOU HAVE THOSE PRECIOUS ACCESS CODES BURIED IN THERE SOMEWHERE, TOO.
BUT WE NEVER GOT IT TO WORK.
BUT *WE* COULD GET IT TO WORK.
WHY NOT JUST BULLY THEM OUT OF ME BACK THEN?
BECAUSE THEN YOU WERE STUPID. THEN YOU MIGHT BETRAY ME. THEN YOU DIDN'T KNOW HIM. BUT NOW. NOW, YOU'RE INVOLVED. NOW, YOU'RE WISER. I'VE DONE MY HOMEWORK ON YOU, LOVERBOY, AND AFTER WHAT I SHOW YOU, YOU'LL WANT TO COME WITH US.

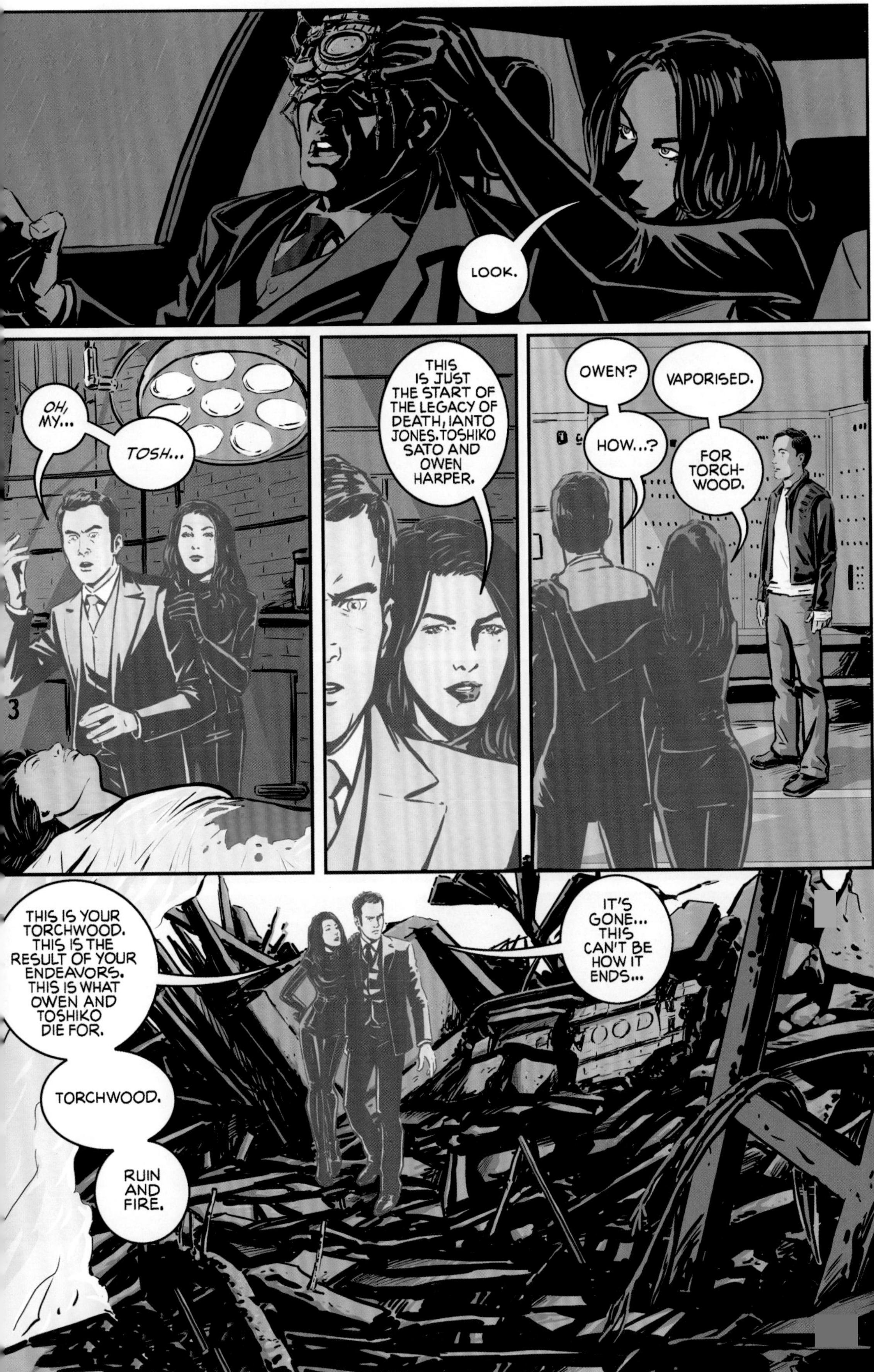
LOOK.
OH, MY...
TOSH...
THIS IS JUST THE START OF THE LEGACY OF DEATH, IANTO JONES. TOSHIKO SATO AND OWEN HARPER.
OWEN?
HOW...?
VAPORISED.
FOR TORCH-WOOD.
THIS IS YOUR TORCHWOOD. THIS IS THE RESULT OF YOUR ENDEAVORS. THIS IS WHAT OWEN AND TOSHIKO DIE FOR.
TORCHWOOD.
RUIN AND FIRE.
IT'S GONE... THIS CAN'T BE HOW IT ENDS...

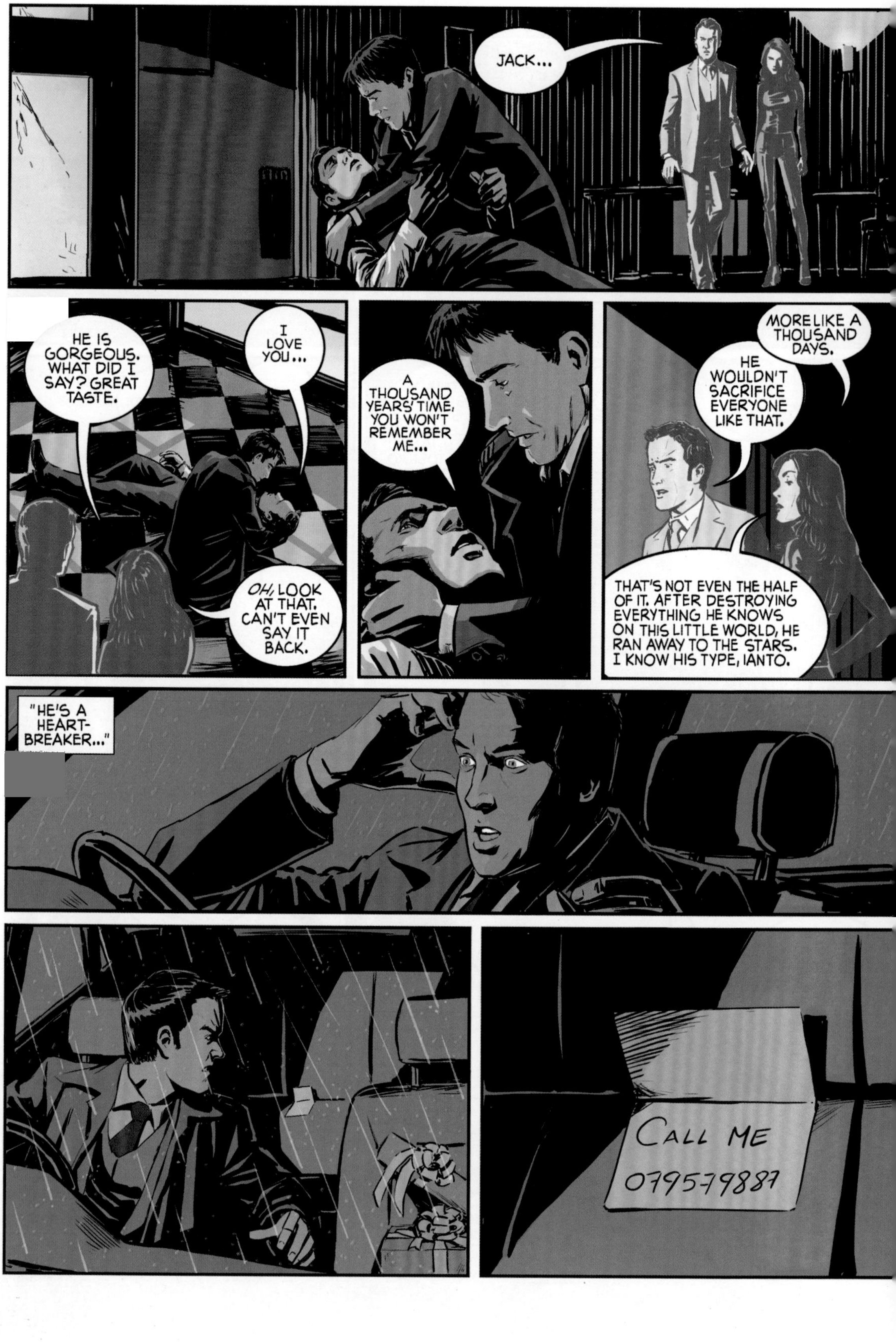
JACK...
HE IS GORGEOUS. WHAT DID I SAY? GREAT TASTE.
I LOVE YOU...
OH, LOOK AT THAT. CAN'T EVEN SAY IT BACK.
A THOUSAND YEARS' TIME, YOU WON'T REMEMBER ME...
HE WOULDN'T SACRIFICE EVERYONE LIKE THAT.
MORE LIKE A THOUSAND DAYS.
THAT'S NOT EVEN THE HALF OF IT. AFTER DESTROYING EVERYTHING HE KNOWS ON THIS LITTLE WORLD, HE RAN AWAY TO THE STARS. I KNOW HIS TYPE, IANTO.
"HE'S A HEART-BREAKER..."
CALL ME
079579887

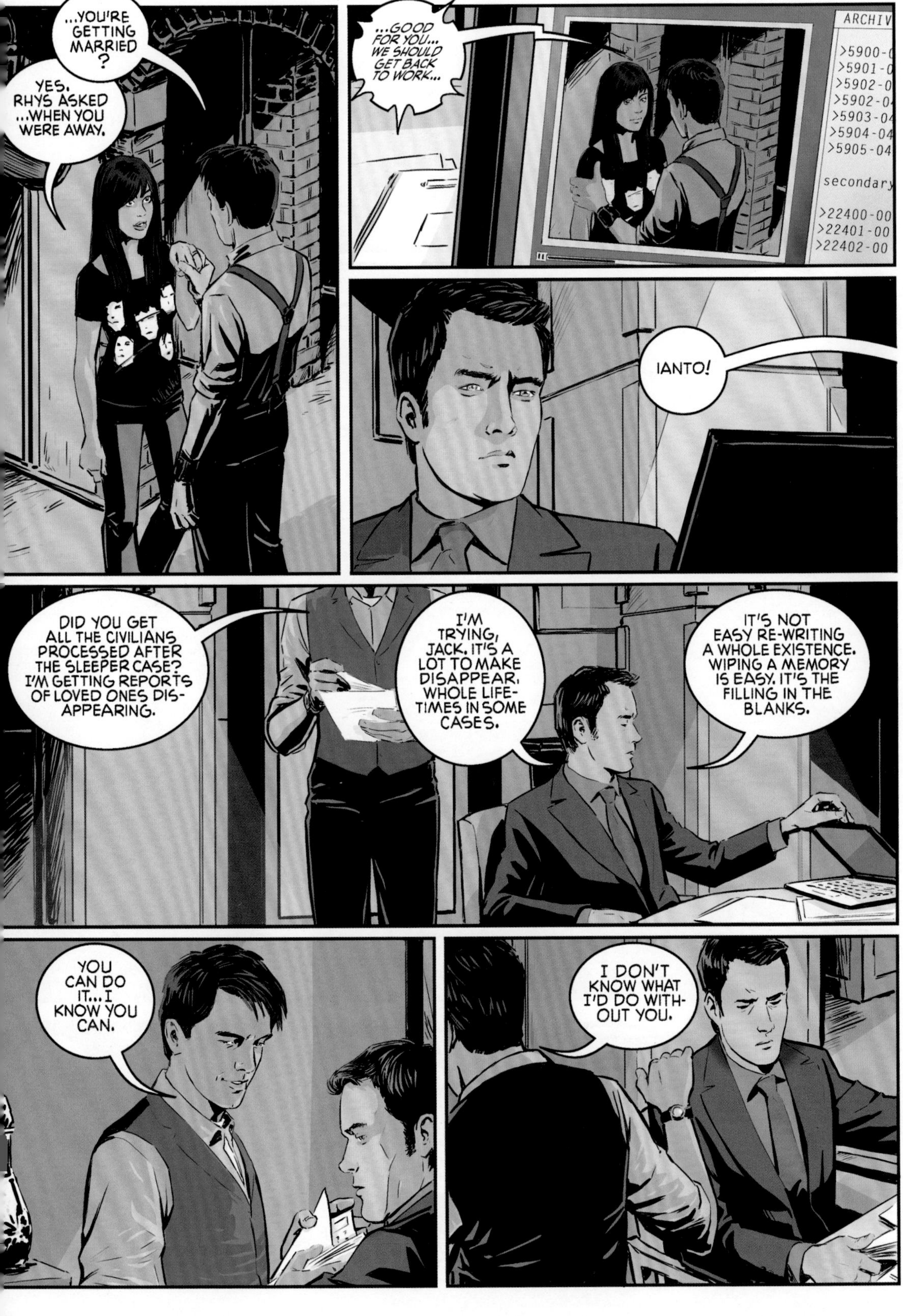
...YOU'RE GETTING MARRIED ?
YES. RHYS ASKED ...WHEN YOU WERE AWAY.
...GOOD FOR YOU... WE SHOULD GET BACK TO WORK...
ARCHIV
>5900-0
>5901-0
>5902-0
>5902-04
>5903-04
>5904-04
>5905-04
secondary
>22400-00
>22401-00
>22402-00
IANTO!
DID YOU GET ALL THE CIVILIANS PROCESSED AFTER THE SLEEPER CASE? I'M GETTING REPORTS OF LOVED ONES DISAPPEARING.
I'M TRYING, JACK. IT'S A LOT TO MAKE DISAPPEAR. WHOLE LIFETIMES IN SOME CASES.
IT'S NOT EASY RE-WRITING A WHOLE EXISTENCE. WIPING A MEMORY IS EASY. IT'S THE FILLING IN THE BLANKS.
YOU CAN DO IT... I KNOW YOU CAN.
I DON'T KNOW WHAT I'D DO WITHOUT YOU.

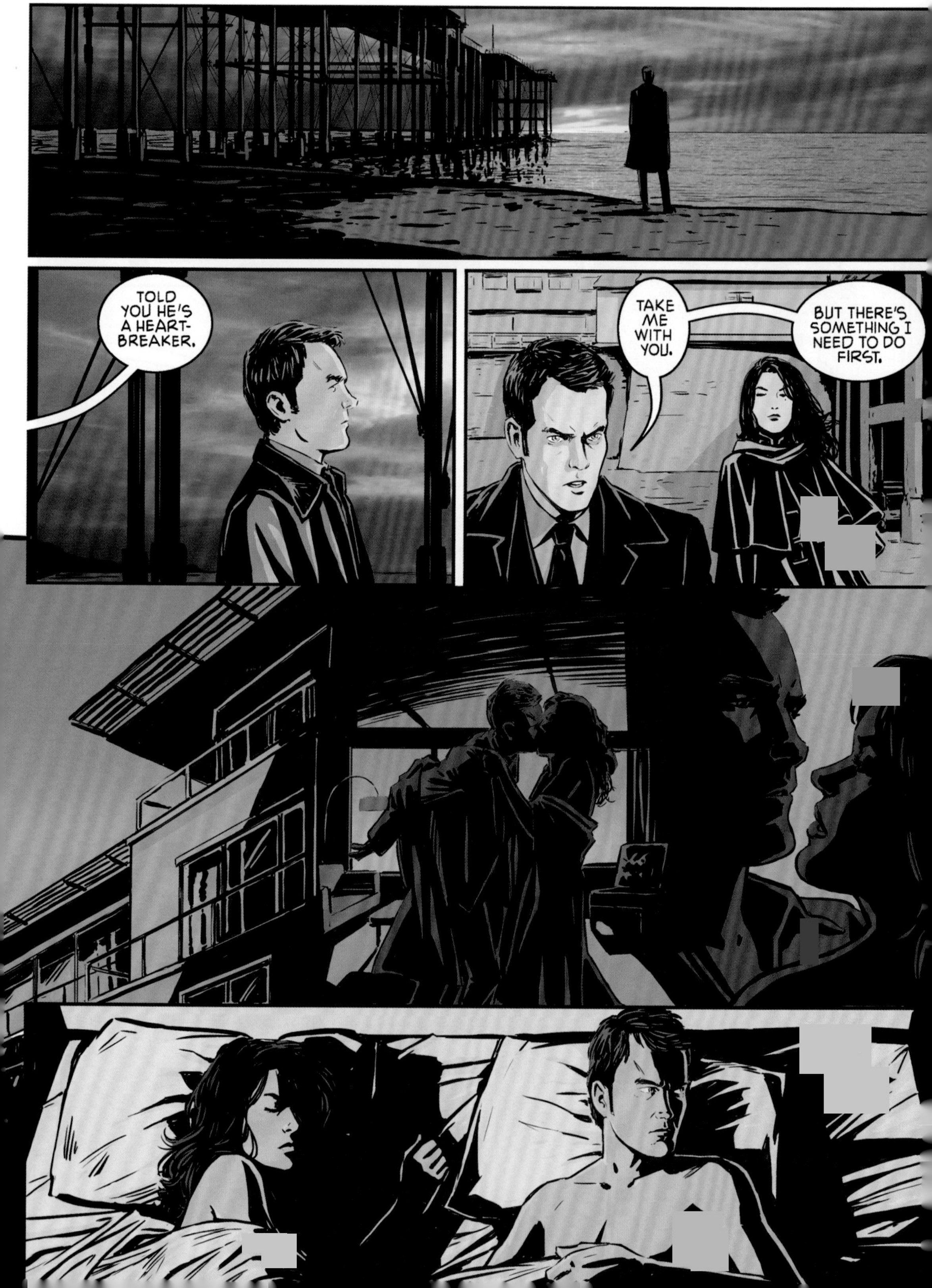
TOLD YOU HE'S A HEART-BREAKER.
TAKE ME WITH YOU.
BUT THERE'S SOMETHING I NEED TO DO FIRST.

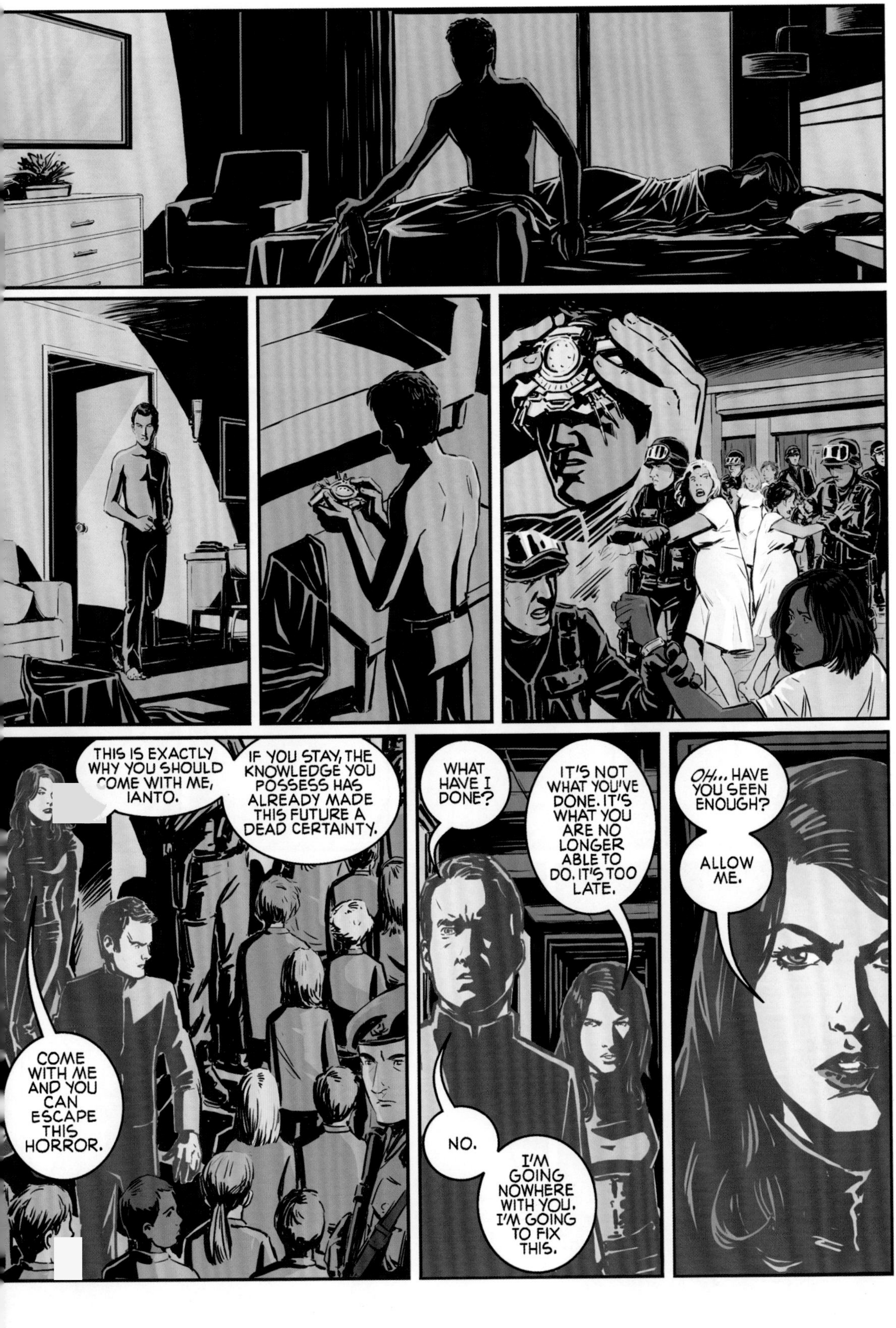
THIS IS EXACTLY WHY YOU SHOULD COME WITH ME, IANTO.
IF YOU STAY, THE KNOWLEDGE YOU POSSESS HAS ALREADY MADE THIS FUTURE A DEAD CERTAINTY.
COME WITH ME AND YOU CAN ESCAPE THIS HORROR.
WHAT HAVE I DONE?
IT'S NOT WHAT YOU'VE DONE. IT'S WHAT YOU ARE NO LONGER ABLE TO DO. IT'S TOO LATE.
NO.
I'M GOING NOWHERE WITH YOU. I'M GOING TO FIX THIS.
OH... HAVE YOU SEEN ENOUGH?
ALLOW ME.

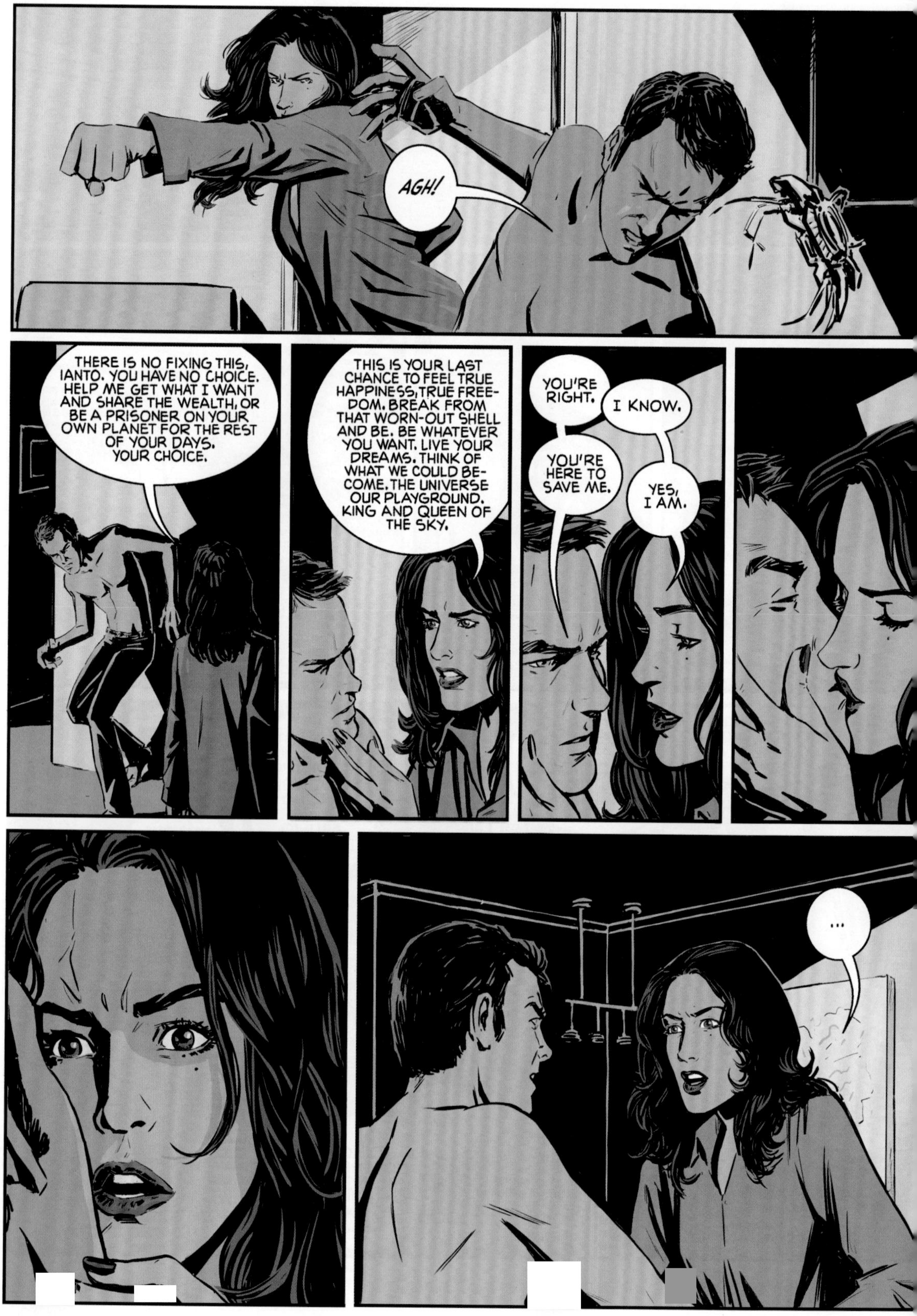
AGH!
THERE IS NO FIXING THIS, IANTO. YOU HAVE NO CHOICE. HELP ME GET WHAT I WANT AND SHARE THE WEALTH, OR BE A PRISONER ON YOUR OWN PLANET FOR THE REST OF YOUR DAYS. YOUR CHOICE.
THIS IS YOUR LAST CHANCE TO FEEL TRUE HAPPINESS, TRUE FREEDOM. BREAK FROM THAT WORN-OUT SHELL AND BE. BE WHATEVER YOU WANT. LIVE YOUR DREAMS. THINK OF WHAT WE COULD BECOME. THE UNIVERSE OUR PLAYGROUND. KING AND QUEEN OF THE SKY.
YOU'RE RIGHT.
I KNOW.
YOU'RE HERE TO SAVE ME.
YES, I AM.
...

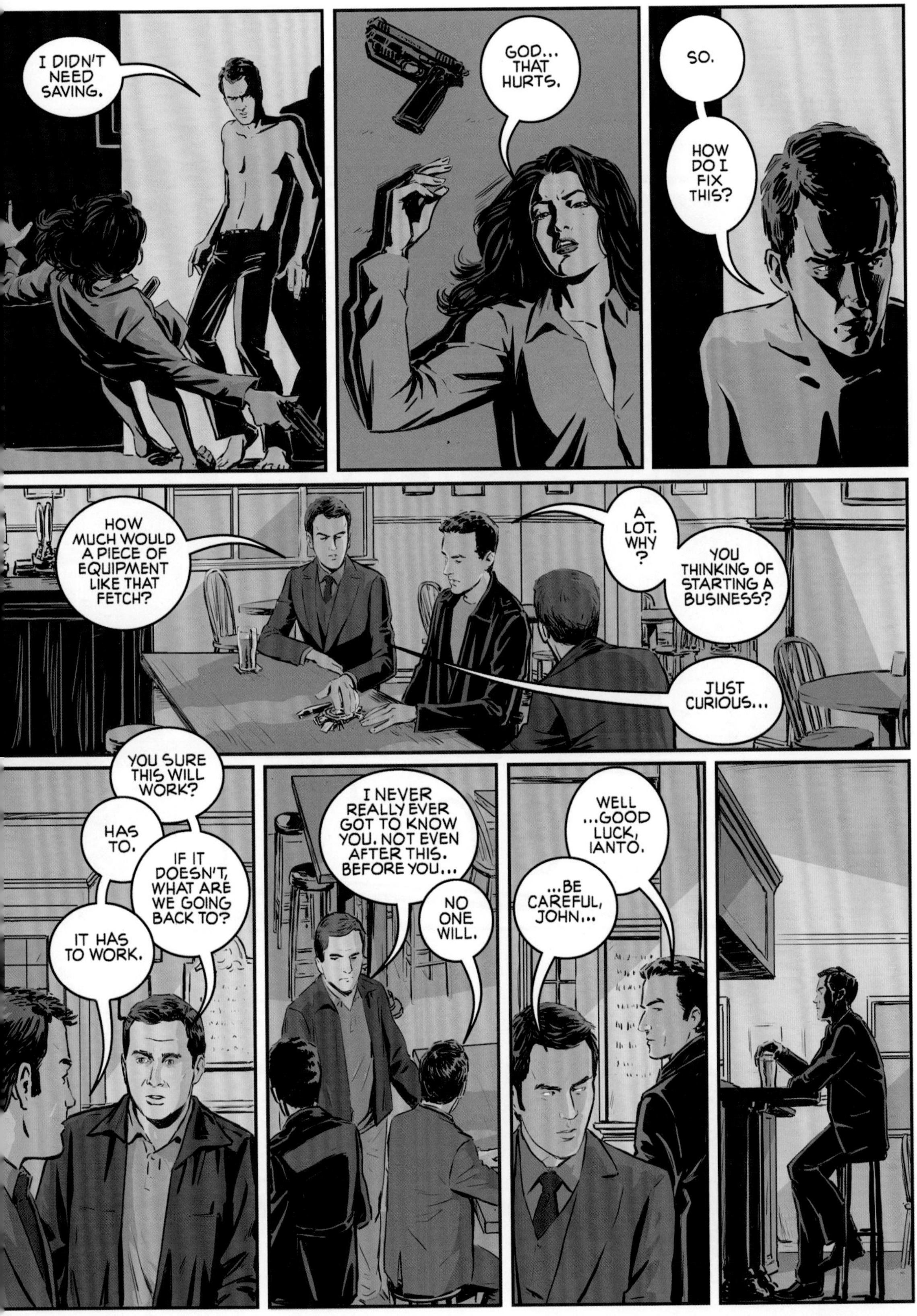
I DIDN'T NEED SAVING.
GOD... THAT HURTS.
SO.
HOW DO I FIX THIS?
HOW MUCH WOULD A PIECE OF EQUIPMENT LIKE THAT FETCH?
A LOT. WHY?
YOU THINKING OF STARTING A BUSINESS?
JUST CURIOUS...
YOU SURE THIS WILL WORK?
HAS TO.
IF IT DOESN'T, WHAT ARE WE GOING BACK TO?
IT HAS TO WORK.
I NEVER REALLY EVER GOT TO KNOW YOU. NOT EVEN AFTER THIS. BEFORE YOU...
NO ONE WILL.
WELL ...GOOD LUCK, IANTO.
...BE CAREFUL, JOHN...

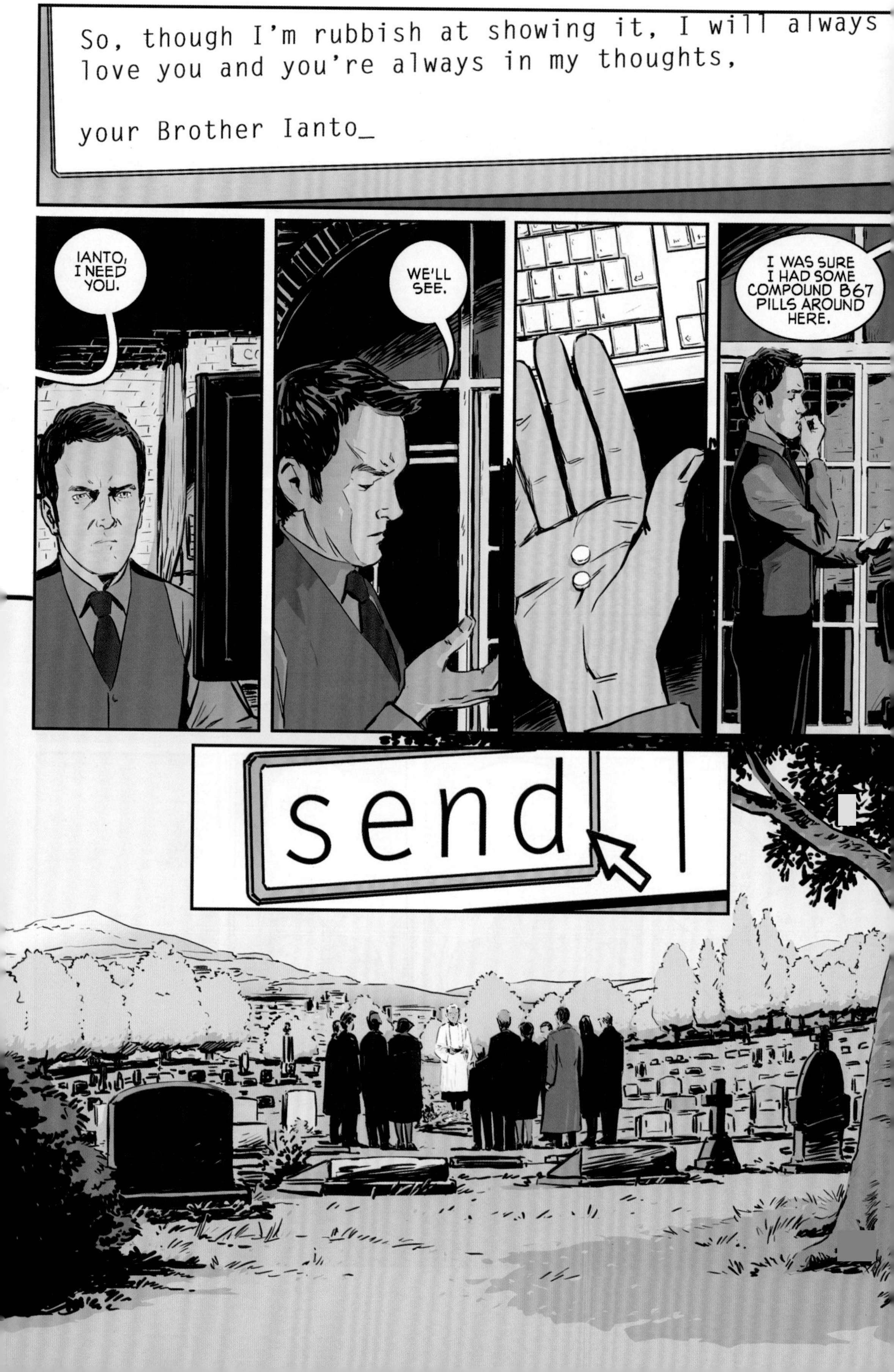
So, though I'm rubbish at showing it, I will always love you and you're always in my thoughts,
your Brother Ianto_
IANTO, I NEED YOU.
WE'LL SEE.
I WAS SURE I HAD SOME COMPOUND B67 PILLS AROUND HERE.
send

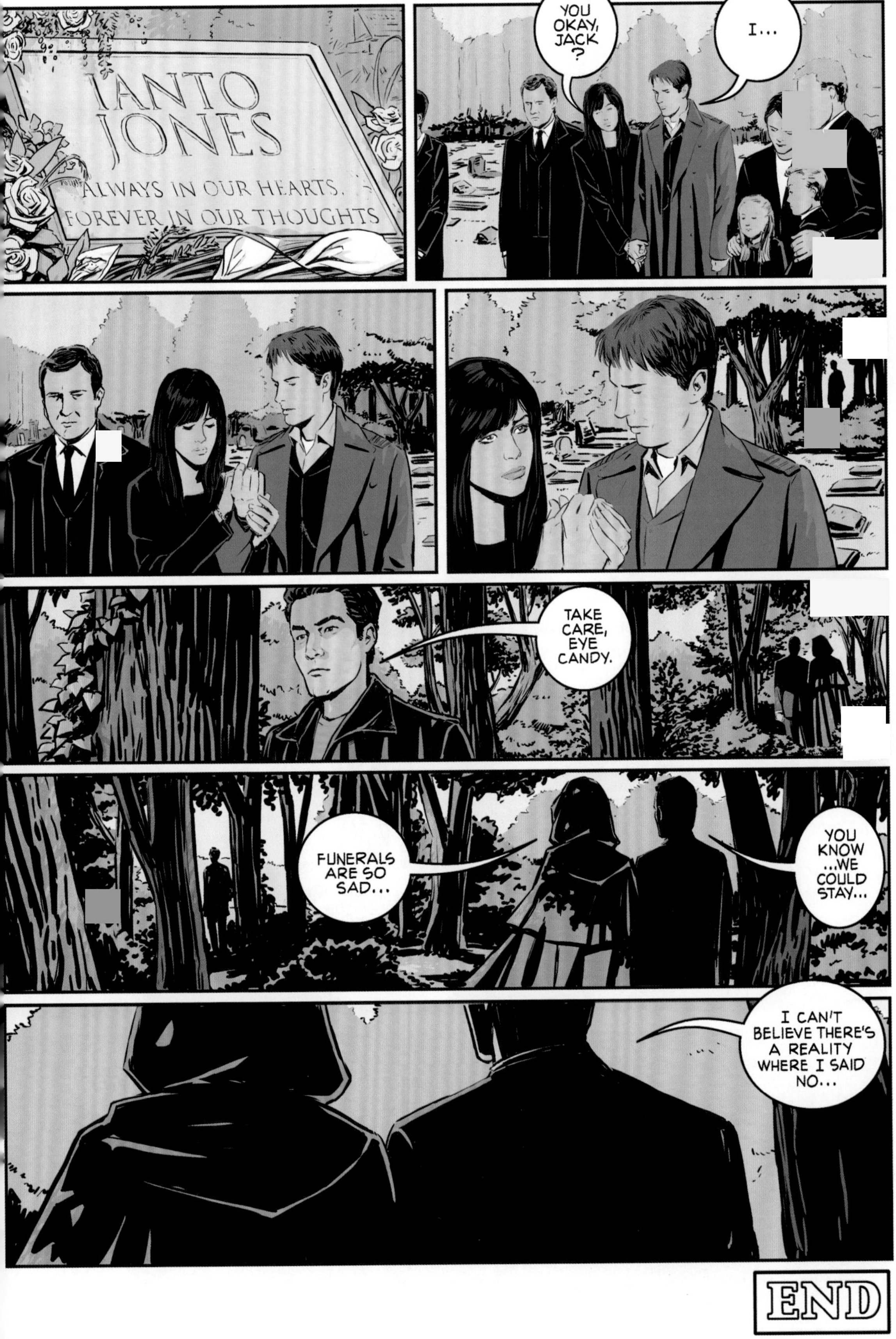
IANTO JONES
ALWAYS IN OUR HEARTS.
FOREVER IN OUR THOUGHTS
YOU OKAY, JACK?
I...
TAKE CARE, EYE CANDY.
FUNERALS ARE SO SAD...
YOU KNOW ...WE COULD STAY...
I CAN'T BELIEVE THERE'S A REALITY WHERE I SAID NO...
END

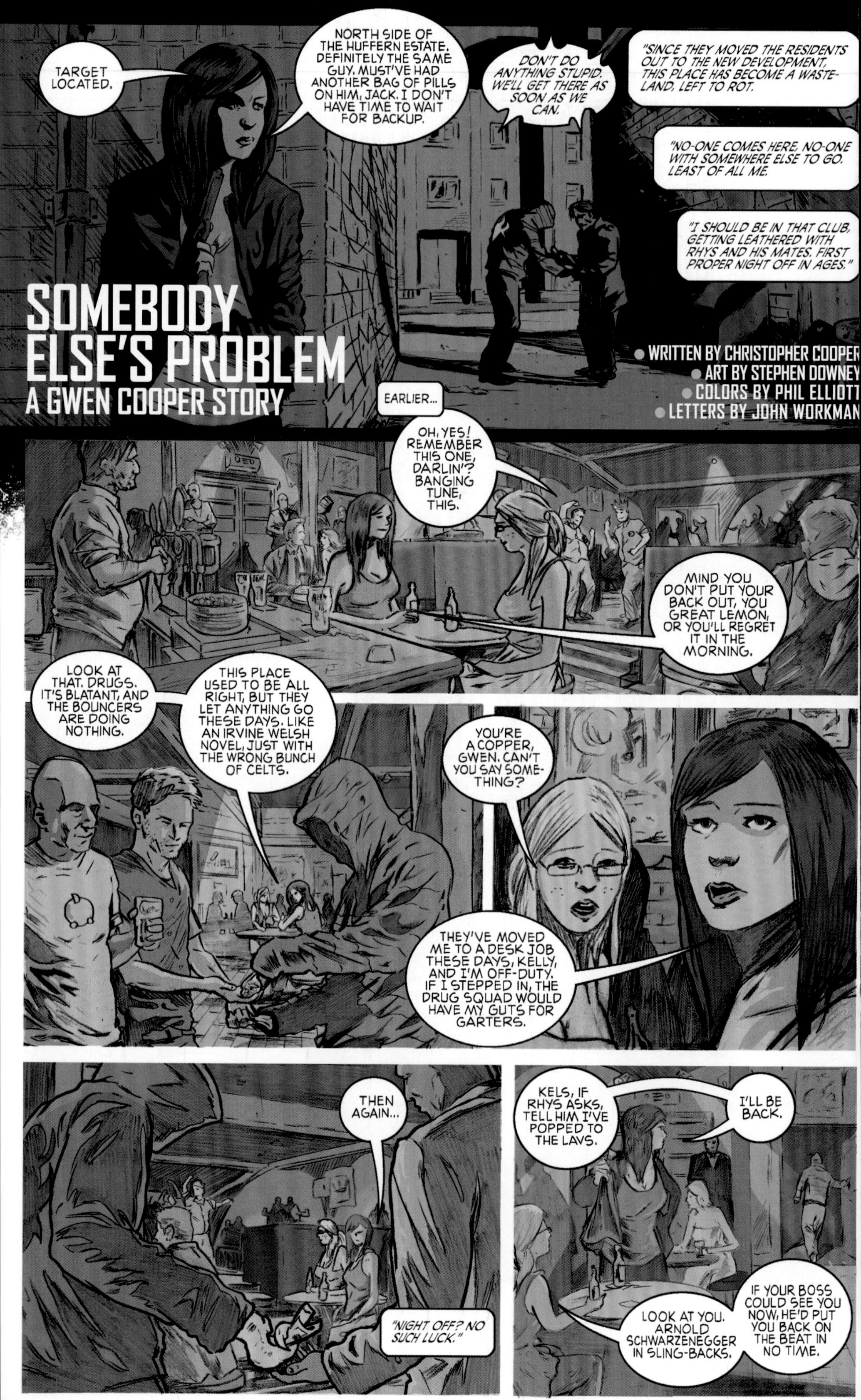

TARGET LOCATED.
NORTH SIDE OF THE HUFFERN ESTATE. DEFINITELY THE SAME GUY. MUST'VE HAD ANOTHER BAG OF PILLS ON HIM, JACK. I DON'T HAVE TIME TO WAIT FOR BACKUP.
DON'T DO ANYTHING STUPID. WE'LL GET THERE AS SOON AS WE CAN.
"SINCE THEY MOVED THE RESIDENTS OUT TO THE NEW DEVELOPMENT, THIS PLACE HAS BECOME A WASTE-LAND, LEFT TO ROT.
"NO-ONE COMES HERE, NO-ONE WITH SOMEWHERE ELSE TO GO. LEAST OF ALL ME.
"I SHOULD BE IN THAT CLUB, GETTING LEATHERED WITH RHYS AND HIS MATES. FIRST PROPER NIGHT OFF IN AGES."
SOMEBODY ELSE'S PROBLEM
A GWEN COOPER STORY
WRITTEN BY CHRISTOPHER COOPER
ART BY STEPHEN DOWNEY
COLORS BY PHIL ELLIOTT
LETTERS BY JOHN WORKMAN
EARLIER...
OH, YES! REMEMBER THIS ONE, DARLIN'? BANGING TUNE, THIS.
MIND YOU DON'T PUT YOUR BACK OUT, YOU GREAT LEMON, OR YOU'LL REGRET IT IN THE MORNING.
LOOK AT THAT. DRUGS. IT'S BLATANT, AND THE BOUNCERS ARE DOING NOTHING.
THIS PLACE USED TO BE ALL RIGHT, BUT THEY LET ANYTHING GO THESE DAYS. LIKE AN IRVINE WELSH NOVEL, JUST WITH THE WRONG BUNCH OF CELTS.
YOU'RE A COPPER, GWEN. CAN'T YOU SAY SOME-THING?
THEY'VE MOVED ME TO A DESK JOB THESE DAYS, KELLY, AND I'M OFF-DUTY. IF I STEPPED IN, THE DRUG SQUAD WOULD HAVE MY GUTS FOR GARTERS.
THEN AGAIN...
"NIGHT OFF? NO SUCH LUCK."
KELS, IF RHYS ASKS, TELL HIM I'VE POPPED TO THE LAVS.
I'LL BE BACK.
LOOK AT YOU. ARNOLD SCHWARZENEGGER IN SLING-BACKS.
IF YOUR BOSS COULD SEE YOU NOW, HE'D PUT YOU BACK ON THE BEAT IN NO TIME.

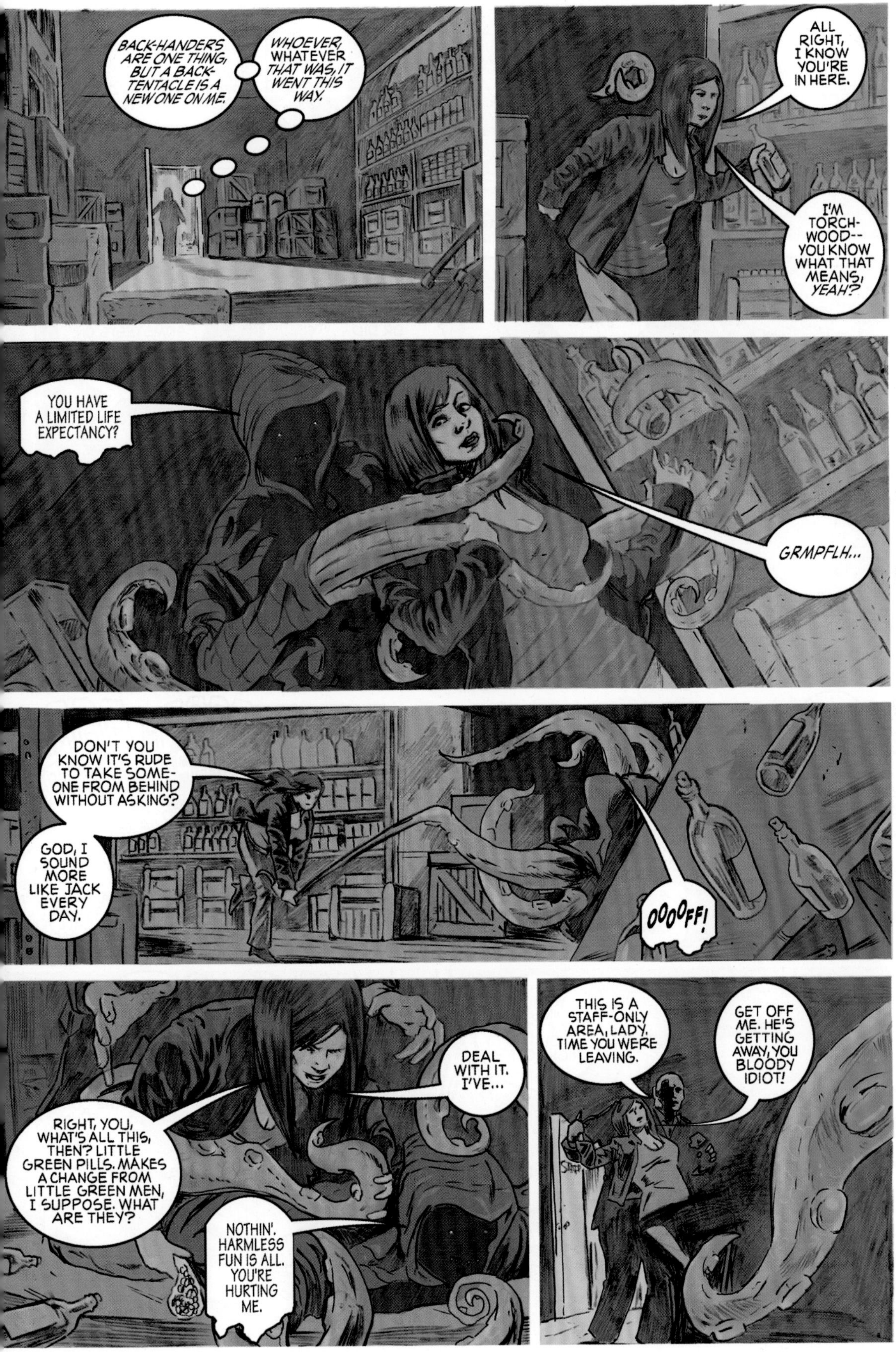
BACK-HANDERS ARE ONE THING, BUT A BACK-TENTACLE IS A NEW ONE ON ME.
WHOEVER, WHATEVER THAT WAS, IT WENT THIS WAY.
ALL RIGHT, I KNOW YOU'RE IN HERE.
I'M TORCH-WOOD-- YOU KNOW WHAT THAT MEANS, YEAH?
YOU HAVE A LIMITED LIFE EXPECTANCY?
GRMPFLH...
DON'T YOU KNOW IT'S RUDE TO TAKE SOME-ONE FROM BEHIND WITHOUT ASKING?
GOD, I SOUND MORE LIKE JACK EVERY DAY.
OOOOFF!
DEAL WITH IT. I'VE...
RIGHT, YOU, WHAT'S ALL THIS, THEN? LITTLE GREEN PILLS. MAKES A CHANGE FROM LITTLE GREEN MEN, I SUPPOSE. WHAT ARE THEY?
NOTHIN'. HARMLESS FUN IS ALL. YOU'RE HURTING ME.
THIS IS A STAFF-ONLY AREA, LADY. TIME YOU WERE LEAVING.
GET OFF ME. HE'S GETTING AWAY, YOU BLOODY IDIOT!

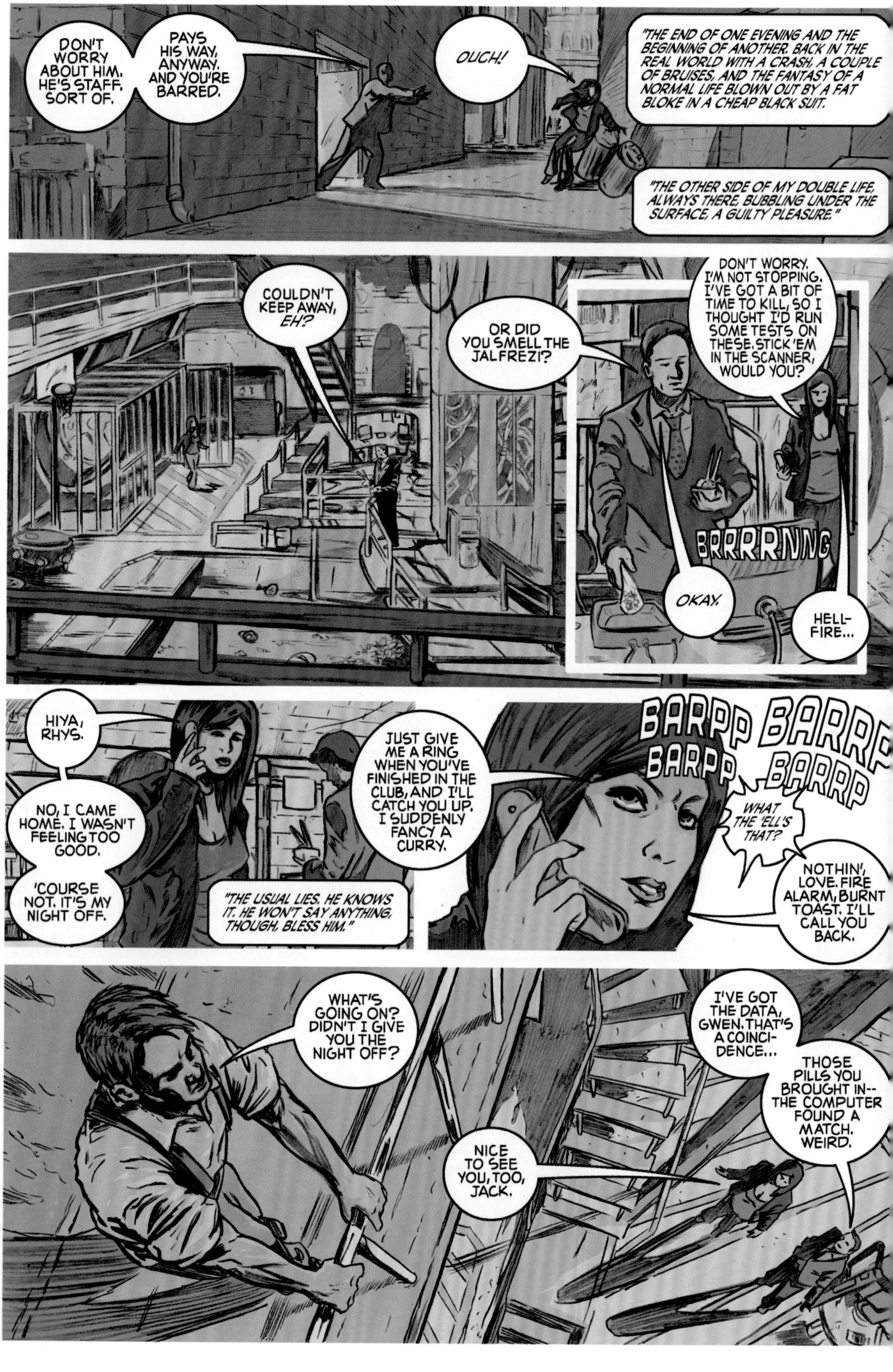
DON'T WORRY ABOUT HIM. HE'S STAFF, SORT OF.
PAYS HIS WAY, ANYWAY. AND YOU'RE BARRED.
OUCH!
"THE END OF ONE EVENING AND THE BEGINNING OF ANOTHER. BACK IN THE REAL WORLD WITH A CRASH, A COUPLE OF BRUISES, AND THE FANTASY OF A NORMAL LIFE BLOWN OUT BY A FAT BLOKE IN A CHEAP BLACK SUIT.
"THE OTHER SIDE OF MY DOUBLE LIFE, ALWAYS THERE, BUBBLING UNDER THE SURFACE, A GUILTY PLEASURE."
COULDN'T KEEP AWAY, EH?
OR DID YOU SMELL THE JALFREZI?
DON'T WORRY. I'M NOT STOPPING. I'VE GOT A BIT OF TIME TO KILL, SO I THOUGHT I'D RUN SOME TESTS ON THESE. STICK 'EM IN THE SCANNER, WOULD YOU?
BRRRRNNG
OKAY.
HELL-FIRE...
HIYA, RHYS.
NO, I CAME HOME. I WASN'T FEELING TOO GOOD.
'COURSE NOT. IT'S MY NIGHT OFF.
"THE USUAL LIES. HE KNOWS IT. HE WON'T SAY ANYTHING, THOUGH, BLESS HIM."
JUST GIVE ME A RING WHEN YOU'VE FINISHED IN THE CLUB, AND I'LL CATCH YOU UP. I SUDDENLY FANCY A CURRY.
BARPP BARRP BARPP BARRP
WHAT THE 'ELL'S THAT?
NOTHIN', LOVE. FIRE ALARM, BURNT TOAST. I'LL CALL YOU BACK.
WHAT'S GOING ON? DIDN'T I GIVE YOU THE NIGHT OFF?
NICE TO SEE YOU, TOO, JACK.
I'VE GOT THE DATA, GWEN. THAT'S A COINCI-DENCE...
THOSE PILLS YOU BROUGHT IN-- THE COMPUTER FOUND A MATCH. WEIRD.

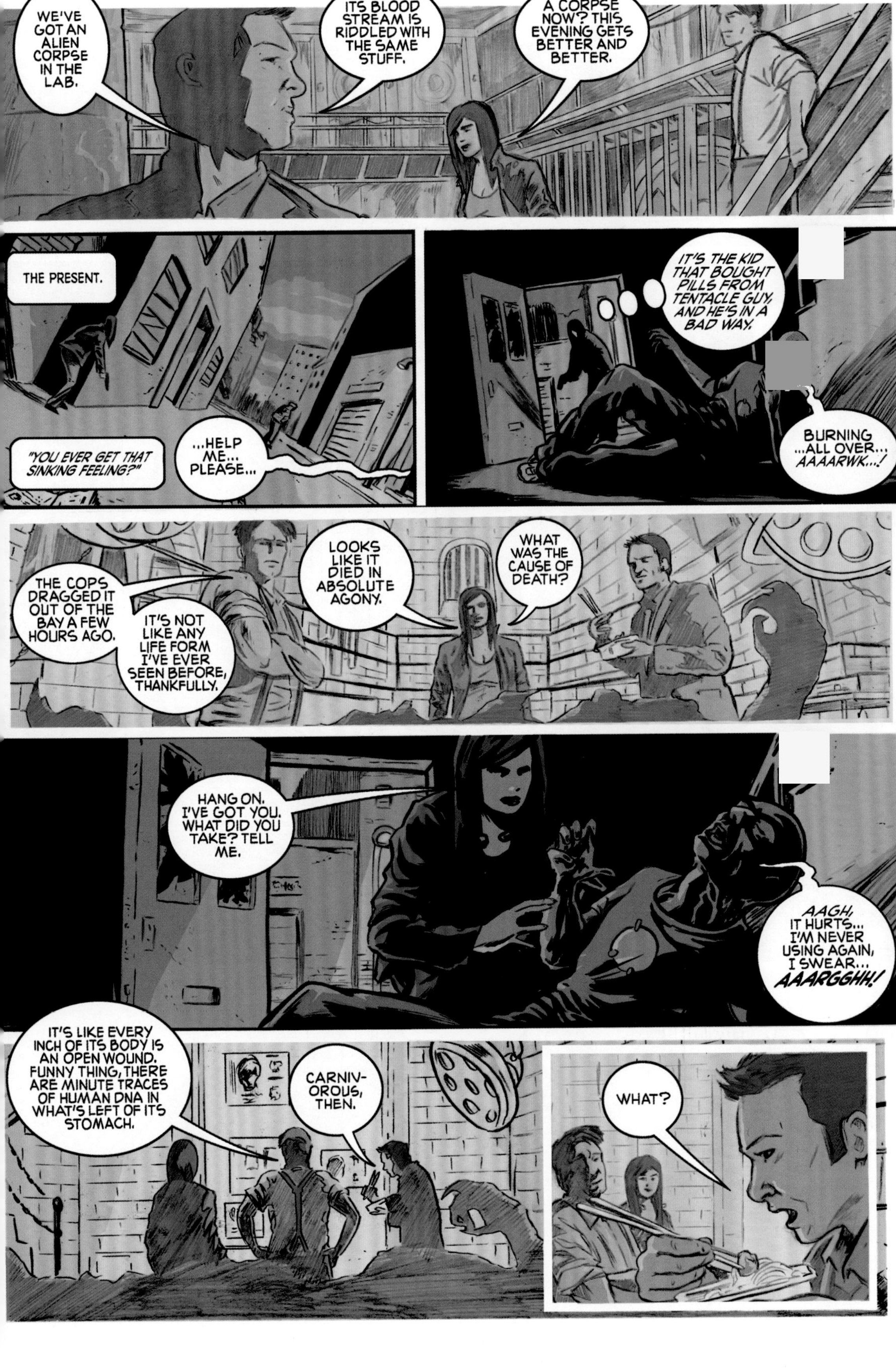
WE'VE GOT AN ALIEN CORPSE IN THE LAB.
ITS BLOOD STREAM IS RIDDLED WITH THE SAME STUFF.
A CORPSE NOW? THIS EVENING GETS BETTER AND BETTER.
THE PRESENT.
"YOU EVER GET THAT SINKING FEELING?"
...HELP ME... PLEASE...
IT'S THE KID THAT BOUGHT PILLS FROM TENTACLE GUY, AND HE'S IN A BAD WAY.
BURNING ...ALL OVER... AAAARWK...!
THE COPS DRAGGED IT OUT OF THE BAY A FEW HOURS AGO.
IT'S NOT LIKE ANY LIFE FORM I'VE EVER SEEN BEFORE, THANKFULLY.
LOOKS LIKE IT DIED IN ABSOLUTE AGONY.
WHAT WAS THE CAUSE OF DEATH?
HANG ON. I'VE GOT YOU. WHAT DID YOU TAKE? TELL ME.
AAGH, IT HURTS... I'M NEVER USING AGAIN, I SWEAR... AAARGGHH!
IT'S LIKE EVERY INCH OF ITS BODY IS AN OPEN WOUND. FUNNY THING, THERE ARE MINUTE TRACES OF HUMAN DNA IN WHAT'S LEFT OF ITS STOMACH.
CARNIV-OROUS, THEN.
WHAT?

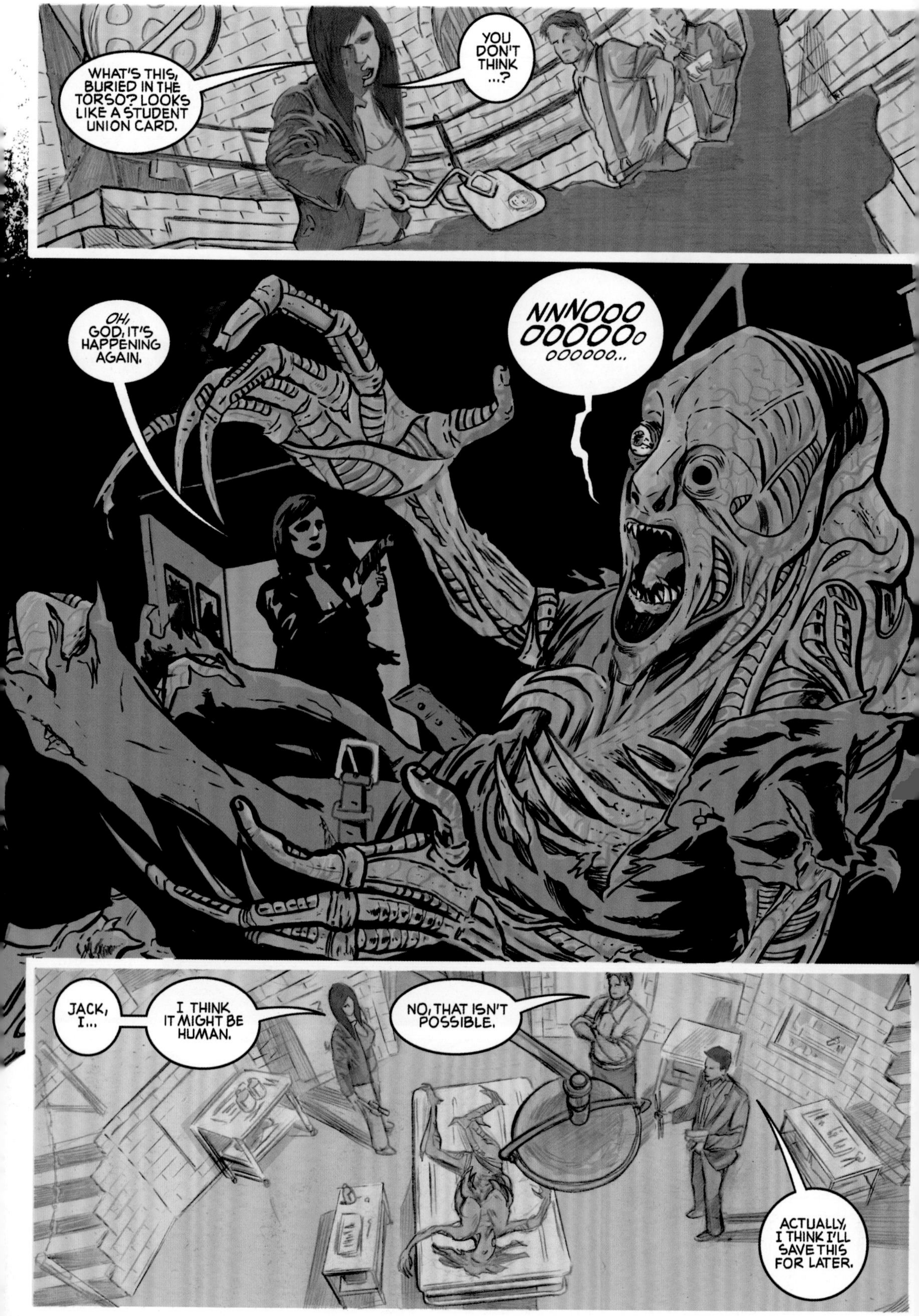
WHAT'S THIS, BURIED IN THE TORSO? LOOKS LIKE A STUDENT UNION CARD.
YOU DON'T THINK ...?
OH, GOD, IT'S HAPPENING AGAIN.
NNNOOO OOOOOo oooooo...
JACK, I...
I THINK IT MIGHT BE HUMAN.
NO, THAT ISN'T POSSIBLE.
ACTUALLY, I THINK I'LL SAVE THIS FOR LATER.

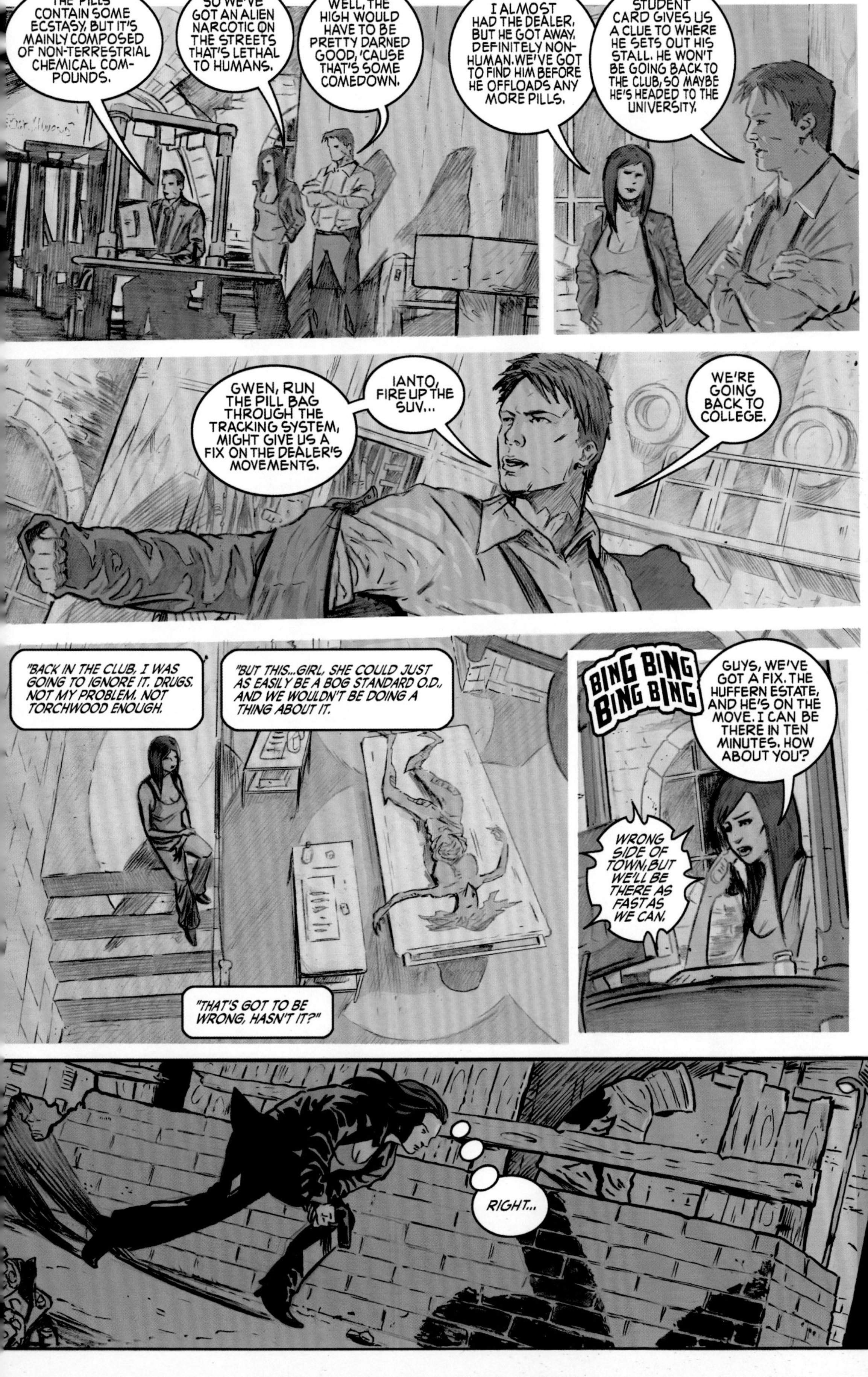
THE PILLS CONTAIN SOME ECSTASY, BUT IT'S MAINLY COMPOSED OF NON-TERRESTRIAL CHEMICAL COMPOUNDS.
SO WE'VE GOT AN ALIEN NARCOTIC ON THE STREETS THAT'S LETHAL TO HUMANS.
WELL, THE HIGH WOULD HAVE TO BE PRETTY DARNED GOOD, 'CAUSE THAT'S SOME COMEDOWN.
I ALMOST HAD THE DEALER, BUT HE GOT AWAY. DEFINITELY NON-HUMAN. WE'VE GOT TO FIND HIM BEFORE HE OFFLOADS ANY MORE PILLS.
STUDENT CARD GIVES US A CLUE TO WHERE HE SETS OUT HIS STALL. HE WON'T BE GOING BACK TO THE CLUB, SO MAYBE HE'S HEADED TO THE UNIVERSITY.
GWEN, RUN THE PILL BAG THROUGH THE TRACKING SYSTEM, MIGHT GIVE US A FIX ON THE DEALER'S MOVEMENTS.
IANTO, FIRE UP THE SUV...
WE'RE GOING BACK TO COLLEGE.
"BACK IN THE CLUB, I WAS GOING TO IGNORE IT. DRUGS. NOT MY PROBLEM. NOT TORCHWOOD ENOUGH.
"BUT THIS...GIRL, SHE COULD JUST AS EASILY BE A BOG STANDARD O.D., AND WE WOULDN'T BE DOING A THING ABOUT IT.
"THAT'S GOT TO BE WRONG, HASN'T IT?"
BING BING BING BING
GUYS, WE'VE GOT A FIX. THE HUFFERN ESTATE, AND HE'S ON THE MOVE. I CAN BE THERE IN TEN MINUTES. HOW ABOUT YOU?
WRONG SIDE OF TOWN, BUT WE'LL BE THERE AS FAST AS WE CAN.
RIGHT...

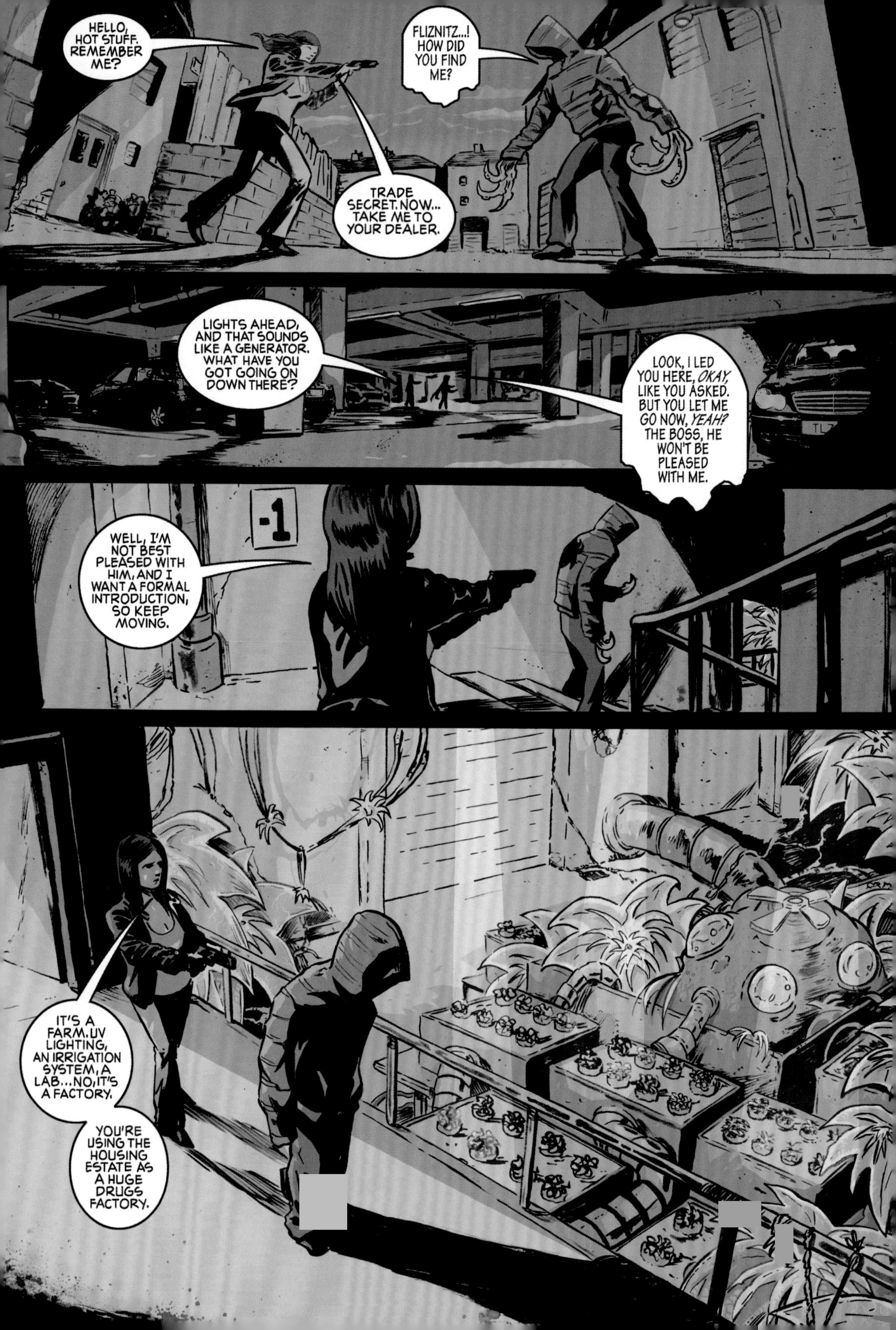
HELLO, HOT STUFF. REMEMBER ME?
FLIZNITZ...! HOW DID YOU FIND ME?
TRADE SECRET. NOW... TAKE ME TO YOUR DEALER.
LIGHTS AHEAD, AND THAT SOUNDS LIKE A GENERATOR. WHAT HAVE YOU GOT GOING ON DOWN THERE?
LOOK, I LED YOU HERE, *OKAY*, LIKE YOU ASKED. BUT YOU LET ME GO NOW, *YEAH?* THE BOSS, HE WON'T BE PLEASED WITH ME.
-1
WELL, I'M NOT BEST PLEASED WITH HIM, AND I WANT A FORMAL INTRODUCTION, SO KEEP MOVING.
IT'S A FARM. UV LIGHTING, AN IRRIGATION SYSTEM, A LAB...NO, IT'S A FACTORY.
YOU'RE USING THE HOUSING ESTATE AS A HUGE DRUGS FACTORY.

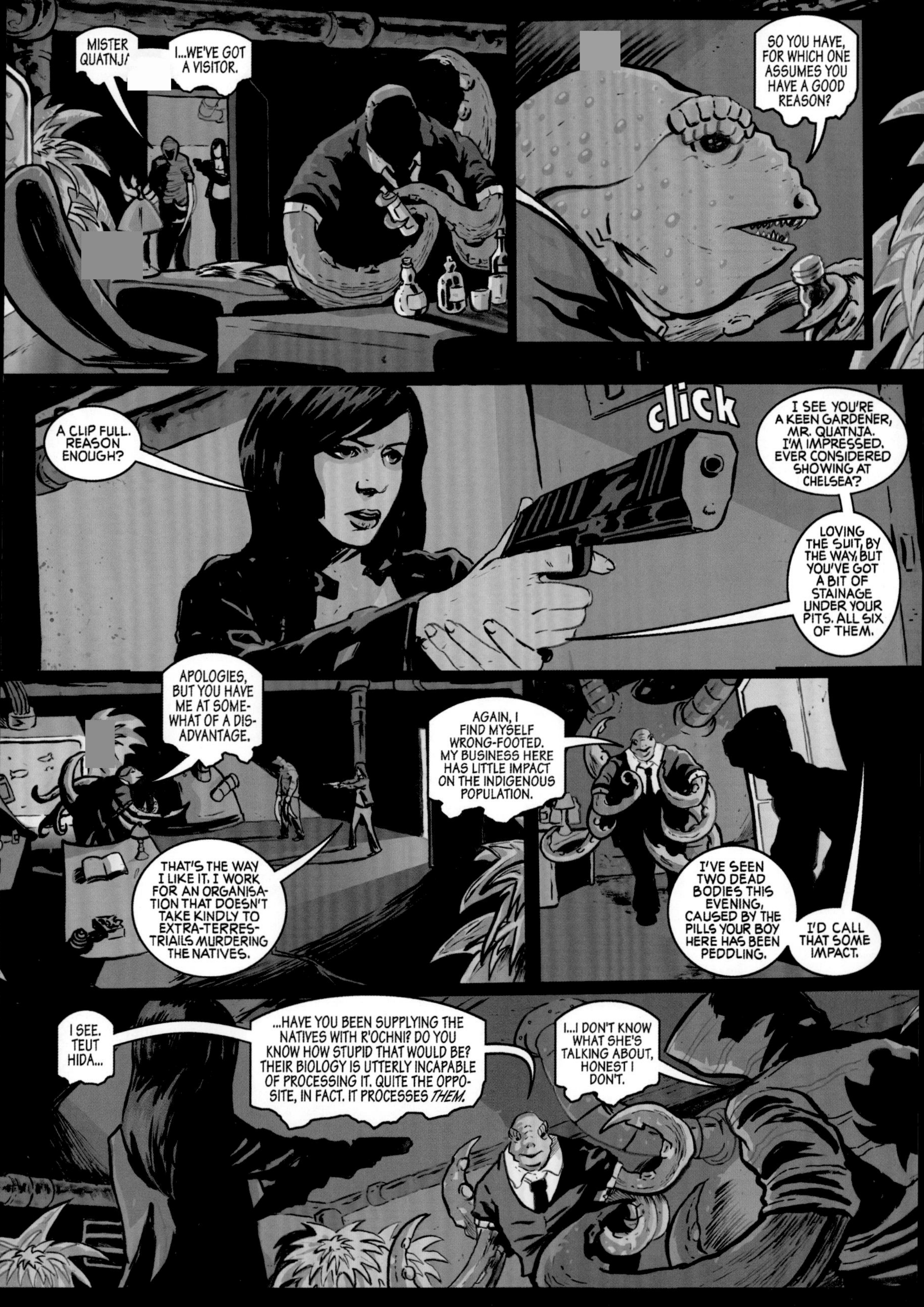
MISTER QUATNJA
I...WE'VE GOT A VISITOR.
SO YOU HAVE, FOR WHICH ONE ASSUMES YOU HAVE A GOOD REASON?
A CLIP FULL. REASON ENOUGH?
click
I SEE YOU'RE A KEEN GARDENER, MR. QUATNJA. I'M IMPRESSED. EVER CONSIDERED SHOWING AT CHELSEA?
LOVING THE SUIT, BY THE WAY, BUT YOU'VE GOT A BIT OF STAINAGE UNDER YOUR PITS. ALL SIX OF THEM.
APOLOGIES, BUT YOU HAVE ME AT SOME-WHAT OF A DIS-ADVANTAGE.
THAT'S THE WAY I LIKE IT. I WORK FOR AN ORGANISA-TION THAT DOESN'T TAKE KINDLY TO EXTRA-TERRES-TRIALS MURDERING THE NATIVES.
AGAIN, I FIND MYSELF WRONG-FOOTED. MY BUSINESS HERE HAS LITTLE IMPACT ON THE INDIGENOUS POPULATION.
I'VE SEEN TWO DEAD BODIES THIS EVENING, CAUSED BY THE PILLS YOUR BOY HERE HAS BEEN PEDDLING.
I'D CALL THAT SOME IMPACT.
I SEE. TEUT HIDA...
...HAVE YOU BEEN SUPPLYING THE NATIVES WITH R'OCHNI? DO YOU KNOW HOW STUPID THAT WOULD BE? THEIR BIOLOGY IS UTTERLY INCAPABLE OF PROCESSING IT. QUITE THE OPPO-SITE, IN FACT. IT PROCESSES *THEM.*
I...I DON'T KNOW WHAT SHE'S TALKING ABOUT, HONEST I DON'T.

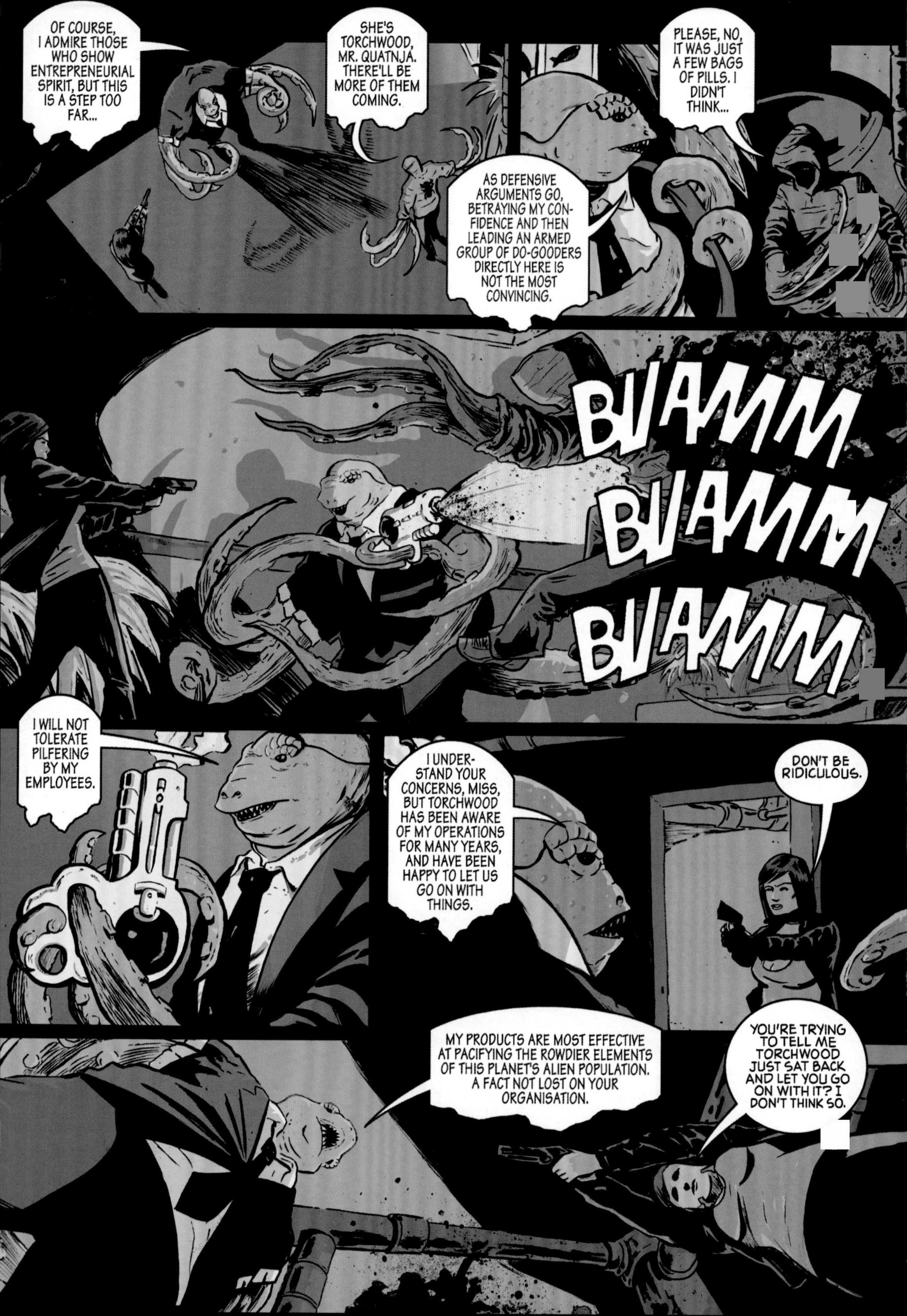
OF COURSE, I ADMIRE THOSE WHO SHOW ENTREPRENEURIAL SPIRIT, BUT THIS IS A STEP TOO FAR...
SHE'S TORCHWOOD, MR. QUATNJA. THERE'LL BE MORE OF THEM COMING.
PLEASE, NO, IT WAS JUST A FEW BAGS OF PILLS. I DIDN'T THINK...
AS DEFENSIVE ARGUMENTS GO, BETRAYING MY CON-FIDENCE AND THEN LEADING AN ARMED GROUP OF DO-GOODERS DIRECTLY HERE IS NOT THE MOST CONVINCING.
BLAMM
BLAMM
BLAMM
I WILL NOT TOLERATE PILFERING BY MY EMPLOYEES.
I UNDER-STAND YOUR CONCERNS, MISS, BUT TORCHWOOD HAS BEEN AWARE OF MY OPERATIONS FOR MANY YEARS, AND HAVE BEEN HAPPY TO LET US GO ON WITH THINGS.
DON'T BE RIDICULOUS.
MY PRODUCTS ARE MOST EFFECTIVE AT PACIFYING THE ROWDIER ELEMENTS OF THIS PLANET'S ALIEN POPULATION. A FACT NOT LOST ON YOUR ORGANISATION.
YOU'RE TRYING TO TELL ME TORCHWOOD JUST SAT BACK AND LET YOU GO ON WITH IT? I DON'T THINK SO.

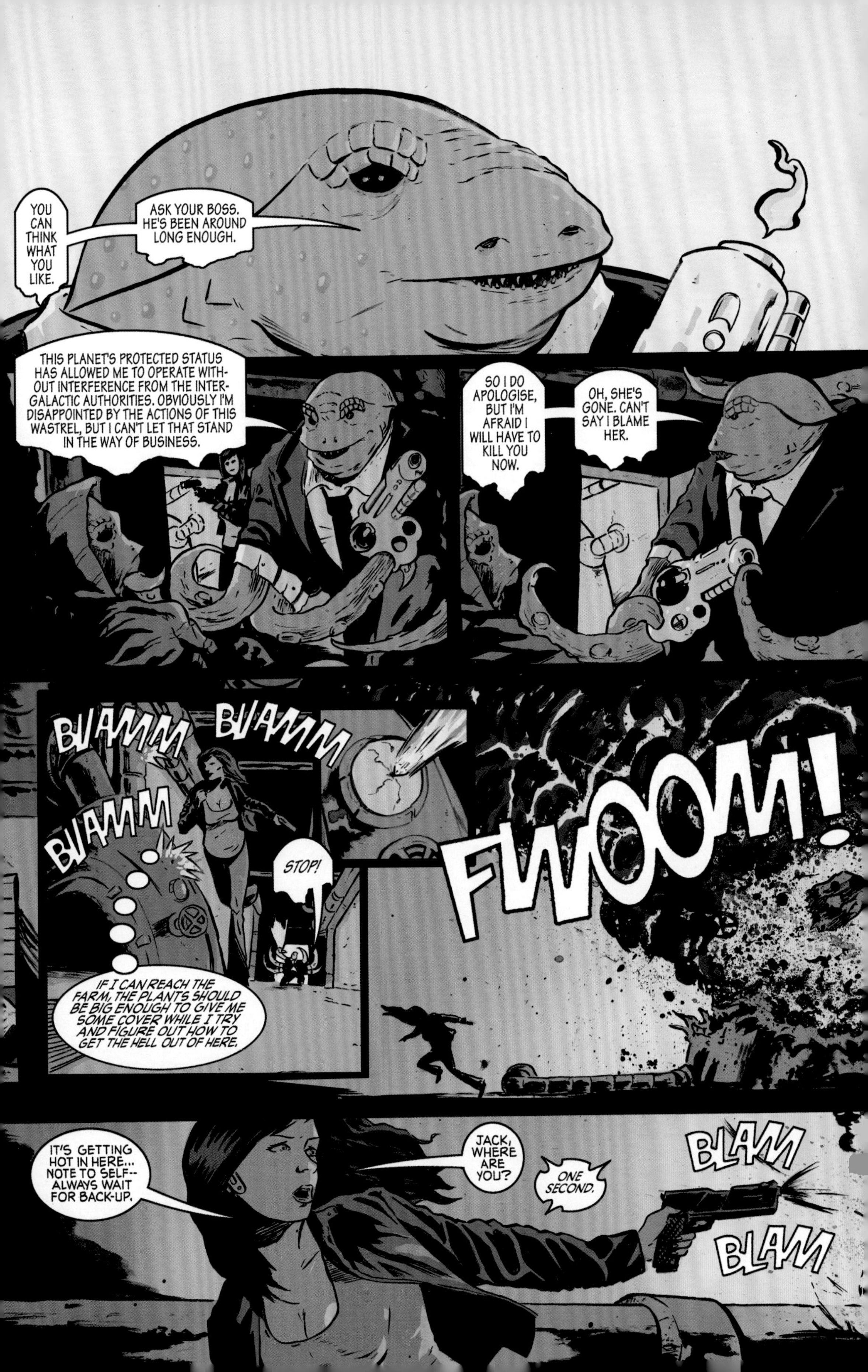
YOU CAN THINK WHAT YOU LIKE.
ASK YOUR BOSS. HE'S BEEN AROUND LONG ENOUGH.
THIS PLANET'S PROTECTED STATUS HAS ALLOWED ME TO OPERATE WITHOUT INTERFERENCE FROM THE INTERGALACTIC AUTHORITIES. OBVIOUSLY I'M DISAPPOINTED BY THE ACTIONS OF THIS WASTREL, BUT I CAN'T LET THAT STAND IN THE WAY OF BUSINESS.
SO I DO APOLOGISE, BUT I'M AFRAID I WILL HAVE TO KILL YOU NOW.
OH, SHE'S GONE. CAN'T SAY I BLAME HER.
BLAMM
BLAMM
BLAMM
STOP!
IF I CAN REACH THE FARM, THE PLANTS SHOULD BE BIG ENOUGH TO GIVE ME SOME COVER WHILE I TRY AND FIGURE OUT HOW TO GET THE HELL OUT OF HERE.
FWOOM!
IT'S GETTING HOT IN HERE... NOTE TO SELF-- ALWAYS WAIT FOR BACK-UP.
JACK, WHERE ARE YOU?
ONE SECOND.
BLAM
BLAM

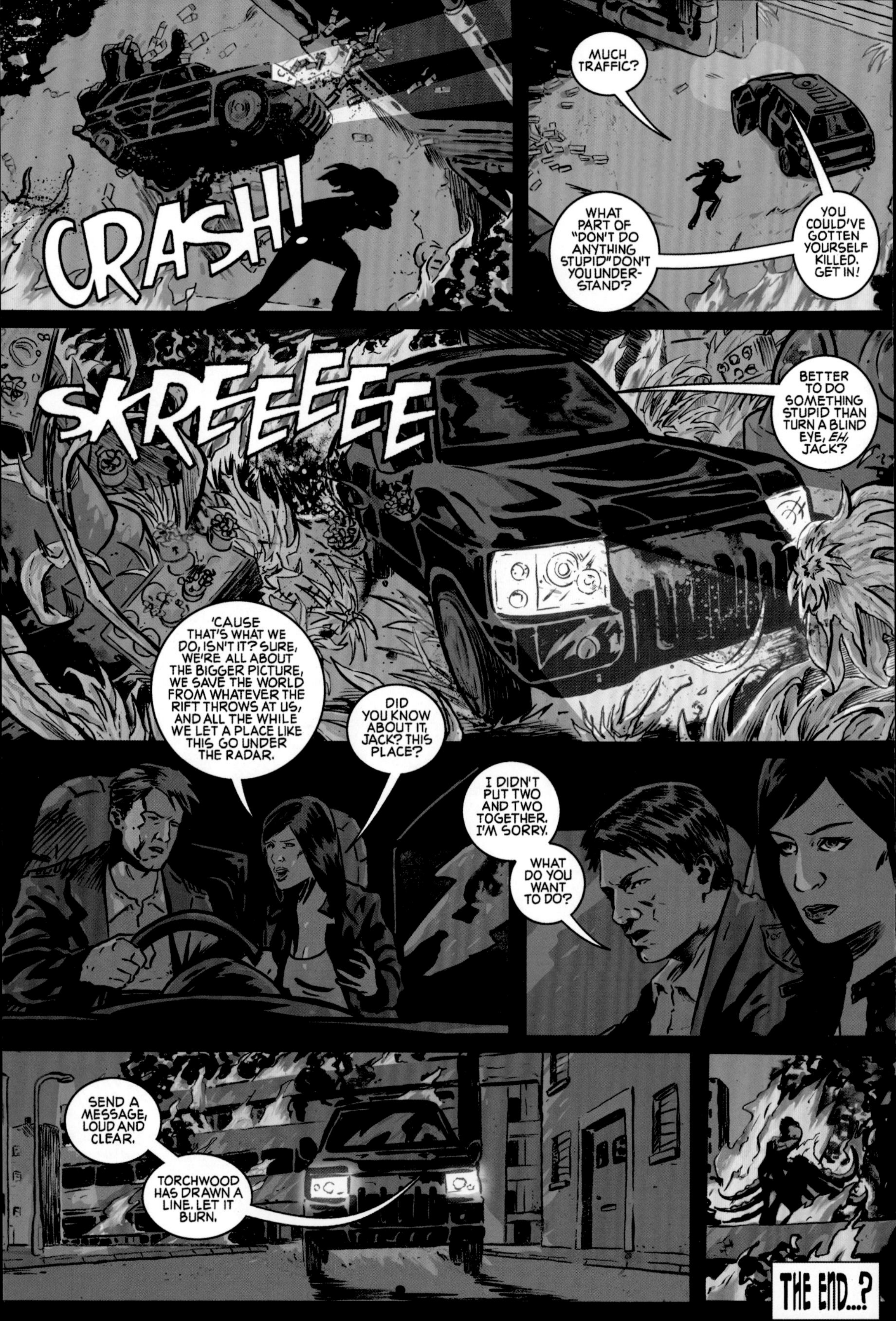
CRASH!
MUCH TRAFFIC?
WHAT PART OF "DON'T DO ANYTHING STUPID" DON'T YOU UNDER-STAND?
YOU COULD'VE GOTTEN YOURSELF KILLED. GET IN!
SKREEEEEE
BETTER TO DO SOMETHING STUPID THAN TURN A BLIND EYE, EH, JACK?
'CAUSE THAT'S WHAT WE DO, ISN'T IT? SURE, WE'RE ALL ABOUT THE BIGGER PICTURE, WE SAVE THE WORLD FROM WHATEVER THE RIFT THROWS AT US, AND ALL THE WHILE WE LET A PLACE LIKE THIS GO UNDER THE RADAR.
DID YOU KNOW ABOUT IT, JACK? THIS PLACE?
I DIDN'T PUT TWO AND TWO TOGETHER. I'M SORRY.
WHAT DO YOU WANT TO DO?
SEND A MESSAGE, LOUD AND CLEAR.
TORCHWOOD HAS DRAWN A LINE. LET IT BURN.
THE END...?

THE RETURN OF THE VOSTOK

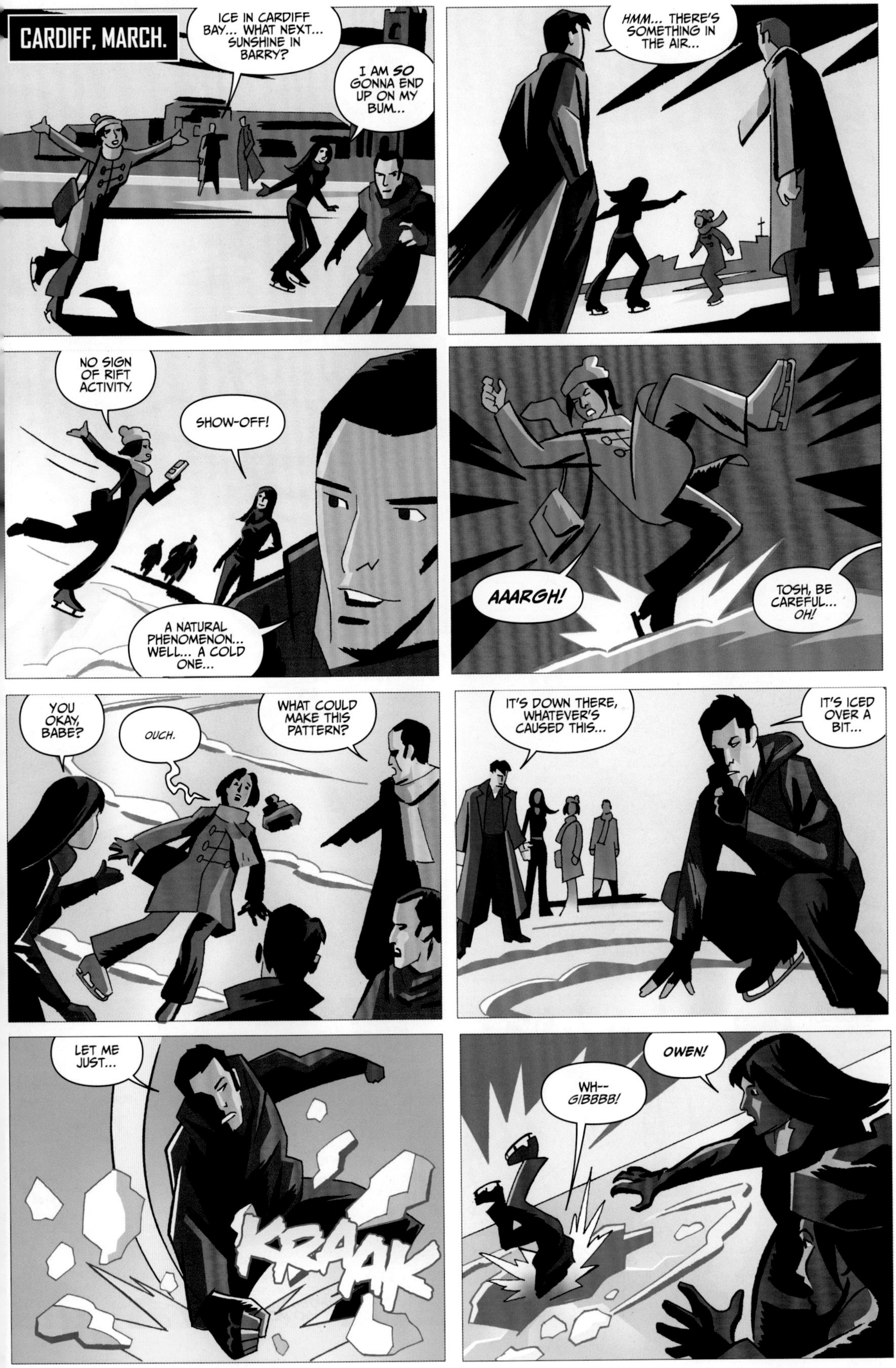
CARDIFF, MARCH.
ICE IN CARDIFF BAY... WHAT NEXT... SUNSHINE IN BARRY?
I AM SO GONNA END UP ON MY BUM...
HMM... THERE'S SOMETHING IN THE AIR...
NO SIGN OF RIFT ACTIVITY.
SHOW-OFF!
A NATURAL PHENOMENON... WELL... A COLD ONE...
AAARGH!
TOSH, BE CAREFUL... OH!
YOU OKAY, BABE?
OUCH.
WHAT COULD MAKE THIS PATTERN?
IT'S DOWN THERE, WHATEVER'S CAUSED THIS...
IT'S ICED OVER A BIT...
LET ME JUST...
KRAAK
OWEN!
WH-- GIBBBB!

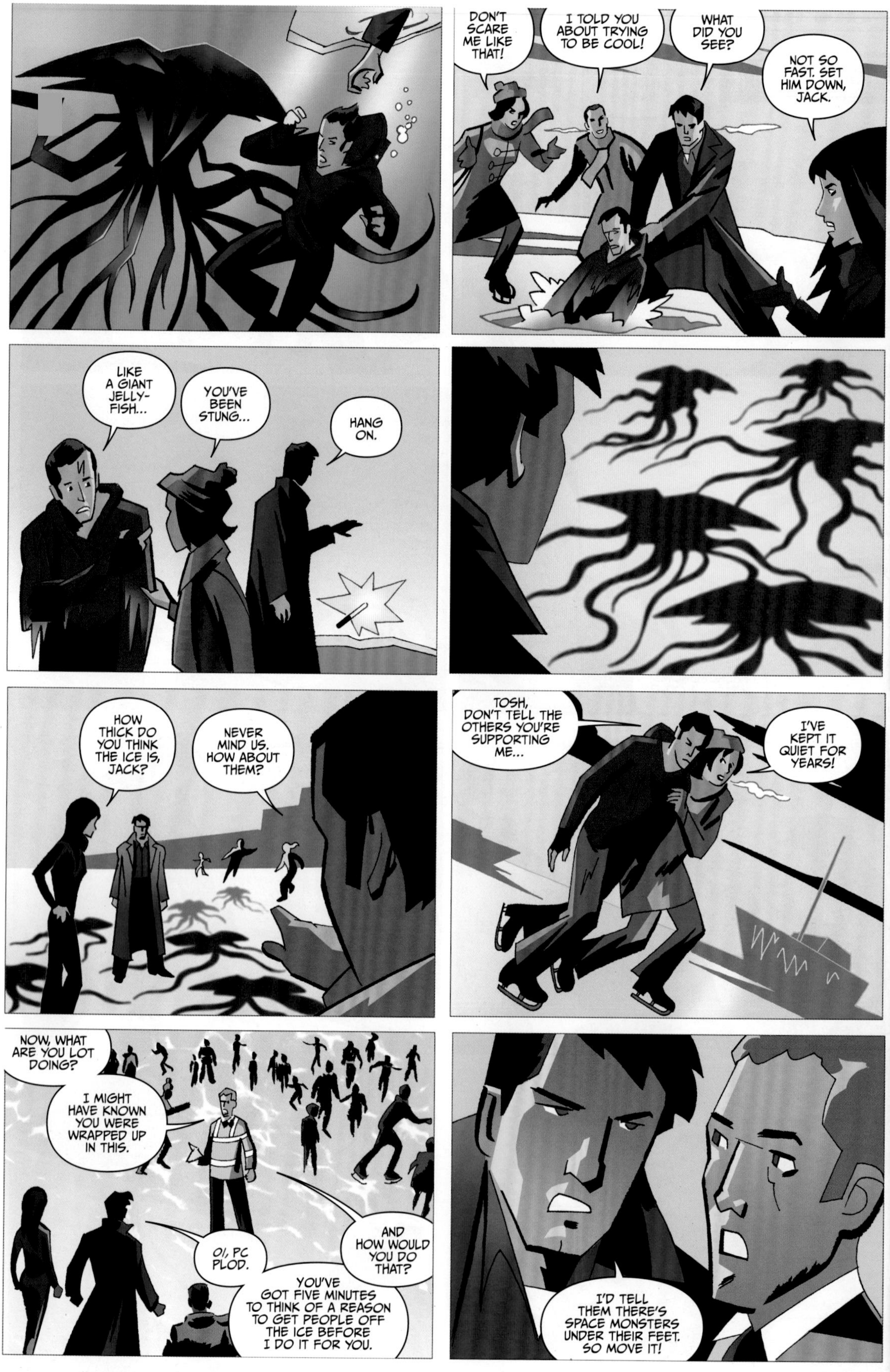
DON'T SCARE ME LIKE THAT!
I TOLD YOU ABOUT TRYING TO BE COOL!
WHAT DID YOU SEE?
NOT SO FAST. SET HIM DOWN, JACK.
LIKE A GIANT JELLY-FISH...
YOU'VE BEEN STUNG...
HANG ON.
HOW THICK DO YOU THINK THE ICE IS, JACK?
NEVER MIND US. HOW ABOUT THEM?
TOSH, DON'T TELL THE OTHERS YOU'RE SUPPORTING ME...
I'VE KEPT IT QUIET FOR YEARS!
NOW, WHAT ARE YOU LOT DOING?
I MIGHT HAVE KNOWN YOU WERE WRAPPED UP IN THIS.
OI, PC PLOD.
YOU'VE GOT FIVE MINUTES TO THINK OF A REASON TO GET PEOPLE OFF THE ICE BEFORE I DO IT FOR YOU.
AND HOW WOULD YOU DO THAT?
I'D TELL THEM THERE'S SPACE MONSTERS UNDER THEIR FEET. SO MOVE IT!

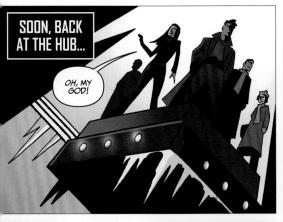

SOON, BACK AT THE HUB...

OH, MY GOD!

SHOULD'VE KNOWN THAT DAMP WOULD BE A PROBLEM...

THE ICEBERGS ARE HEADING FOR CARDIFF...

ARE THE POLAR BEARS FINALLY GETTING THEIR OWN BACK?

SOMEHOW, I DON'T THINK SO...

HERE, PAGE 31.

"BARK OF RIVERS, ROOF OF THE WAVES, DESTRUCTION OF THE DAMNED..."

EH?

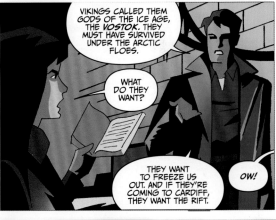

VIKINGS CALLED THEM GODS OF THE ICE AGE, THE VOSTOK. THEY MUST HAVE SURVIVED UNDER THE ARCTIC FLOES.

WHAT DO THEY WANT?

THEY WANT TO FREEZE US OUT. AND IF THEY'RE COMING TO CARDIFF, THEY WANT THE RIFT.

OW!

LOOK AT THIS! HOW CAN IT GET SO COLD DOWN HERE? HEATING'S ON FULL BLAST!

KCHAKT

THE VOSTOK CAN SUCK THE HEAT OUT OF THE AIR. YOUR ECONOMY 7'S NOT GONNA WORK.

IANTO, HISTORY QUIZ... WHAT DEFEATED NAPOLEON?

THE RUSSIAN WINTER.

TOP MARKS. VERY CLEVER SPECIES. THE ALIENS, NOT THE FRENCH. THEY LOWER THE TEMPERATURE UNTIL NO ONE ELSE CAN SURVIVE. IF THEY LATCH ONTO THE RIFT, THEY'LL SEND A NEW ICE AGE ECHOING BACK THROUGH TIME.

WOOLLY MAMMOTHS? NICE!

HUB LOCKS SHOULD HOLD THEM, BUT IT'S MINUS 20!

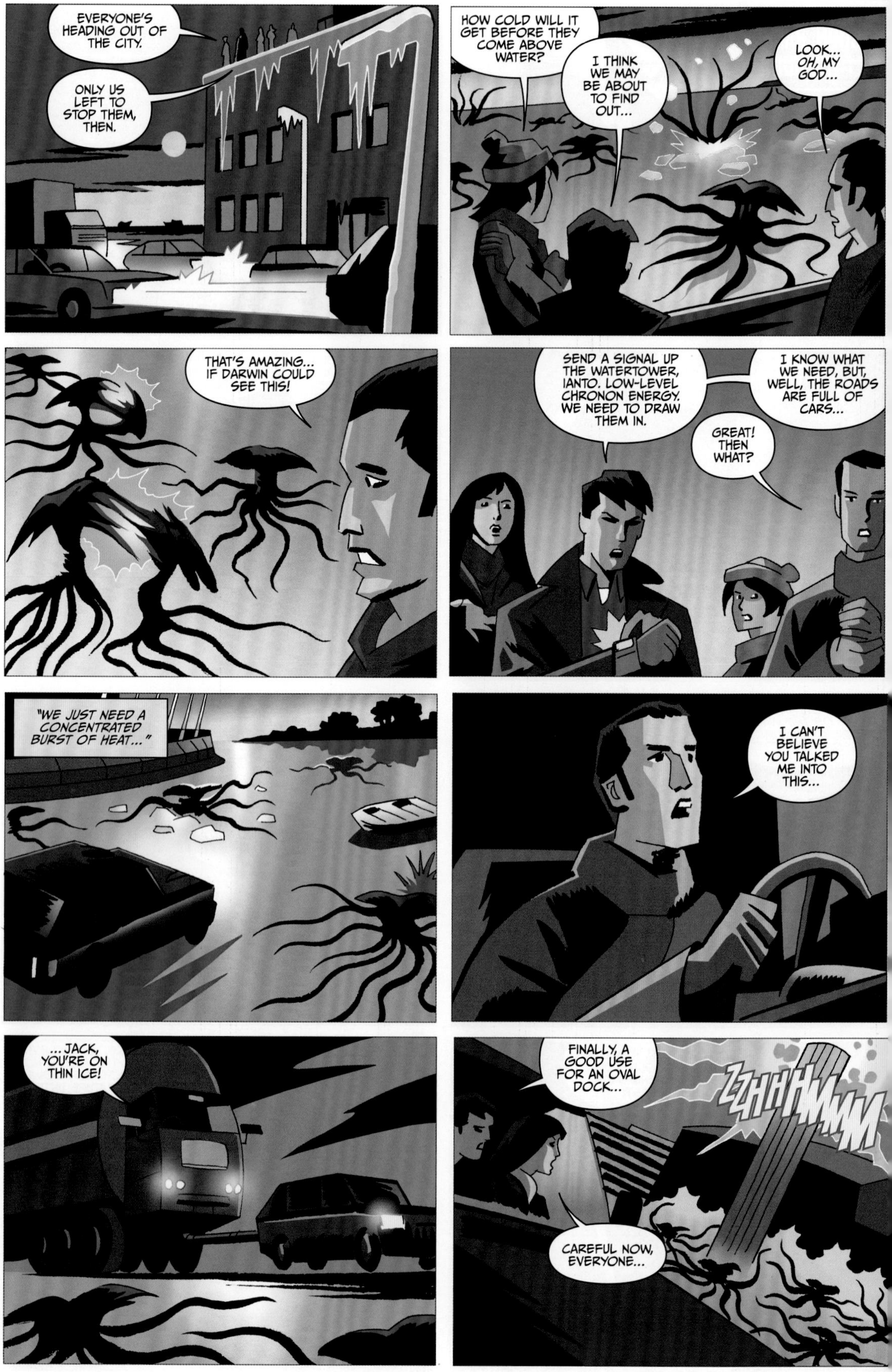
EVERYONE'S HEADING OUT OF THE CITY.
ONLY US LEFT TO STOP THEM, THEN.
HOW COLD WILL IT GET BEFORE THEY COME ABOVE WATER?
I THINK WE MAY BE ABOUT TO FIND OUT...
LOOK... OH, MY GOD...
THAT'S AMAZING... IF DARWIN COULD SEE THIS!
SEND A SIGNAL UP THE WATERTOWER, IANTO. LOW-LEVEL CHRONON ENERGY. WE NEED TO DRAW THEM IN.
I KNOW WHAT WE NEED, BUT, WELL, THE ROADS ARE FULL OF CARS...
GREAT! THEN WHAT?
"WE JUST NEED A CONCENTRATED BURST OF HEAT..."
I CAN'T BELIEVE YOU TALKED ME INTO THIS...
... JACK, YOU'RE ON THIN ICE!
FINALLY, A GOOD USE FOR AN OVAL DOCK...
ZZHHHMMMM
CAREFUL NOW, EVERYONE...

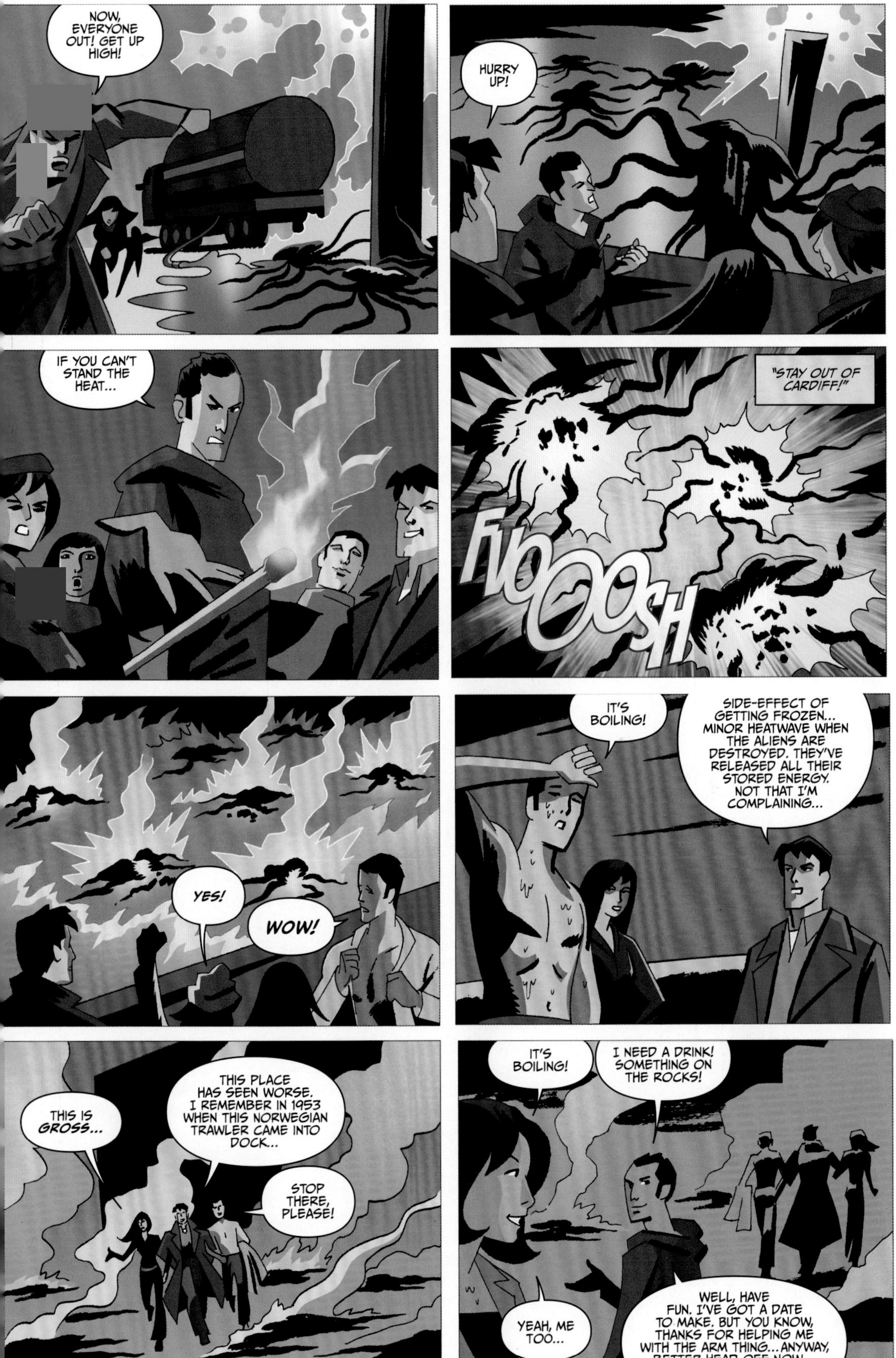
NOW, EVERYONE OUT! GET UP HIGH!
HURRY UP!
IF YOU CAN'T STAND THE HEAT...
"STAY OUT OF CARDIFF!"
FWOOOOSH
YES!
WOW!
IT'S BOILING!
SIDE-EFFECT OF GETTING FROZEN... MINOR HEATWAVE WHEN THE ALIENS ARE DESTROYED. THEY'VE RELEASED ALL THEIR STORED ENERGY. NOT THAT I'M COMPLAINING...
THIS IS GROSS...
THIS PLACE HAS SEEN WORSE. I REMEMBER IN 1953 WHEN THIS NORWEGIAN TRAWLER CAME INTO DOCK...
STOP THERE, PLEASE!
IT'S BOILING!
I NEED A DRINK! SOMETHING ON THE ROCKS!
YEAH, ME TOO...
WELL, HAVE FUN. I'VE GOT A DATE TO MAKE. BUT YOU KNOW, THANKS FOR HELPING ME WITH THE ARM THING... ANYWAY, BETTER HEAD OFF NOW...

END

CULTURAL FIRSTS

A NEW SHORT STORY BY RICHARD STOKES

ART BY MIKE DOWLING

Jack could feel the tears pricking at his eyes. This always happened. Barely into Act One and the soprano's high notes of *Chi Il Bel Sogno Di Doretta* got to him. His broad shoulders relaxed back into the velour of the Cardiff Millennium Centre seat as he let Puccini's aria wash over him.

Some weeks ago he had suggested to Gwen and Ianto that they try and indulge in a few entertainments out of their comfort zone. They rarely got downtime and had decided to treat each other to a 'cultural first'. Ianto's invitation to the pantomime last Christmas had proved a disaster after Jack had been convinced to go on stage and lead the children in a chorus of 'The Time Warp.' So Puccini was a welcome change. However, the moment was broken as an elbow dug into his arm. He turned to see Gwen mouthing "Sorry" at him.

She fidgeted for a few seconds and then pushed back into the seat. Jack kept an eye on her as she opened her mouth in an almighty yawn.

He leaned over. "You can't be bored already."

"Sorry, Jack. I did say you should have brought Ianto. Opera's not really my thing"

"I thought that was the point," replied Jack. "Ianto's done opera. You haven't."

An irritated shush coming from behind them halted the whispered exchange. The music continued for a few seconds until a very tinny, but unmistakable Rhys-like voice came from Gwen's jacket pocket.

"Come on gorgeous, answer your phone... Come on gorgeous, answer your phone..."

Gwen cursed under her breath and scrambled in her jacket pocket as several people around her tutted in disgust. Jack just looked at her, disbelief bordering on anger in his eyes. "Bloody Rhys keeps playing with my phone," she offered as an excuse then, looking at the phone, silenced the ringtone and showed the call-ID to Jack.

"Ianto."

Jack sighed. They both knew he would only call in an emergency.

Ianto wiped the frothy excess milk from the lip of his coffee cup and tipped a light dusting of cinnamon on his drink. He sipped at it, tilting his head as he rolled the taste around his mouth. Then he nodded in appreciation at his own efforts and took a larger mouthful as the gate began to swing open behind him, lights flashed and the big round door rolled to the side, revealing Jack and Gwen in mid-argument.

"...1917 when I first saw that opera. And that was interrupted by an air raid. I've still never seen the end."

Ianto smiled as Gwen rolled her eyes at Jack. "La Rondine?" he asked.

Jack nodded, "It's not the greatest opera but it has certain personal memories for me. Monte Carlo, a certain tenor..."

"And we'll leave the rest of that story to our imaginations," interrupted Gwen. "Ianto, you called?"

Ianto put down his coffee and walked over to the computer display at Gwen's desk, tapped at the keyboard, and stood back. The others gathered around the display and looked at the readings. They both knew instantly what it meant

"There's been rift activity in the last few minutes," said Jack. "And right here in the Hub."

"What came through? Where is it?" asked Gwen.

"It wasn't a what. It was a who." Ianto tapped at the keyboard again, and several images of the Hub's cell complex came up on the CCTV display.

"I think he's from Italy. I put him in a cell."

"Any idea who he is?" said Gwen.

"Difficult to be sure," Ianto continued. "My Italian stops at 'Prego' and 'Quanto costa per un'ora?'"

"Quanta what?"

"How much by the hour," Jack answered Gwen's question with a smile. "Best not to ask."

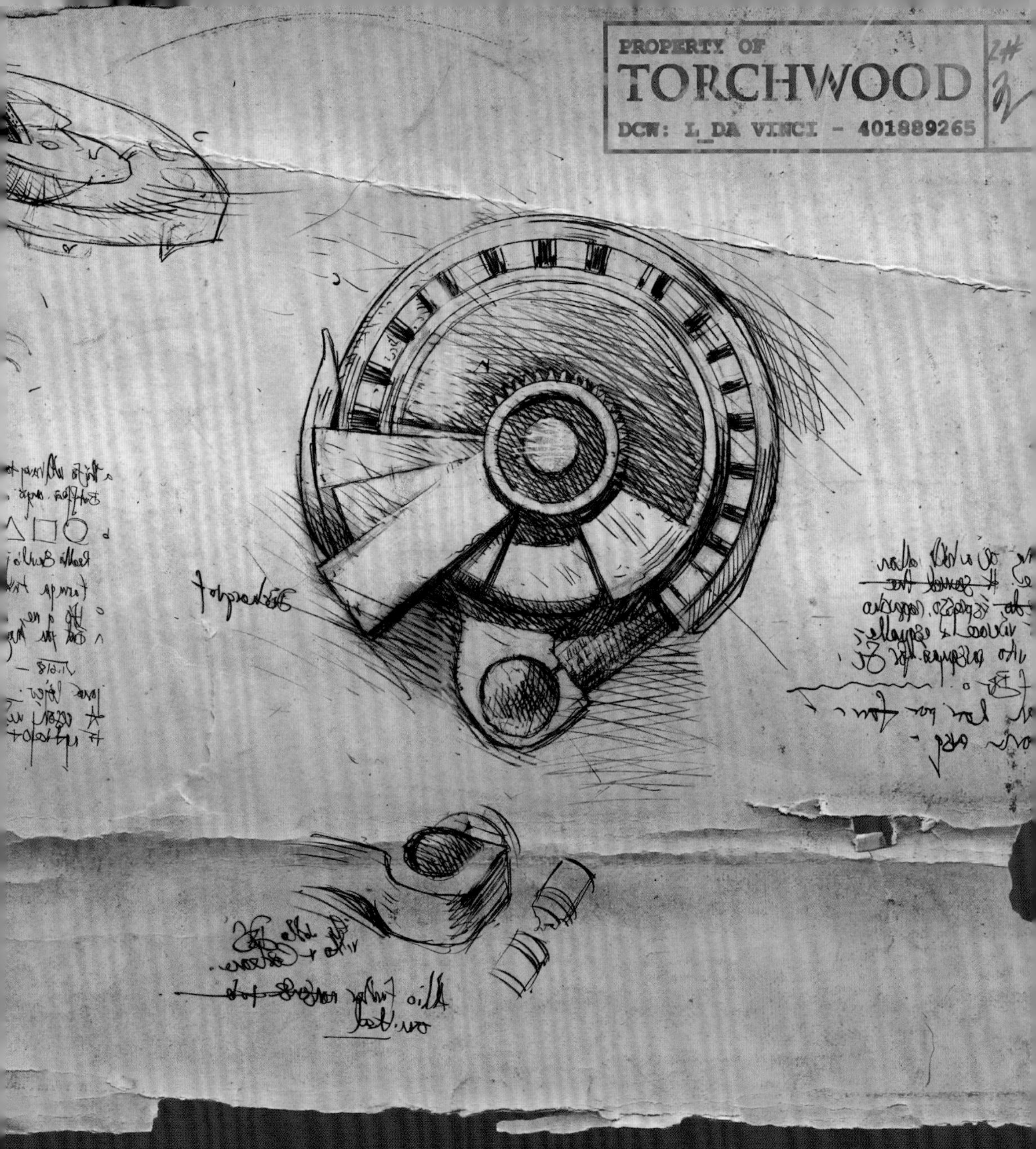
PROPERTY OF
TORCHWOOD
DCW: L_DA VINCI - 401889265

Gwen was alone in the cell corridor. She leaned towards the glass and looked into the large green eyes of the man on the other side. They seemed immediately disarming, paternal even. They were framed by a shock of greying hair and a short beard, and he was dressed in simple leathers and cloth.

"Hello," she said. No answer. "Buon journo," she added with an accompanying gesticulation. He smiled at her, and that provoked an involuntary smile from her.

She turned as she heard the door at the end of the corridor, and Jack and Ianto walked in.

Ianto nodded at the prisoner, "Has he said anything?"

"No, not yet. What do you think, Jack? What form of torture should we use on this evil monster? Deny him his five a day?"

But Jack wasn't listening. He approached the window of the cell and put this hand up against the glass.

"Good to see you again, Jack," said the man in a stilted fashion, the words tripping over a heavy accent.

Jack stared back at him, eyes growing wider in surprise and wonder.

"Leo?"

The man smiled and nodded.

"Who's Leo?" asked Ianto, curtly.

In the boardroom, Gwen and Ianto sat at the big mahogany table as Jack paced in front of the flatscreen monitor, on which was a familiar pencil sketch of an old man with a long white beard.

"Leonardo," announced Jack to his audience. "The original Renaissance man. Polymath. Genius. Call him what you will, but he's 500 years out of his time and we have to get him back. Now."

"Sorry," said Gwen in that tone of voice Jack knew was going to lead to the $64,000 question. "Are we talking Leonardo da Vinci? Mona Lisa and all that?"

Ianto answered on Jack's behalf. "Yes, though da Vinci isn't actually

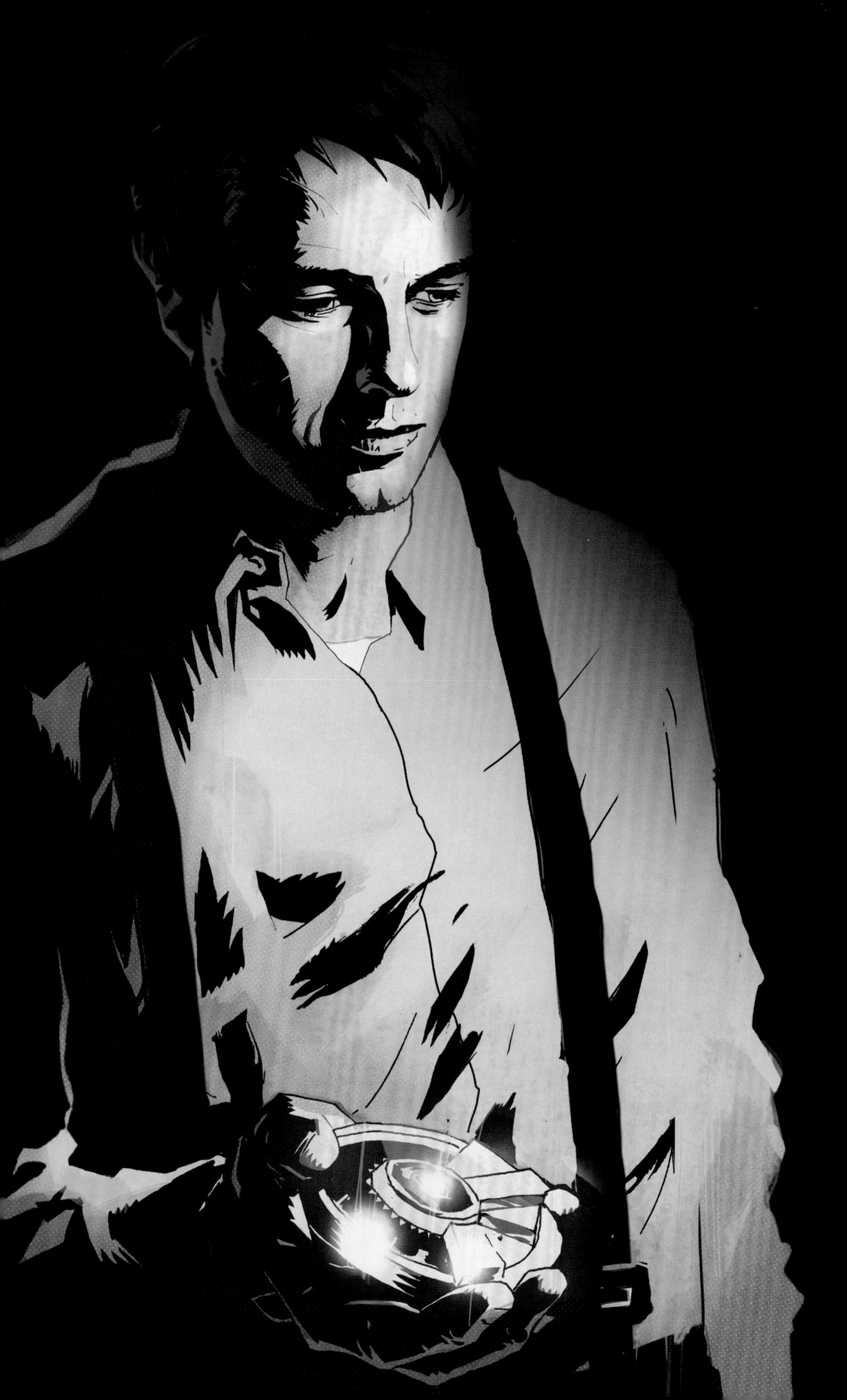

if Shirley Bassey was called 'Dame Shirley Splott.'"

"I rather like that."

Jack raised his hand to silence them. "That's not the point. We need to send him back."

"Oh, can't we keep him for a little bit?" asked Gwen. "What's he going to do? Paint us to death? I've never met one of the real Ninja Turtles before."

Jack sat down, his tone of voice dictating the seriousness of the situation. "He's a genius. That word is splashed around today like cheap cologne, but back then? We're talking mind-of-the-century, change-the-course-of-humanity genius. Think about where he is, what he's surrounded by. He can't be allowed to see or touch anything. Not this time."

Ianto nodded, before a frown slowly descended. "What do you mean, 'Not this time'? And how did he know who you were, anyway?"

Jack stood up and went to the monitor by way of a reply. He picked up the remote at the side of the screen and started flicking through pages of old pencil sketches.

"To the modern world, Leonardo is known for a handful of paintings, some pencil sketches and his detailed anatomical notebooks. He also drew concepts of ideas way ahead of his time, including helicopters, calculators... And this."

He stopped flicking the remote and the extraordinary drawings stopped whizzing by, leaving one image on the screen: a detailed pencil sketch surrounded by cross-sections and scribbling. Jack could see from the two wide-eyed expressions in front of him that he had made his point.

"This drawing has never been seen by anyone outside Torchwood. It's held in our archive, here in the Hub."

Ianto and Gwen were open-mouthed as they stared at the screen. It showed a perfect 500-year-old drawing of a Rift Key.

In the cell Leonardo held the Rift Key in his hands. He turned the dull golden object over, admiring once more its beauty as he had done the first time he had seen it, nearly 40 years ago. A teenager

had struck him, and he awoke in a magical place like nowhere he had ever seen before. The Hub. He had spent part of that time in this very cell.

Recalling the memory, he looked around and smiled. He stood and stroked the hard stone wall with the palm of his hand. He never thought he'd made it back.

Little seemed to have changed. The girl and the boy were new, but Jack looked the same. Forty years had passed since he was last here – but how many for Jack? The question excited him. It was a new theory to ponder, but not now. Now he needed to start what he had come here to do.

He placed the Rift Key back in the pouch he had made for it, which he kept around his waist, and dug around inside his leather jerkin for the other essential item with which he had returned. It was a thin rectangular card made of a substance he had never been able to identify. Plain on one side, with a dark rust-coloured strip on the back – or the front. He did not know. He had yet to deconstruct the object, as there were no moving parts and there seemed no way inside the thin strip of hard material.

What he did know, however, was if he held it close enough to the lock in his cell, the door opened obediently before him.

Jack held court in the boardroom. "In 1967," he said, "a 17-year-old kid from the late 15th Century got swept up in a Rift storm and deposited here. It took us a while to work out exactly who he was, but he charmed us all and was super-smart. He just wanted to learn and know everything. We all fell in love with him a little bit, and then it clicked exactly who he was. Leonardo – the man who thought centuries ahead of his own time."

Ianto leaned forward, "So you're saying that he's the Leonardo we know now because he came to the Hub all that time ago? The helicopters, the anatomy, is all because of Torchwood? That's a bit disappointing."

Jack shook his head slowly. "No. It wasn't like that. We may have lit the fire under his imagination, but

"So how, precisely," asked Gwen "was he able to draw the detailed inside workings of a Rift Key?"

"He had it with him when we sent him back. The Rift manipulator was more stable then. If you knew exactly when and where someone came from, you could send them back with a Rift Key and some very high-grade math. With most people it was hard to get a precise temporal fix, but in Leo's case, he actually helped us with the equations."

"So he dismantled the Rift Key when he got home?" asked Ianto. "Found out what made it tick?"

"Shouldn't its self-destruct function have kicked in?" added Gwen.

"Yes it should. He must have stopped that, too. Like I said: mind of the century."

Ianto raised a hand. "What's that noise?" he asked.

A distant, low whirring was coming from somewhere in the Hub. Ianto had become attuned to the noises the place made throughout the day, and prided himself on being able to identify the various clicks, thuds, bangs and hums that came from the machinery, the locked-up Weevils and the distant buried chambers, barely visited. But this one was so faint, all three of them struggled to discern it.

"I sort of recognise it," said Gwen, straining to hear.

Jack suddenly realised what it was and ran for the door.

The recognition hit Ianto like a hammer-blow at the exact same moment.

"It's the hydraulics on the invisible lift!"

Jack came running into the main chamber of the Hub at full speed and looked skyward at the lift platform as it ascended. He flipped open the vortex manipulator on his wrist and pressed a button, but to no avail. In frustration he pushed it again and again. Nothing. Ianto arrived out of breath beside him.

"Why's nothing happening?" Jack barked.

'Too late," gasped Ianto. "Past the safety zone. Override won't work." They stood and watched the lift reach its destination, and the big metal doors below it close with an echoing clang.

"Guess it's the old-fashioned way, then," said Gwen who'd come in behind them. All three of them ran for the stairs.

Leonardo stood by the fountain, gazing at the wonder of the world. Now this had changed since he was last here. This was bright, shiny, lots of people. Last time he was here it was dark and cold, and he remembered being shouted at by a large man with a crowbar, and approached by a woman who must have been freezing, judging by how few clothes she had worn.

But this was amazing. This would provide him with everything he could possibly need. He took in the Millennium Centre, a huge bronze beetle of a building, and the wide expanse of the Plass leading to the Bay. He stepped off the lift. A passing couple jumped slightly at his movement and stared at him as they continued their journey. Odd, he mused. Must be his clothes. Now, he thought, where to begin?

Down by the Bay, Jack, Gwen and Ianto came running out of the door below an evening crowd of happy summer drinkers. They continued at full pace under the footbridge and on to Roald Dahl Plass, heading for the fountain. A few minutes later their exhausted reflections danced in the silvery pillar as they looked around in the fading light.

"How far could he have gone?" asked Gwen. Ianto did a quick calculation. "Sixty-something man, normal fitness, at pace, no more than 800 metres. Approximately."

"But he could have gone in any direction. What's he after? Is he heading away from the crowd, or into it?"

Jack shook his head, frustrated at the turn of events. What was Leonardo after? Why would he come back?

Gwen was realistic. "We could waste hours looking for him on foot. Better to use the CCTV feeds in the Hub and then pick him up in the SUV."

"Or," said Jack, beginning to grin, "if he's still carrying the Rift Key we can lock on to the residual temporal radiation..."

"And drag him back!" finished Ianto.

Leonardo wandered among the busy summer crowds, watching them eating and drinking. So many people! Nearly all were talking, yet very few to the people around them. The majority seemed to have a small black device clutched in their hand and pressed to their ear. Perhaps it was a way of depositing a spoken message one could retrieve later, like a spoken letter?

As he began sketching this idea in his mind, a group of young women walked past, laughing together, and all carrying similar devices. He watched as one of them stood apart from the others and held the device at arm's length while the others all posed in a line. A flash of light from the device momentarily blinded him, then the girls laughed some more and carried on their way.

As they passed, he was able to catch a quick glimpse of the device, now showing an instant miniature painting of the very scene he had just observed. Extraordinary. As he contemplated this, he began to feel an odd sensation in his stomach, like something was pulling at his insides. He felt nauseous very quickly and staggered back, bumping into a group of men who jumped to one side and began to shout about their spilt drinks.

And then he was on the floor, being dragged by an invisible force as more and more people leaped out of his way. He went clattering through tables, bumping over steps and rebounding off walls as he lost all control. His legs and back began to burn with pain as he was pulled along the rough concrete. Too late he realised what was happening – something to do with the Rift Key that was still attached to his waist. He grappled at the pouch, but at the speed he was travelling he couldn't get his fingers around the clasp. As he sped through Roald Dahl Plass, failing to avoid bemused bystanders, there was nothing left to do but scream.

He hit the silver

fountain with some force and let out a cry of pain. He stayed there, suspended about midway up, unable to move, looking down at Gwen, who smiled up at him.

"Gwen Cooper one, timeless genius nil," she said.

Jack stood in the corridor, leaning against the perspex of Leonardo's cell door. He looked at the old man who sat in the cell, rubbing his back in some pain. In Jack's pocket was the master key Leonardo had used to escape and in his hand was the Rift Key.

He turned to Ianto. "Translator switched on?" he asked.

Ianto nodded. "It's as accurate as I could make it. I've made a few adjustments to differentiate modern Italian from the language spoken five centuries ago."

"Nice touch," said Jack.

"I thought so," nodded Ianto.

And with that he left Jack alone with Leonardo.

"Sorry about the undignified lift back, but you know why we had to, don't you?"

Leonardo heard the translation instantly and shook his head. "All I want to do is explore."

Jack nodded his understanding. "I just want to know

how it works,' Leonardo continued. "How everything works. You don't understand what that visit did to me all those years ago. The hunger, the desire to come back and learn more is... overwhelming. Have you any idea what it's like to visit a place so extraordinarily beautiful, so different and wondrous compared to your own, that the thought of never going back is like physical pain, an emptiness that grows in intensity every day of your life? Have you any idea what that's like?"

Jack nodded. "Yes. I have."

Leonardo stood and looked into Jack's eyes. There was an age and a pain to him Leonardo had never seen in any other man. "I believe you," he said. "And yet... You take it all for granted."

Jack smiled. "Believe me, we don't. If anyone understands the wonders of the world it's us, here at Torchwood. Every day we're confronted by stuff we don't understand. Most of it blows our minds if and when we figure out what it is or what it does. The marvels of the universe will never end for us."

"Nor for me," said Leonardo.

They stared at one another for a moment, both knowing what must happen next.

"You have to go back, Leo. You can't stay here. It's too dangerous. You've already seen too much."

"But what danger could it bring? I want to see, to understand –"

"Things you should never see or never come close to understanding," Jack interrupted. "Time isn't something you can play with. To control it is a power beyond any of us. No human should ever be able to use it. Using knowledge of the future to change the past is something that can change a whole world!"

Leonardo nodded. "Yes. For the better."

"You can't know that."

Jack let the thought hang there, knowing, hoping Leonardo was one of the few who could genuinely grasp the monumental dangers he had left unspoken. Slowly, Leonardo nodded. Jack opened the cell door and handed the Rift Key back to him.

"We've reprogrammed this," explained Jack, "to take you back to where and when you came from. If it makes you feel any better, we had to use the same math equation you left us with 40 years ago in order to be this accurate."

Leonardo smiled. He remembered doing the calculus in his head, to the amazement of the Torchwood team. But the truth was no, it didn't make him feel better.

Jack didn't wait for an answer. "This time, the internal workings will burn out when you get back, Leo. There'll be no tampering and no return trips."

Leonardo took the burnished gold object and felt the comfort of its weight in his hand.

"Goodbye, Jack," he said and offered his hand. "I shall never forget you or the glimpse of this world I have seen."

Jack shook his hand. He reached down and picked up the pint glass of water that had been sitting hear his feet and offered it to Leonardo.

"Drink this," he said. "Time travel can dehydrate you."

Back in the heart of the Hub, Jack walked up to the coffee machine where Ianto was prepping a particularly potent brew.

Gwen was sat at her workstation, busy tapping away at the keys of her computer.

"Did he take the Retcon?" Ianto asked.

Jack nodded. "Every last bit of it came from him."

"Yes!" shouted Gwen in triumph from her desk.

Jack and Ianto looked over with a mix of curiosity and dread.

"I've been hanging onto this website since this morning," she explained. "Finally!"

"Finally what?" asked Jack.

"Tickets for the international between Wales and Italy. Six Nations! Come on!"

Ianto frowned. "That doesn't qualify as a cultural first. We saw that last year."

"I know," said Gwen. "But they played here in Cardiff. This match is in Rome, which I've never been to. And guess which airport we have to fly into?" Jack smiled.

"Leonardo da Vinci," he said. •

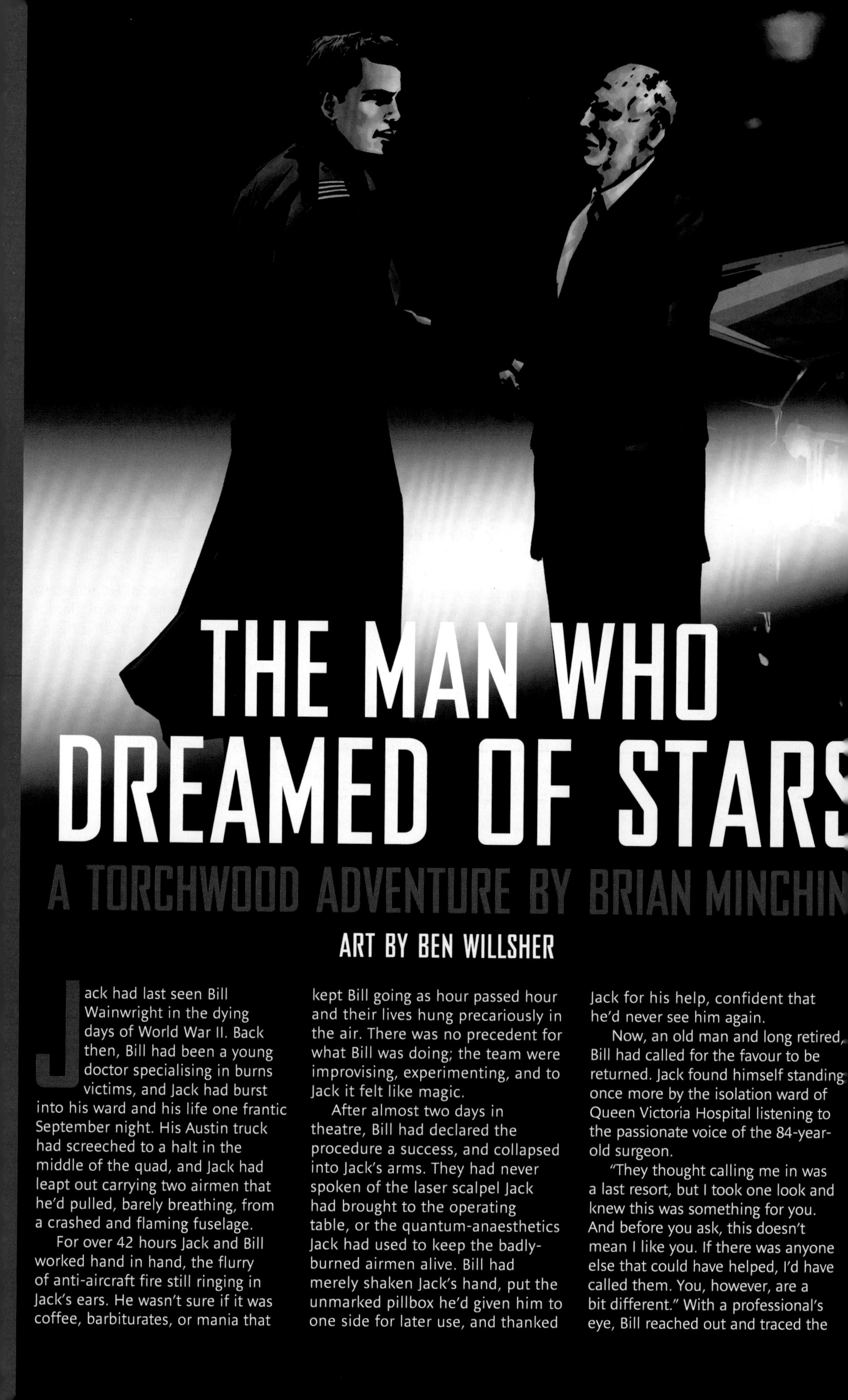

THE MAN WHO DREAMED OF STARS

A TORCHWOOD ADVENTURE BY BRIAN MINCHIN

ART BY BEN WILLSHER

Jack had last seen Bill Wainwright in the dying days of World War II. Back then, Bill had been a young doctor specialising in burns victims, and Jack had burst into his ward and his life one frantic September night. His Austin truck had screeched to a halt in the middle of the quad, and Jack had leapt out carrying two airmen that he'd pulled, barely breathing, from a crashed and flaming fuselage.

For over 42 hours Jack and Bill worked hand in hand, the flurry of anti-aircraft fire still ringing in Jack's ears. He wasn't sure if it was coffee, barbiturates, or mania that kept Bill going as hour passed hour and their lives hung precariously in the air. There was no precedent for what Bill was doing; the team were improvising, experimenting, and to Jack it felt like magic.

After almost two days in theatre, Bill had declared the procedure a success, and collapsed into Jack's arms. They had never spoken of the laser scalpel Jack had brought to the operating table, or the quantum-anaesthetics Jack had used to keep the badly-burned airmen alive. Bill had merely shaken Jack's hand, put the unmarked pillbox he'd given him to one side for later use, and thanked Jack for his help, confident that he'd never see him again.

Now, an old man and long retired, Bill had called for the favour to be returned. Jack found himself standing once more by the isolation ward of Queen Victoria Hospital listening to the passionate voice of the 84-year-old surgeon.

"They thought calling me in was a last resort, but I took one look and knew this was something for you. And before you ask, this doesn't mean I like you. If there was anyone else that could have helped, I'd have called them. You, however, are a bit different." With a professional's eye, Bill reached out and traced the

ontours of Jack's face, marvelling
t how untouched he was by the
ndignities of time. "And quite
mpossible, as you well know."

Jack gently took Bill's hand away
rom his face. "What made them
all you back? Did the club need a
ew barman?" Bill shook his head.
Hardly any of the boys left now,
ack. Still, we managed to marry most
f them off in the end." The Guinea
ig Club of injured servicemen had
net every Thursday for 60-odd years,
ll of them long-term patients of
ill's and happy to meet where they
vouldn't draw attention.

But Bill's thoughts were
lsewhere. "I was hoping you could
oring some of that space quackery
of yours to bear on this new patient.
We've had to re-open Ward 11. We
lidn't even do that for the Falklands."
ack was intrigued that after all these
ears something had the power
o make Bill uneasy. There was
omething about burns victims that
nade people turn away: the way the
edness of the flesh drew in the eye,
he sinews shining through
he tattered skin. But if Bill wanted to
nide someone away, then they must
oe a special case indeed.

"He was found outside Worthing,
oy Totnes Weir. They think he
crawled into the water himself,
trying to lessen the pain." Bill
oaused before opening the solid
green door. "He's in an isolation

containment unit, for all the good
it's doing him." Jack knew exactly
what Bill meant and grimaced.
"What do you think I can do?"

Bill didn't answer straight away.
"His dog tags were burnt into his
chest," he said eventually. "His
name's Silas. I told the chaps here his
date of birth was illegible. But I saw
it, and he's more like you than me."
Bill paused. "It's a hope, I suppose.
Maybe he'll talk to you. Maybe he's
got something we can use." Jack put
a hand firmly on Bill's shoulder. "You
know I'll need to see him alone." He
was touched that Bill's burning desire
to discover the new hadn't faded, but
his first responsibility was protecting
the present, and he couldn't let the
future casually stride in.

Bill attempted to put a note of
command into his voice: "Just tell me
what you find. Might be something
in this for us." Seeing Jack's stony
reaction he continued, softer. "Take
care. Last man in Ward 11 was
involved in a chemical spill and lost
83 per cent of his skin. He looked
like James Dean compared to that
man in there. 49th Century or not,
Jack, folk still burn the same."

Jack's watch showed 09.38 when
he sat down beside the ward's
only patient – less a man than
a tattered silhouette, his scorched
features casting sharp shadows in
the gloom of the ward. As his eyes

got used to the dark, he saw Silas'
body was blackened and cauterised
by the heat. Yellow-white bone jutted
through the thin covering of his
scalp, and where his ears should
have been there was only a gooey
mess of cartilage and bone. Silas'
face had been protected, and Jack
could make out the rough shape
of two clasped hands. All the
skin surrounding them had gone.
Glancing down, Jack could see that
the backs of the man's hands were
also little more than bone. On his
arms, the heat had gone further still,
and had scorched away muscle and
bone itself, leaving him pitted and
eroded. Whatever had done this had
burned long and deep.

Bill had updated the containment
unit since World War II, but it was
essentially the same – a tank of salt
water, charged with electric currents
and an oxygen-rich atmosphere
enclosed in glass. Looking at Silas'
charts, Jack could see Bill had
given him everything – pethidine,
diamorphine, codeine, tramadol –
plus a few things Jack didn't know
Bill had. He took a small ampoule
out of his pocket and attached
it to the stent in Silas' hand, the
painkillers sparkling as they ran
down the canula and into his veins.
This close, Jack could see the man's
heart quicken, and the tension in his
muscles slump. He'd just given him
30 minutes without pain.

Temporarily released from his suffering, Silas' eyes flicked open and latched onto Jack, his pupils widening with excitement. Silas lifted a damaged finger, and traced a number on the clear plastic wall. Jack was no longer calm. "That's my age. My REAL age!" he hissed. "Who are you?" Silas' hand had dropped down, and for almost a minute Jack heard nothing in reply but the sounds of breathing. Then a raspy voice coughed out, "Who are you, more to the point. A Time Agent, perhaps?"

Jack shook his head. "I used to be. Got a vortex manipulator and everything. But right now I'm not really working, if I'm honest."

Silas shut his eyes for a very long time. When he opened them again Jack could see tears hitting the raw skin on his cheeks. Holding Jack's gaze he begged, "Hold me." When Jack didn't move, he asked again, "Please."

Jack couldn't see a reason for keeping the air sterile. The man had lost all the skin on his body, and Bill wasn't about to try a 100 per cent skin graft. He slid the doors of the containment unit apart and took Silas' hand in his. He was surprised at how warm it felt, and the effect it had on Silas. As if sparked into life, Silas moved jerkily in his saline bath, his dry tongue sliding along his teeth, eyes darting around the dark of the ward. His fingers tightened on Jack's, and he craned his neck conspiratorially towards him: "Get me out of here, Time Agent."

Jack shook his head. "I have painkillers, but that's all." Silas' eyes bulged greedily and he attempted to move his body towards Jack. "Let me out." Jack shook his head again. "The saline is keeping you alive," he said. Silas sank back into the tank. His brief surge of hope had passed and he was sinking even lower than before. Jack knew that he had a short time before the pain returned and overwhelmed Silas for good.

"Tell me who you are." Silas looked at Jack for a second, weighing him up. Something prickled in Jack's mind, and he had the unsettling impression he was being probed. Ignoring the sensation, Jack went on: "I don't think they called me in to help

you, Silas. I think they got scared you might turn into something else." Silas spoke again. "So you're my final guard?" Jack nodded. Silas seemed to almost smile. "Here in your long coat, escorting me over..." A terrible hacking laughter came out of his mouth. "I'm dying with a Time Agent by my side!"

Silas came to a decision. He lifted his other hand and clasped Jack's in a skeletal grip. As Silas shut his eyes, the skin around Jack's forehead started to tingle, and as it grew warm, Jack started to feel Silas' thoughts entering his head. Keeping his voice calm, Jack spoke out loud, "You're a low-level empath, right? That's how you know how old I am, but you don't know my name." Silas answered inside Jack's head. "So, show me where you're from. I want to know." And with an almost imperceptible squeeze of his hand, Silas transported Jack into his memories.

He was miles above Earth, hanging in the vacuum of space. After the close confines of the ward, the vastness of the heavens stunned Jack, and he wondered why

he'd stayed Earthbound for so long. All around him stars burned and roared, not still and peaceful but a cauldron of activity. Silas' memory was so real that Jack could feel the solar wind buffeting his body and ruffling his hair. And looking around he could see in awful clarity how Silas had ended up drifting in space.

Silas was in a spacesuit, tumbling away from the aftermath of an explosion. Behind him, the heavens were full of the remnants of a Class Five space cruiser, tangles of wires and twisted metal littering the sky. Crueller still, near to Silas, the wreckage of an escape pod was cartwheeling slowing away from him, its padded seats drifting sadly apart. Looking to his left, Jack could see another spacesuit, its visor filled with a dead, bloated face. Silas was letting Jack feel what he'd felt as he floated, and Jack was filled with a dread he hadn't felt in a very long time: an expectation of finality – of death. It dominated his mind and made his thoughts pulse with anger and injustice.

As the spacesuit turned in the vastness of space, Jack could see the blue and green of Earth far

below. Twinkling beneath them, a satellite locked into its final descent began to brush the atmosphere, before its solar panels glowed orange and broke off, fluttering down into oblivion. Freed from any impeding shape, the lump of metal plunged deeper, turning into something so bright Jack had to shut his eyes. He thought for a second how wonderful it was to see the heavens at work – the tiny moments of beauty as a hundred pieces of space debris sent shooting stars over an unsuspecting world.

When the gentle tug of gravity began to take Silas, Jack was surprised by the calmness of the moment. The dread was evaporating inside Silas' mind. The final decision had been made, and his life would soon be over. All Silas expected was a final switching-off of experience. There would be no continuation of doubt and worry. His body had become no different from the other debris around him: he had become an inevitability. Jack could feel Silas' heartbeat slow. This was what it really meant to be carefree. Free of caring for anything anymore, even himself.

Silas began to feel the resistance to his fall. Faster and faster he fell, his silica-cell suit scant protection against the burn of the thickening atmosphere. In his saline tank, Silas was speaking. Jack kept his eyes shut and listened to the story. Images came to his mind like little explosions. As weak as he was, Silas still had abilities to touch and create.

"I fell from the stars, through the higher reaches of your world. At 100 miles my suit began to crack, and at 80 miles my boots burnt up. I used the pads on the knees against the burn, and when they went I used my feet." Jack could see him, face contorted behind the mask, as one thousand and six hundred degrees centigrade tore against him.

"But the death I expected never came. By the time my suit started to rip away, I was in the upper atmosphere. Under my suit I was wearing neo-thermal fabric. It burnt, but only at the very last. One more minute of heat and I'd be dead. My oxygen lasted until I was able to breathe." And Jack could see it all. The rushing and the wonder, as Silas passed through the dark layers of the stratosphere, into lighter and lighter shades of blue. Silas felt like a man who had defeated death. He felt like he had achieved the impossible.

It was a miracle, I guess." Jack opened his eyes. Silas was smiling a lipless smile as he went on. "So instead of dying with the stars behind me, I get to pass away in a salt water tank in a tin hut." Jack had known men like Silas in World War II: pilots so used to losing those around them that they began to take pride in their fate, glorying in the manner of their own eventual deaths.

Silas talked on, his voice dry, but feeling no pain. "I'm the navigation officer of the spaceship *Taurus X*. We were a convoy mission, two thousand of us in three ships, returning from the New Earth colonies. Our colony had been deemed too expensive, and we were being brought home. There was a fire on the oxygen decks, my cabin was directly above it. My wife was there. My boys..." Jack could see the tears running down Silas' cheeks, but he didn't pause, eager to share his story. "Our escape pod was a new design – equipped with an emergency time-jump." Jack knew what Silas was talking about. Instead of escaping a wrecked ship, the pod leaped a week into the future, arriving at a point in time when the danger had all passed, and with rescue ships primed to await your arrival.

"Something went wrong. We got caught in the blast as we made the jump. The pod disintegrated and I was left floating in space –

falling down and down. Everything I know has gone, Jack. You can make this better. In 200 years they'll be able to cure this, you know they will. Take me there, Jack. I know you can."

Jack knew that Silas was right. In the 23rd Century the best surgeons could encase him in metal and call him a success story. A few hundred years later and the Bill Wainwrights of the day would be able to graft geo-skin to his body, encasing him in a soft green carapace. Eventually they'd be able to give him everything back – unblemished, taut and toughened. Superskin: a process so expensive they made patients serve four years on the front lines in order to pay it back.

"All we can do is freeze you, Silas." But they both knew where that would lead. Jack thought sadly about the fate of the 21st Century dreamers – the men and women who were cryo-frozen, only to find that when they awoke they were condemned to life in their giant freezers, wheeled around and transmitting their thoughts as tinny little electronic voices, their bodies never fully able to defrost entirely.

And now Jack felt very tired. Silas' story had been beautiful. And if anyone deserved saving, it was a man who had lost everything. Silas was still talking; clinging to the new hope he had found in Jack. "I have immunisations, you know. Compounds in my blood. You could use them to destroy malaria, to destroy..." But Jack cut him off. "I can't let that happen Silas." Jack let go of his hand and stood up.

The room was silent. Jack gazed at the pictures of surviving servicemen hanging on the walls. These were soldiers whose lives had been saved in this hospital: men who had defended their country, and in return had been left disfigured. They had left cheery signed messages to Bill and his team. "My darts have improved. Your glass eye works a treat! Love 'Eye-too-high Tom.'" Jack controlled the emotion in his voice. "You make me wonder, Silas. Whether everyone deserves saving."

In the silence that followed, Jack thought about when it was that he had come to play God with

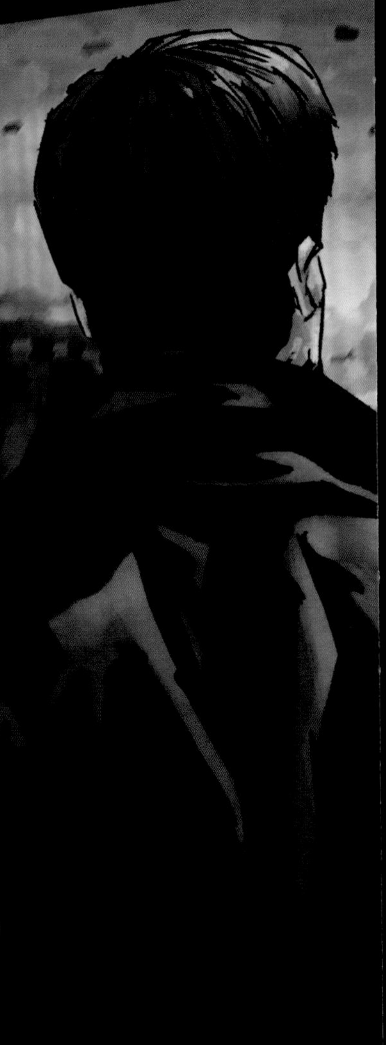

people's lives. He'd never meant to become the arbiter of whether people deserved to live. But looking around th[redacted]ward he realised it was[redacted] him that carried the burd[redacted] Jack was thankful for Silas. For once, here was a man who was going to make it easy for him.

[redacted]e brought Silas into his confidenc[redacted]ou know, last time I was here[redacted]ot of people were unhappy [redacted]th me," he said. "I brought in two injured bombers. German airmen. The British surgeons knew – I didn't hide it and we never talked about it. Afterwards, Bill told me he'd carried out the most experimental surgery of his career. Something he'd never try on a British serviceman. It saved their lives. They didn't go back to fight, and they have families now. I still get postcards sometimes. But you, Silas, you weren't a soldier, and you weren'[redacted] navigation officer. You were a [redacted]reamer, and sometimes you have to let those dreams die."

Silas was attempting to sit upright now.

[redacted]You showed me almost everything[redacted]ilas. And you were good, oh [redacted], you are very good at hiding. Bu[redacted] been here before, and I know that under that calm, you were angry when you fell. You'd been betrayed. You weren't even surprised to be floating in space. Your mind didn't even flicker when you saw your co-pilot dead. But you weren't ex[redacted]ting to be in the 21st Century. And the reason is that you planned it all, didn't you? Every single last detail. So show me again." This time it was Jack grabbing hold of Silas' hand. "I want to see the truth."

All too willingly, Silas took Jack back – th[redacted]images in his mind blurring and settling. Now Jack could see the *Taurus X* floating above Earth in all its glory, its two sister ships alongside. Silas was far away, sitting in a separate ship, cloak[redacted]m the *Taurus*. Silas drew Jack closer in. He could see Silas sitting with controls in his hands, pressing a sequence of buttons, and he could see the *Taurus* exploding: gouts of flame obscuring everything that Silas could see, the reflections bright agains[redacted]ilas' black visor. The time-jump drive kicked in, taking Silas and all the debris with it. Here was the moment of disaster! The settings were wrong. Silas had been betrayed. Such fear, such anger. Silas was free and falling.

Jack's grip was growing tighter, and he could feel the last remaining flesh giving beneath his fingers. "SHOW ME MORE!" he growled at Silas, and the dying man obliged. In snapshots, he saw Silas placing the explosives on the outside of the hull; he saw Silas on a colony planet, surrounded by blue mountains and white chalk roads that shone under the light of several stars; he saw him arguing in a restroom, shouting his heart out: "The colonies must stay separate!" He saw the slogans scrawled across the newsgroups: "There shall be no return to Earth!" He saw Silas drinking alone in his room, fingers racing across a keyboard – long, pain-filled rants of the Free Colony Movement. And before all this, Jack saw Silas standing inside a vast geo-dome, ecstatic in his home, the only place he'd felt safe, a land that was his with the stars all around him. And Jack felt Silas' rage, his impotence. His world was being taken from him.

"They called us back like we were cattle returning from the fields." While Jack saw nothing but low-ceilinged dorms and rationed water, Silas' thoughts floated through the cramped base, singing and happy, imagining freedom.

But Silas' truths were hard and angry. Bitterness loomed over them, and death had been the result. "You were conned," said Jack. "They'd programmed the time drive to dump you here – the backwaters of the 21st Century. Somewhere no one would know what you'd done and no one would know your name. If you died in the 49th Century it would have started a war. But this was a perfect burial ground for just another piece of space trash. You'd disappear from time. An unmarked corpse. No record of what happened. I guess they knew you'd be defenceless – that you'd fall through the atmosphere unguarded. It must have hurt. Oh, it must have stung. They probably calculated exactly how far to let you fall. Couldn't risk you floating off into space – they wanted your body burnt. All you'd risked and they didn't even try to get you home."

Silas looked at Jack with defiance in his eyes. "I did what was right," he said. But Jack was angry [redacted]self now and barely listening. "You killed your own people! People you'd grown up with! You blew them up so you could make a point?" Silas had heard these arguments playing over and over in his head and wasn't going to be persuaded now. He had no regrets. "Sometimes, Jack, people achieve more in dying than they do in living. I had to make a stand."

"Let me tell you now, Silas, that you did not succeed. What you did was ignored; never studied. It's not in a single history book. The colonies returned, Earth remained united, and you were no hero. Not even a villain." Silas smiled – his blackened teeth murderous in the gloom. "Your anger is very touching..." He rested his bony finger on Jack's hand and suddenly he was back on the Boeshane Peninsula, running and runn[redacted] and running. His mother so angr[redacted]his father gone. Then it all went black. Momentarily blinded. Jack opened

ever more painful. "I'm a hero, Jack! Everything changes because of me. I know it happens! I can feel it!" But Jack was still impassive.

When the pain came, Silas' eyes showed it first. The painkillers drained from his body as quickly as they'd entered it, and the feeling returned to every nerve ending with brutal impact. Silas was quivering with shock, his body unable to take what he was feeling. With his last breath, Silas whispered, "I'm proud of what I did," and then his knees buckled and he collapsed on the floor. Jack wasn't sure at what point Silas died.

Bill was still standing outside the ward, and was surprised to be caught up in a massive embrace from Jack. "It's been really good to see you again Bill. I don't think I ever thanked you all those years ago." Jack reached into his jacket pocket and handed Bill five ampoules of his shimmering serum. Bill nodded gratefully and pocketed it. "Never did manage to replicate that stuff, no matter how much I tried. Got a few things out of it, though." Jack couldn't help but smile at the old man's determination.

"And that man in there — Silas — who was he?" Jack paused for a while before answering. "He was no one." Bill hurried after Jack, who was all too keen to get away. "Should we put him with the servicemen?" Jack thought for a second, "Better not — him being from the future. Put the remains in the incinerator. Forget he was ever here." Bill was looking at Jack in surprise. He hadn't expected him to be so affected by what he'd seen in there. "You OK, Captain?" Jack nodded. "You did the right thing calling me, Bill. Now back home with you, and that's an order." Bill gave a mock-salute as Jack stepped into the SUV. "Thank you Captain." Jack smiled back, "Take care, Bill."

As the car pulled away from the ramshackle Victorian building, Jack wondered what his last story would be, and who he would be telling it to. Would he end up like the man that dreamed of stars, full of conviction to the very end? Or did the cosmos have other fates in store for him? •

his eyes, and saw that Silas had achieved the impossible.

Silas was standing outside the tank, unsteadily walking on bloodied feet. He was heading for the door, the painkillers making him feel invincible. He saw Jack had regained consciousness and spoke down at him, all traces of humility gone. "I'm like the men on the wall: a hero, a soldier. My cause was true. More true than theirs. And you saved all of them, even the ones that bombed you while you slept. So you can save me, Time Agent. I've seen inside your mind!" Silas took a lurching step towards the door. "You have it in you, so call your surgeon! I'll tell them who I am. They can keep me alive." Silas took another few steps, bloody footprints marking his sorry progress. Jack watched quietly, there was no way Silas could reach the door in time. "I'll tell them so much, Jack! I'll show them ways to heal they've never dreamed of! I'll save so many lives!"

But Jack felt sad. So very sad. "I think it would destroy Bill," Jack replied, "to find out that centuries from now, with all that will have been achieved, people are still planting bombs, and innocent people are still dying." He strode to where Silas was unsteadily walking, and looked him in the eye. "I honestly don't know if he'd be able to go on. All the people working in this hospital Silas — they're hoping for a better future. One without men like you. Because if it's all about new bombs and new ways to patch people up, then it's all a bit pointless, isn't it?"

Silas was still yards from the door, and was staring at his feet in horror. "Jack, I'm starting to feel them!" he cried. Jack looked at his watch: it was now 10.02. The dose he'd given Silas didn't have long. "Give me more! I can live like this. I don't need to die". In the face of Jack's silence, he started to rant, his mouth slowing as sensation returned and movements became

THEY KEEP

Gwen shone a light over the corpse. Thirty-ish, blond. Black jeans, white shirt. Face down at the end of the alleyway, crumpled like a piece of litter. Life, love, dreams, hopes... Everything screwed up and thrown away.

The handle of the knife stood up from between the narrow shoulder blades, the blade buried deep in a bright flower of blood. You never get used to the sight of a dead body. Gwen had seen quite a few, both as a police officer and a Torchwood operative. She'd seen messy deaths, tragic deaths, brutal, silent, ugly, alien deaths – the lot. But you never really got used to it. And that was a Good Thing. Because, as Jack Harkness had often told her, when death no longer bothers you, life's really not worth living. But this one really stopped her in her tracks. For one thing, she knew the victim. She knew him very well. His name was PC Andy Davidson. He was face down, but she recognised him easily enough. Gwen drew in a deep breath and let it out very slowly, counting to 10. She had to steady herself for this. Her mouth felt dry and her heart was beating heavily. "For Pete's sake, Andy," she said eventually. "That's the fifth bloody time this week."

"So let me get this straight," said Andy. He fixed Gwen with a steady glare as they sat in a café overlooking Roald Dahl Plass. "I've been killed."

"Murdered."

He blinked. "Murdered. With a knife. Stabbed in the back."

"Five times so far. It's getting to be a habit."

Andy looked down at his tea and uneaten biscuit. "I dunno what to say. I mean, normally, I'd call you a bloody liar and a nutcase. But you're not normal, are you?"

Gwen stiffened. "Of course I'm normal."

"I mean what you do isn't normal."

Andy rolled his eyes. "Torchwood and everything."

A waitress hovered nearby, waiting to see if they'd finished yet. Gwen smiled at her. The café was nearly empty, and the girl was just looking for something to do. "Could we have some more water, please?"

"Sure." The waitress headed off and Gwen turned back to Andy. His eyes were full of worry.

"I can't just ignore it, can I?" he asked. "Not when it's you telling me that I've been murdered..."

"Five times..."

"Five times this week. Although I think I would prefer it if I'd been abducted by aliens five times this week. That I could understand. You know, taken away in a spaceship, experimented on, cloned or whatever, and then returned to Earth."

Andy sat back in his chair, arms folded. "But murdered? How can I keep coming back from that? Dead is a pretty permanent state of affairs in my line of work. How about yours?"

Gwen bit her lip.

"No, of course not. Nothing's normal in your line of work, is it?"

"You're not making this easy for me," Gwen said irritably. She bit aggressively into a shortbread biscuit.

"Easy for you?" Andy gasped. "I'm the one who's been murdered here!"

He'd raised his voice, and the waitress was back with more water. She looked uncertainly at Andy, smiled at Gwen, then moved quickly away.

"We're doing our best," Gwen hissed. "Somehow your personal timeline is looping back over the last 24 hours. We don't know how or why but we need to find out."

Andy sighed, defeated. "Five times this week, right?"

"Same wound. Same knife."

"Same murderer?"

Gwen frowned. "What do you mean?"

"I mean," Andy said slowly, "that it seems to me – whichever way you

KILLING ANDY

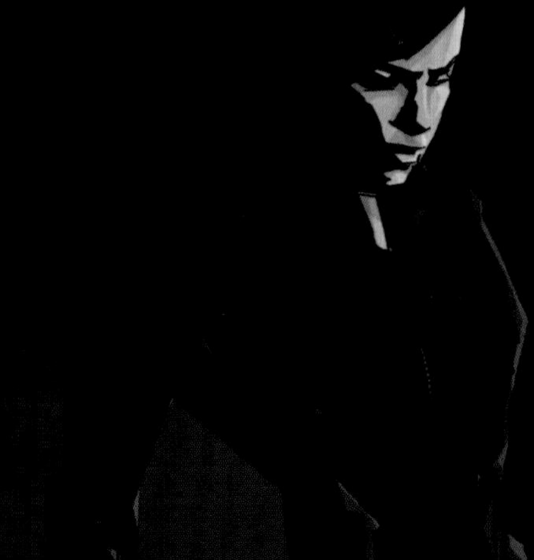

A NEW SHORT STORY BY
TREVOR BAXENDALE

ART BY BEN WILLSHER.

look at it – that a murder has been committed. OK, it's been committed over and over again, but essentially it's the same crime, isn't it? Therefore we should apply the same techniques to find the murderer that we would in any crime. For example, start with the facts."

"OK, that's good..." Gwen nodded, hesitating. "Because I do need to bring you in for questioning."

Andy was dimly aware that Torchwood had a vast, secret headquarters somewhere beneath the Cardiff Bay area. In his imagination it was a sprawling network of chrome and glass corridors, gleaming laboratories and flickering workstations. In reality, there was a lot of concrete and Victorian tiling that reminded him of nothing so much as a public convenience.

"Stop staring," said Gwen. "You'll soon get used to it."

Then a confident American voice called out from an upper level.

"Impressed?" said Captain Jack Harkness as he jogged down a flight of metal steps, a broad, white grin on his handsome face.

Andy smiled back at him. "Yes," he said. "Very impressed."

"Get over it," Captain Jack advised.

Andy sat on the long table in the conference room, his hands sweating.

"What's going on?"

"That's what we're here to find out."

"You can do that?"

Jack smiled wolfishly. "Hey – I'm a glass-half-full kinda guy."

Ianto Jones – immaculate in three-piece suit and tie – stepped up, placing a fresh cup of coffee down in front of Andy. "Five times murdered – that's got to be a record. In fact, it's got to hurt. Don't you remember any of it?"

Andy screwed up his eyes. "Nothing. Well, nothing of any use. I'd been following my normal routine all week. No one's said anything to me about it. Except you lot."

"That's because we're the only ones who noticed," Ianto told him. Jack Harkness tapped a nearby computer monitor with a knuckle. "Routine chronon displacement scan. Zeroed in on you at oh-five-

thirty last Tuesday."

"You were just coming out of the Brewery Quarter," Gwen said. "Do you remember that?"

"Yeah." Andy nodded. "Minor disturbance. We'd been clearing up after a party. Funny night for a party, though. Who'd have a party on a Tuesday?" He frowned. "Was it someone at the party? Are they the murderer?"

"No, nothing like that," Jack said. "Gwen found you dead in the gutter on Galt Street at oh-five forty-four."

"Lucky it was me who found you," Gwen said. "Though it was the biggest shock of my life."

Andy smiled at that. He felt genuinely touched. "And then I came back to life?"

"No," Jack said emphatically. "You did not."

"What we think happened," Ianto explained, "was a basic time loop. By the time the paramedics arrived, you'd disappeared."

"There one second," said Gwen. "Gone the next."

"Where to?" Andy asked.

"When to," Jack corrected.

"Back along your own personal timeline," Ianto said. "Everything that had happened to you in the previous 12 or so hours completely erased."

"That's impossible. What about all the people I met? Places I went to? Are you trying to tell me those things never happened?"

"It's not as simple as that," Jack said.

"You call this simple?"

"You looped back along your own personal time line, no one else's," Ianto explained. "If it sounds complicated, then that's because it is. Even I don't fully understand it, and I'm brilliant."

"He is good," added Captain Jack. Andy looked at them all in turn. The three of them sitting around the table, arms folded. They were completely serious. "You're all completely potty, you know that, don't you?"

"Is this really necessary?" Andy's voice filtered through the plastic screen of the holding cell. "I think you ought to know that I am well and truly out of my comfort zone."

Gwen smiled reassuringly. "Trust me, it's the best way we can be sure of monitoring you."

"By locking me up?"

"It's an observation process. You'll be safe in here."

Andy looked around the cell. "It's a lock-up. I should know. I've been on the other side of that kind of door often enough. You know this is completely against my human rights!"

Gwen rolled her eyes. "We're doing our best, Andy. You've got to believe that. We've got pretty sophisticated devices for measuring temporal anomalies, and the one surrounding you at the moment is contracting."

"Meaning?"

"Meaning the times between your murders are getting shorter. The first took place in the early hours of Tuesday morning. The second one – when we found you just outside the Arms Park – was on Wednesday night at 11:41pm. Then it was Thursday evening in Butetown. Then just past midnight on Saturday morning..."

"OK, I get the picture," Andy sighed, irritably. "You can put me at the scene of every murder. You've got me bang to rights. I'm the victim. A serial murder victim! Now all you have to do is find the killer."

"Andy..."

"Look, Gwen." He spoke through gritted teeth. "You used to be a good copper. So tell me what good does this do? Treating people like lab rats! You can show me that I'm getting murdered more and more frequently. But what does that prove?"

"We need to see it happen."

"Well that's every copper's dream isn't it? That would make the conviction rate shoot right up!"

"Just settle down and let us handle this."

He took a deep breath. "Okay... So you know when the last five murders took place. Can't you work out when the next is due to happen?"

"Not yet. The temporal contractions aren't regular. But they are getting more frequent. This is the first stage in finding out exactly what's happening to you in a controlled environment."

"Can't we just work out who the murderer is?"

"You're thinking like a policeman."

"Well, duh."

Gwen touched the plastic gently, her fingers pressed against his on the other side. "Sorry Andy. I mean it's no good thinking in normal terms. Not with something like this. It's a Torchwood problem. Leave

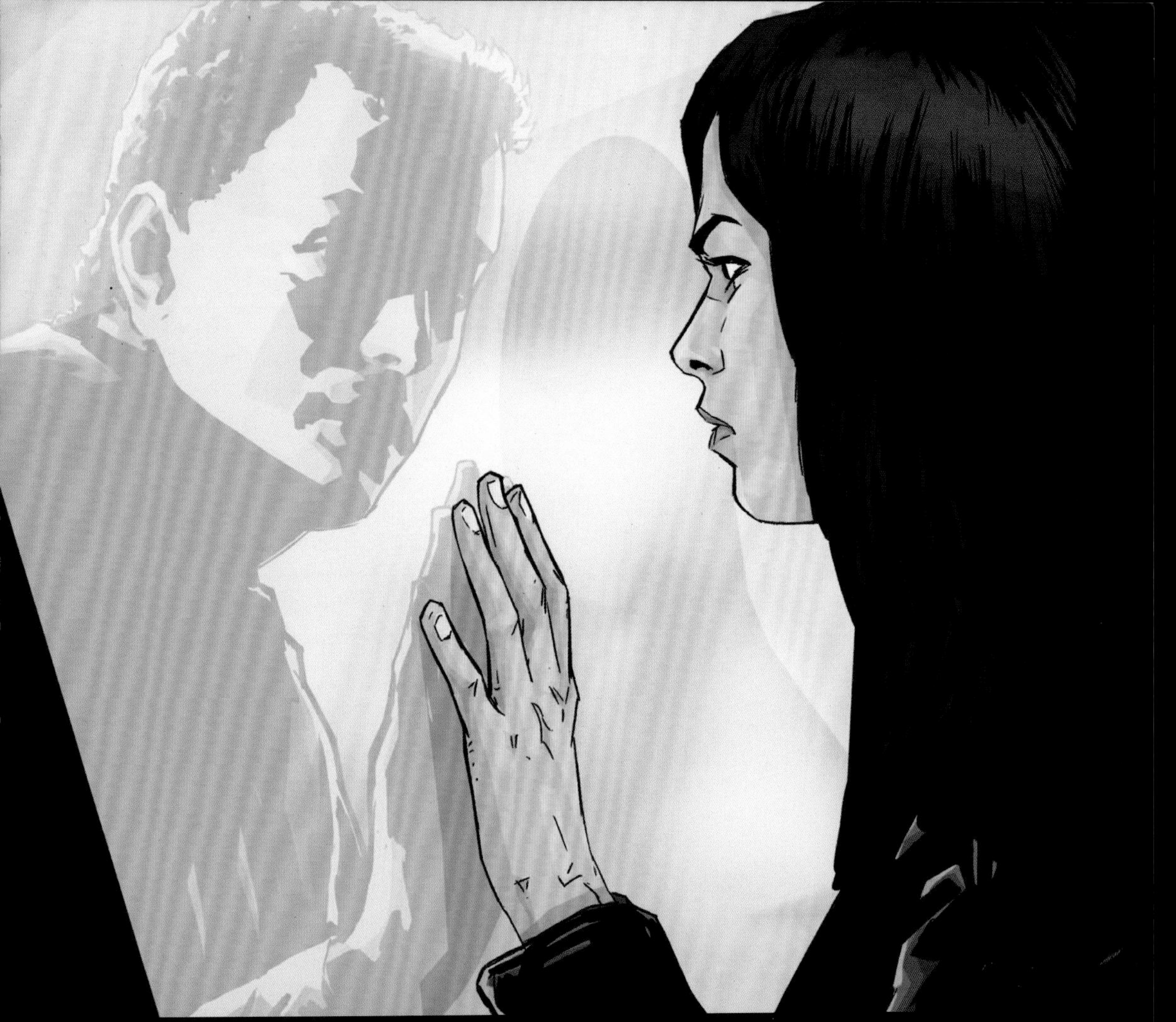

it to us."

"What did he say?" Ianto asked as soon as Gwen walked into Jack's office.

"He agreed he doesn't have much choice."

"He's being pretty cooperative," Jack said appreciatively. "I like him. I like blonds."

"You leave him alone, Jack," Gwen ordered. "You'd eat him alive."

"Given half a chance."

"Hey!" said Ianto.

"Joking," Jack grinned. He winked at Gwen and she rolled her eyes.

"Well, I should think – hey, look!" Jack and Gwen followed Ianto's gaze to the CCTV screen showing the holding cell. On the floor, Andy was lying in a pool of blood, a knife in his back glinting in the low light.

"Bloody hell!" Gwen dashed out of the office, knocking over chairs and equipment as she went.

When they reached the cell, it was empty. No Andy, no blood, no knife.

"And no murderer," Ianto noted. "So much for Plan A."

Gwen was furious. "Oh shut up, Ianto!"

She stormed out of the cell and ran all the way back to Jack in his office. He was leaning over his desk, staring at the monitor. "Ianto's right," he told her without preamble. "It didn't work."

"There must be something!"

Jack clicked his tongue. "I've already run the recording back. There's nothing. One second Andy's sitting there, the next he's dead on the floor. It just switches from one frame to the next, like something out of a badly edited movie."

"Not that a digital recording has frames, of course," said Ianto as he walked into the room.

"It doesn't matter," said Jack. "Same result. Whatever's happening to Andy is happening in a sliver of time too small to capture on any recording equipment.

There's a small delay, when he's actually dead – and then he just disappears as the time loop resets. Wherever he is now, it's not Heaven or Hell. It's Cardiff."

Gwen was already speed-dialling Andy's mobile. "Come on, come on..." she muttered, pacing across the office. "Pick up, Andy."

"Gwen?"

"Andy! Where are you?"

"Erm... St Mary Street. Anything wrong? You sound a bit... Flustered."

"What are you doing?"

"I'm just on my way home. Stopping off at the bookshop. Why, what's up?"

"Nothing. I'll catch you later."

She closed the phone and pressed the cold metal against her lip, trembling.

Jack put a hand on her shoulder. "He's okay. He's still with us."

"For how long?" Gwen asked. "The times between each murder are getting shorter and shorter. That must mean something."

"It does," said Ianto. He was typing rapidly at a computer, his attention fixed on the screen. "And now we know the exact second that the last murder took place... It's safe to assume that Andy will be killed again within the next four hours. And after that, within the next two to three hours. Eventually, it will become a fixed point in time and Andy will be dead for good."

"We're running out of time," said Jack.

"Andy's running out of time," said Gwen.

"We should get him back here," Jack said. "Back in the cell. This time I'll stay with him."

"It won't work," Ianto put in. "It's only Andy's timeline that's looping. You won't be able to do anything, and you won't see anything more than the CCTV."

"Then I'm open to suggestions," Jack snapped back. "So start coming up with some!"

"Maybe Andy was right," Gwen said suddenly." He wanted to know why we didn't just find the murderer. I told him off for thinking like a copper, but that's exactly what you want when you're looking for a criminal. It's obvious now I think about it. Find the killer and stop the killing!"

"So we turn it over to the boys in blue? I don't think so!" said Jack.

"No need," said Gwen. "You just leave it to the lady in leather."

Gwen spent the next three hours trawling through police and news archives. Ianto cross-checked and referenced every file he could find on violent criminals in Cardiff since records began. Andy's murder must be connected to the Rift, they reckoned, so there was every chance of something similar turning up in the Torchwood archives. Something that could give them a lead.

"I hope you're right," said Jack. "But if there's one thing we've learned about the Rift, it's that it's hardly predictable. It rarely pulls the same stunt twice."

"I thought you were a glass-half-full kinda guy?" Ianto remarked.

"That's the thing with half-full glasses. Damned things are always half-empty too, too."

"At least we're trying to do something," said Gwen. "Besides, I think I've found something."

Jack and Ianto gathered round her screen. There, amid archive police records, was a blurry photograph of a heavy-set man with a large moustache and whiskers, and deep-set, angry eyes. His shaved head showed a wide, pucked scar running right across the top of his scalp and down to his bristling right eyebrow.

"This is the arrest card of one Roderick Simonsen," Gwen told them. "Notorious in his day, he was a Cardiff cop killer whose modus operandi exactly matches Andy's murder. He killed four police officers

with the same weapon — and here's a picture of it. Look familiar?"

A mouse click revealed a carving knife with a worn, black handle. The evidence label was dated 1919.

"Exhibit A," murmured Ianto.

"Last seen in Andy's back," Gwen nodded.

"Hang on, I remember this case," said Jack. "Roderick Simonsen went to the gallows the year he was caught. He came back from the Great War with a crack in his skull and a psychotic personality. A disaster waiting to happen. He had a pathological hatred of authority figures, and he took out his frustrations on policemen. When they caught him, he confessed to all four murders."

"Actually," Gwen corrected him, "he confessed to five. It was never made public, but it's here on the records. Though he was tried and hanged for killing four policemen, he went to the gallows insisting he'd killed a fifth. He was proud of it."

"So what happened to the fifth body?" Ianto wondered.

"There wasn't one," said Gwen. "Simonsen said it happened in the alleyway where they found him, but there was nothing. The police just put it down to his madness."

There was a short, uncomfortable silence. The three of them looked at each other. “Are you both thinking what I’m thinking?” asked Ianto eventually.

Gwen nodded. “The fifth murder was Andy Davidson.”

“And they didn’t find a body, because it wouldn’t be there for another 90 years,” said Jack.

“But why?” Gwen shouted. “How did Andy’s timeline come to cross over with Simonsen’s?”

“I don’t know,” said Jack, softly. “But if Simonsen said he killed another cop... It looks like Andy’s death might already be a fixed point in histo[redacted]”

“No[redacted]screamed Gwen. “I won’t believe[redacted]at. Simonsen was a murdering bastard with an inch-wide crack in his head! He is not the final authority on this case, and it’s up to us to prove him wrong!”

“That’s[redacted]t going to be easy,” said Ianto[redacted]We can keep track of Andy, but[redacted]w do we keep tabs on a man who was hanged nearly 100 years ago?”

Gwen’s mobile trilled, making her jump. She took a sharp breath when she saw the name flashing on the display[redacted]ANDY D.

“Gwen[redacted]His voice crackled through th[redacted]phone, distorted, panicky. “Gw[redacted]e been stabbed!”

She heard[redacted]all to the ground, followed by a harsh, wet cough. She waited until there was silence, and then sh[redacted]closed the phone.

“It’s [redacted]ppened again,’ she said.

Andy was killed for the seventh time in his own flat, stabbed in the shower, just like Janet Leigh in *Ps[redacted]ho*. There was blood everywhere[redacted]brilliantly stark against the white e[redacted]amel and tiling. Gwen almost vomited when she saw his body, face down, the knife projecting from the bare flesh. The skin was [redacted]ollen and angry around the blade[redacted]eacting automatically even as A[redacted]dy’s life drained away down the plug hole in a red river.

His mobil[redacted]was lying on the bathroom flo[redacted]r, where it had slipped from his lifeless fingers.

Gwen screwed up her eyes, feeling dizzy. When she opened them again, the body, and the blood, had all vanished.

“He’s in here,” Ianto whispered, pointing to the bedroom.

Andy was in bed, half-hidden by the duvet. His clothes were hanging over the back of a chair. His snores wafted gently from the depths of a pillow.

“Cute,” said Jack, before turning his attention to the vortex manipulator on his wrist. Lights flashed rapidly, illuminating his face in the dark. “And kinda interesting. Time has tried to correct itself by returning him to exactly where he would have been now if he hadn’t been murdered.”

“Which, of course, he wasn’t,” said Ianto. “Although he was. And he will be again very shortly.”

“Time travel is so confusing,” said Gwen, dully. She was finding it all hard to take in. How many times in a week can you see one of your best friends dead?

Ianto went through to the bathroom. “No trace of the murder weapon of the killer, of course,” he called out. “Mr Simonsen is long gone – by about 90 years.”

“If it is him,” said Jack. “Let’s find out... PC Davidson! Rise and shine!”

Andy was dazed and confused after being woken from bad dreams about knives and cop killers. For some reason, Torchwood were in his flat, and now Gwen had taken him somewhere that looked like a big Victorian toilet.

“What am I doing here, Gwen?” he asked for the fifth time.

“Staying safe,” said Gwen. “I hope so, anyway. I’ve explained all this to you already, but you don’t remember because your timeline has reset itself again. You got cross with me before, so please just trust that I’ve got your best interests at heart.”

Andy frowned a deep, worried frown. “What are you talking about?” he persisted.

“Here’s the deal, Andy,” Jack took up the story. “We think your timeline has gotten tangled up with that of a murderer from 1919. No real reason for it. Just bad luck, I guess. Anyway, in about an hour, he’s going to kill you. Again.”

“For the eighth time, to be precise,” added Ianto, helpfully.

“This is all made possible by a Rift in time and space that runs through your good city and adds to the local colour. However, even the Rift seems to find the temporal repercussions of an early 20th Century cop killer killing an early 21st Century cop hard to swallow, so the whole sequence of events keeps repeating, like a bad meal.”

“You’ve given the Rift indigestion.” Ianto again.

“Sorry, can you start again?” pleaded Andy.

“No. The point is, as Ianto says, the Rift is struggling to keep you down. You get killed, but then time vomits you back up again. Eventually, however, you’re gonna stay swallowed.”

“By which he means dead, if you weren’t keeping up with the metaphor.”

“I think I’m going to be sick.”

Gwen stepped in before Andy could get any paler. “The thing is, Andy, we think we can save you, but we don’t have much time.”

“You mean I don’t have much time.” Andy was sweating and his mouth was grit dry.

“You see that column over there?” Gwen indicated where the water tower in the Bay descended down through the Hub, like the hidden mass of an iceberg. “That’s our very own Rift manipulator.”

Andy recognised the familiar form of the tower from above ground, but not the vast, complex apparatus that he could now see inside it. He thought it looked like a cross between a homemade boiler and a nuclear bomb, and hoped it was the former.

“As the name suggests,” Gwen went on, “we can use it to manipulate the Rift to a small extent.”

“And I’ve tuned it to the right frequency, using my own vortex manipulator and the readings I picked up in your flat,” Jack held up his left wrist, to indicate the wide leather strap. “You’re not following this at all, are you?”

“I think you’re all bonkers,” Andy replied. “I mean, I know you’re all a bit kooky, but this is just... I mean, this is nuts.”

Gwen touched his arm. “I know it sounds mad, but with the data we’ve built up, we reckon we can anticipate the next murder attempt.” She paused. It felt better when she called it a murder attempt. “We can lock onto the precise fluctuation in the Rift, and we can isolate the moment your time line intersects with Simonsen’s.”

“Who the hell is Simonsen?” Andy’s eyes were pleading.

"He's the insane killer who's coming for you," said Ianto. Gwen shot him a look.

"Or not," added Ianto, meekly.

"And then what are you doing to do?" Andy scoffed in disbelief. "Arrest him?"

"If we can isolate the moment your lives intersect," said Jack, "then we can snip it out." He made a scissor motion with his fingers. "Cut the link between the two of you."

"Like a badly-edited movie," said Ianto.

"And then?"

"And then it's over," Ianto replied, before Gwen could speak. "You're either saved, or you're dead for good."

Things happened fast after that. Gwen monitored the Rift manipulator while Jack made some last-minute adjustments to his wrist strap. Ianto, rather worringly, was keeping a close eye on a stopwatch. "Ten seconds," he intoned, and Andy felt the sweat run down the back of his neck.

Sudden[redacted]he wasn't in the Hub any longer[redacted]cold, wet evening descended on him from nowhere, rain falling into dark puddles around his feet. Gasping, he turned, reaching out to the brickwork of a nearby wall. He was in an alleyway. It was night time. And there was a dim, yellow light coming form the far end.

He staggered forward, panicking, shaking, his stomach in knots. In front of him there was a man in a long, wet duster. He turned, his face silhouetted by the gaslight. Andy saw the thick moustache, the scar, and the sharp glint of metal in the man's hand.

There was blood on the knife. It had already been used.

Andy's h[redacted]rt raced. The man saw him staring[redacted]turning to run, and Andy's inst[redacted]cts took over. "Stop! Police! Hold it right there!"

He raced down the alley, reaching for the baton clipped to his belt. As he flicked open the baton, he ran through the techniques for disarming an armed assailant. Splashing through puddles, he shouted again, as the man with the knife turned down a narrow cobbled street, and then into a darkened alleyway.

It was a dead end. The man was cornered.

"All right," said Andy, trying to keep the stress out of his voice. "There's nowhere to go. Drop the knife, why don't you? Then we can do this nice and civilised."

The man's beetle-bright eyes sized up Andy in an instant: tall, willowy, incredibly young. Carrying a truncheon.

"You a copper?"

"Just put the knife down and then we can talk."

"You don't look like any copper I've ever seen. You don't look old enough to shave. Still... All the same to me." He lunged forward with the knife, aiming it straight for Andy's throat.

Andy staggered backwards in

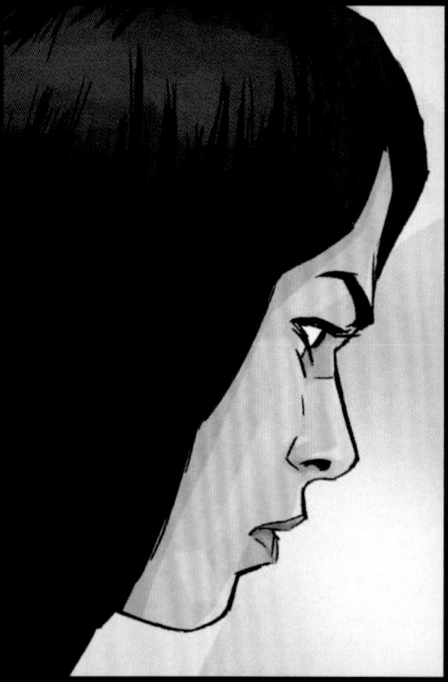

shock, flailed with the baton, and knocked the slashing arc of the knife to one side before he fell to the floor. The man snarled angrily, and grabbed Andy as he tried to stand, shoving his face hard into the alley wall.

Andy heard the sweep of his attacker's coat as he raised his knife-hand once more. He tried to break free, but was pinned fast to the rough brickwork.

He could only wait for the killing stroke.

But it didn't come.

Instead he felt a soft hand in his, and saw Gwen looking at him in the Hub. It was light and dry and he felt no pain.

"Are you okay?" said Gwen. "Speak to me, Andy!"

He nodded, his mouth open but no sound coming out. He looked around and blinked twice. He looked back at Gwen. And then he fainted.

"He's bound to be disorientated," Jack told Gwen as they carried Andy into his flat. "Shunting back and forth in time like that, it can be overwhelming for a beginner. He needs rest an[redacted] sleep. He won't remember anything in the morning."

"That's good," said Gwen. "No need for Retcon."

"I shouldn't think so," Jack agreed. "Shall we take him through to the bedroom?"

"I'll do it," said Gwen, taking her friend's weight.

"He'll be annoyed to have missed that," smiled Jack. "But still... It's a good result all round. Ianto's been digging into the archives again, and it seems Roderick Simonsen was only arrested that night because of Andy."

"How so?"

"Seems that Torchwood interviewed Simonsen after they got wind of the mystery fifth mur[redacted] he claimed to have committe[redacted] didn't pick it up before because it was filed under false leads – in other words, nothing he told them was useful in defending the British Empire."

"But?" Gwen prompted him.

"But what he told them was that the fifth policeman disappeared the moment he thrust the knife into his back. At least, that's how it appeared to Simonsen. In fact, he must have disappeared a split-second before. Simonsen was so shocked, he just slumped down right there in the alley. That's where the police found him, still clutching the murder weapon. Kept saying he'd sent a man to heaven in a brilliant flash of light."

"So if Andy hadn't been there..."

"Simonsen might have killed again. In fact, he might never have been caught."

"Good old Andy. Fighting crime before any of us were born."

"Speak for yourself," said Jack.

"I thought you were born in the future?" asked Gwen with a frown.

"You're right," he said. "Time travel is confusing, isn't it?"

Gwen shot him a grin, and the two of them walked out arm in arm. •

COVER GALLERY

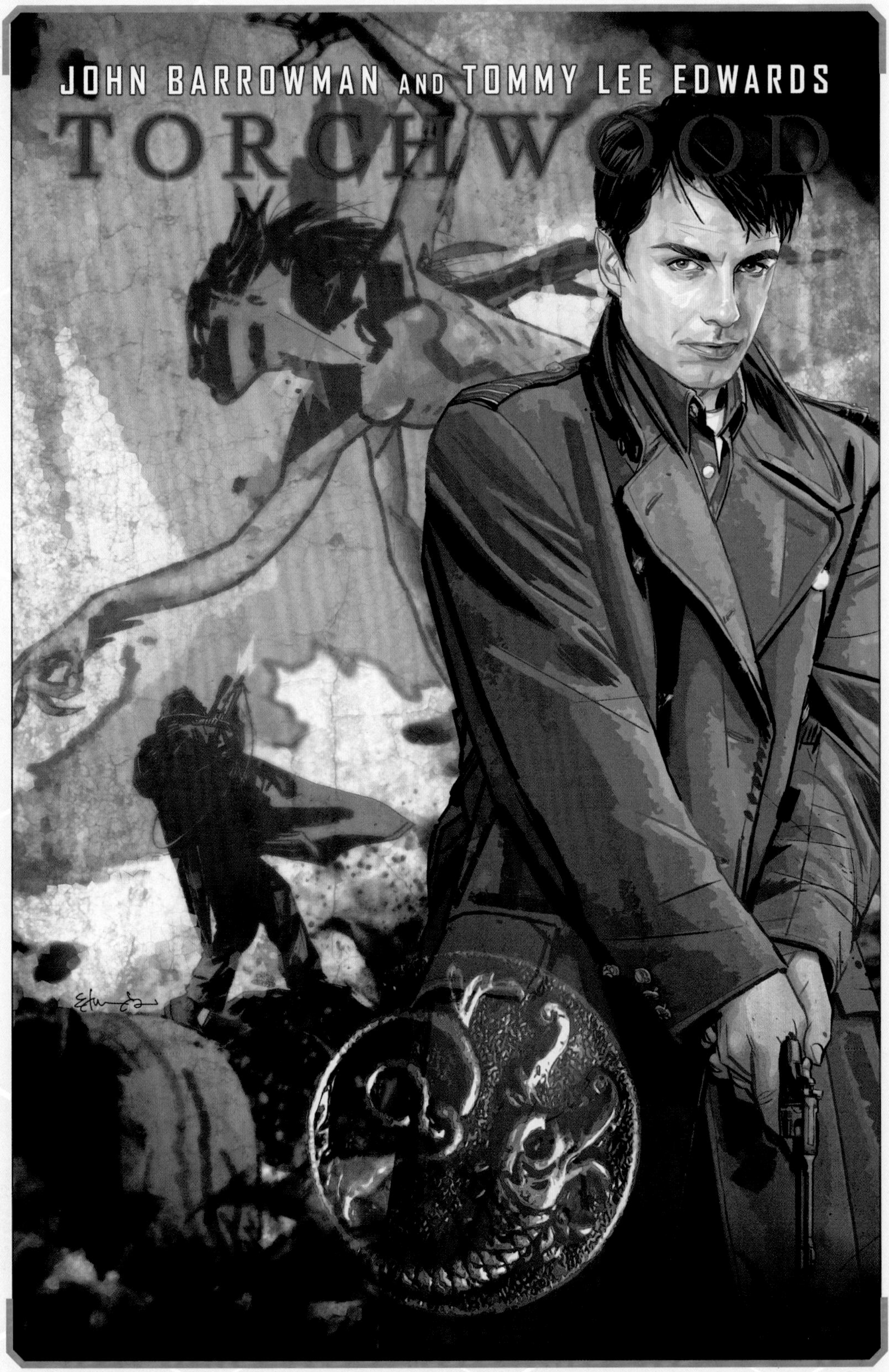
JOHN BARROWMAN AND TOMMY LEE EDWARDS
TORCHWOOD

ISSUE 1 COVER
BY TOMMY LEE EDWARDS

COVER GALLERY

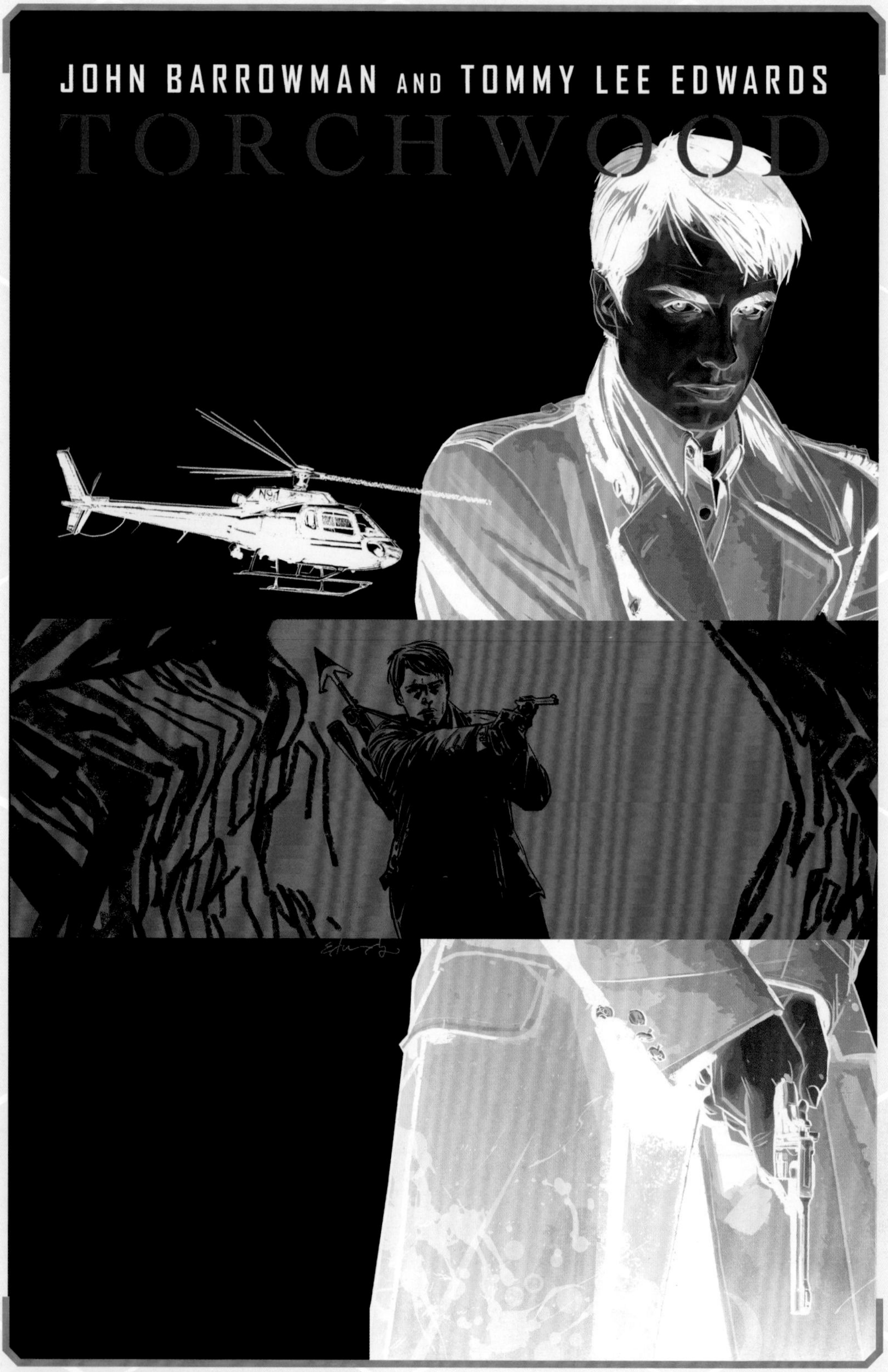
JOHN BARROWMAN AND TOMMY LEE EDWARDS
TORCHWOOD

SAN DIEGO COMIC-CON 2010 EXCLUSIVE COVER
BY TOMMY LEE EDWARDS

COVER GALLERY

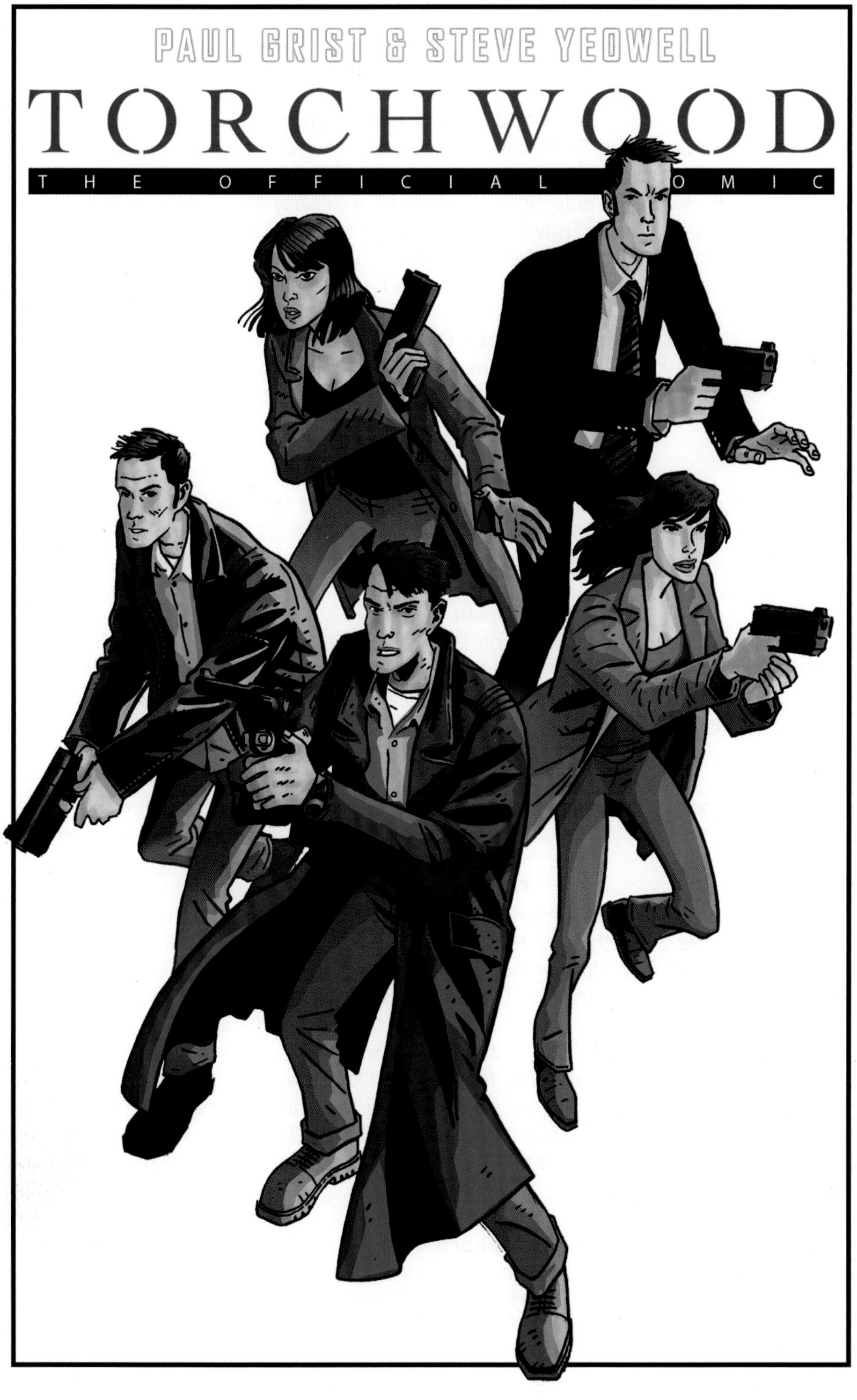

PAUL GRIST & STEVE YEOWELL
TORCHWOOD
THE OFFICIAL COMIC

ISSUE 2 COVER
BY PAUL GRIST

WRITER BIOS

WRITERS

John and Carole Barrowman
Siblings Carole and John Barrowman have collaborated on a number of projects including their latest novel, *Conjuror*, John's autobiographies, the first of which, *Anything Goes*, was a *Sunday Times* bestseller, a fantasy series *Hollow Earth*, and *Exodus Code*, a *Torchwood* novel. They also currently write the official *Torchwood* comic. John's career includes theatre, television, music and film, and he is highly acclaimed for his portrayal of Captain Jack Harkness in *Torchwood* and *Doctor Who*.

Gareth David-Lloyd
Gareth David-Lloyd played Ianto Jones in *Torchwood* seasons 1-3, and in guest appearances in *Doctor Who*. He has reprised the role in the Big Finish *Torchwood* audio series.

Simon Furman
Simon Furman is a British comic book writer most famous for his work on *Transformers*. Other works include *Alpha Flight*, *Northstar*, *What If?* and *The Sensational She-Hulk* for Marvel Comics.

Brian Minchin
Brian Minchin is Executive Producer on *Doctor Who* and its spin-off, *Class*. Previously, he was script editor for *Doctor Who* and *Torchwood*, and a producer on *Sarah Jane Adventures* and *Torchwood: Miracle Day*. Other writing includes *Doctor Who* novel *The Forgotten Army*, and a *Torchwood* audio drama *The Sin Eaters*.

Christopher Cooper
Christopher Cooper is a UK-based writer and editor. Other work includes the *Doctor Who* novel *The Krillitane Storm* and the Big Finish audio series *Bernice Summerfield*.

Trevor Baxendale
Trevor Baxendale is an author who has written many *Doctor Who* novels, and the *Torchwood* novels *Something in the Water* and *The Undertaker's Gift*. He has also written for the Big Finish *Doctor Who* audio range, and has contributed many comic stories to *Doctor Who Adventures*.

James Goss
James Goss has written for the *Torchwood* and *Doctor Who* Big Finish audio stories, and is also a producer for Big Finish. Other work includes novelizing the Douglas Adams-penned scripts for *Doctor Who* stories *City of Death* and *The Pirate Planet*. He also commissioned the *Doctor Who* animated stories *Scream of the Shalka* and *The Infinite Quest*.

Richard Stokes
Richard Stokes is a BAFTA-nominated producer who is perhaps best known as a producer on *Torchwood*. Other work includes *Broadchurch*, *Silk* and *Law & Order UK*.

TORCHWOOD

TORCHWOOD

ARCHIVES VOL.2

COMING SOON!

AVAILABLE IN PRINT AND DIGITALLY
WWW.TITAN-COMICS.COM